D1432601

LIBERALISM AND AMERICAN EDUCATION
IN THE EIGHTEENTH CENTURY

LIBERALISM AND AMERICAN EDUCATION

IN THE EIGHTEENTH CENTURY

BY

ALLEN OSCAR HANSEN

WITH AN INTRODUCTION BY
EDWARD H. REISNER

1965
OCTAGON BOOKS, INC.
New York

Originally published 1926 by The Macmillan Company

Reprinted 1965

OCTAGON BOOKS, INC.
175 FIFTH AVENUE
NEW YORK, N. Y. 10010

LIBRARY OF CONGRESS CATALOG CARD NUMBER: 65-25567

Printed in U.S.A. by
NOBLE OFFSET PRINTERS, INC.
NEW YORK 3, N. Y.

PREFACE

The degree to which American life and institutions were influenced by the liberal movement of the eighteenth century has not yet been adequately set forth. The characteristic ideas of this movement were: that creativeness was inherent in the individual; that the creative genius of man could be directed for social progress; that the lines of human progress could be determined; and that the continuous development of the human race through scientific control was the only valid function of institutions.

In the past institutions had been the result of chance or accident. In America there existed an opportunity for the scientific development of institutions that would be flexible, modifiable, plastic, and directly related to the forwarding of whatever interests might arise. Initiating, refashioning, innovating, creating,—all of these could be scientifically developed and fused in the motif of societal welfare.

Democracy implied the creating of intelligent citizens who would see clearly their responsibility for developing such a government and other institutions. Hence there must be instituted a system of education for creative democracy. To this task many of the best minds of the period turned their energies. The American Philosophical Society, of which Benjamin Franklin and Thomas Jefferson were presidents, offered a prize for the best plan for such a system of education, and published two of the plans submitted, those by Samuel Knox and Samuel H. Smith. Other plans were published by Benjamin Rush, Robert Coram, James Sullivan, Nathaniel Chipman, Du Pont de Nemours, Lafitte du Courteil, and Noah Webster.

v

The present volume is intended to be both an exposition of sources and a source book. As yet the sources for the period of which this volume treats are scattered in various libraries, and even where they are best organized, such as in the New York Public Library, they are difficult of access on account of the absence of an adequate index. In many cases but one copy exists, since the sources were largely the ephemera of the period. Again, as in the case of some of Noah Webster's works, the marginal notes made by the author at a later date are most definitive of the viewpoint held at the time of the original writing. It has been the practice in this volume to quote somewhat at length in order to make available for other students of this period the sources from which the conclusions are drawn. Students of history in the fields of social, political, and economic theory, it is believed, will find much here that will throw new light upon this period. The special contribution toward a reinterpretation of education will indicate how far we have failed to see the real problems of this period and the suggested solutions.

The scholarship and sympathetic support of Drs. Paul Monroe, Isaac Kandel, Edward Reisner, William Heard Kilpatrick, as well as the criticism of John Dewey, were the inspiration during a long period. Dr. Robert Francis Seybolt was the one who gave to me the first impulse to attempt this research. My gratitude is to all of them for criticism that challenged each position taken, and for their fine support even when our opinions differed.

The courtesy of the New York Public Library in providing every service is one of the hopeful signs in the furtherance of research. Also, the manner in which Victor Hugo Paltsits made available the resources of the manuscript division and aided in every way through his almost unlimited knowledge of Americana, made possible the consulting of many obscure sources. Like services were freely extended by the New York Historical Society, the Wisconsin Historical Society, and the Columbia University Library. The private collections of many individuals were put at the disposal of the author. Among these collections was that of William Washington, who generously permitted the use of materials from the library of George Washington.

Acknowledgment is due to Madeleine Monroe Hansen, who labored unceasingly and whose spirit of service made possible the accomplishment of this task.

ALLEN O. HANSEN.

New York City,
August, 1926.

INTRODUCTION

Dr. Hansen has placed students of the intellectual and educational history of the United States in his debt by reason of his intelligent and thorough study of the late eighteenth century period. The liberal influences upon American educational thinking which emanated from France at that time have probably never been estimated at their full importance. Certainly there can be no question regarding the almost complete neglect of these influences in the existing treatments of the history of American education. Jefferson's plan of education for the state of Virginia has, of course, been well known and the French influence has long been recognized in the system adopted for the administration of higher education in the State of New York. The educational views of Benjamin Rush have been somewhat appreciated; the plan of Du Pont de Nemours had previously been made generally available by the translation from the University of Delaware Press published in 1923,[1] and the vigorous Americanism of Noah Webster has received some attention. But until Dr. Hansen's study was made we had had no comprehensive and systematic account of the extent to which eighteenth century French and English liberalism affected the educational thought of the Revolutionary and post-Revolutionary generation of American intellectuals.

There is an extremely engaging quality in much of the eighteenth century theorizing on social and educational problems. It is full of faith in mankind and particularly in

[1] The original was used by the author in this research before 1923, but the references were made to this translation when it appeared, for convenience of reference.

the possibilities that were thought to be latent in the great mass of the uneducated workers and peasants. Eighteenth century liberalism dared exceedingly in those days that preceded the Terror and the general reaction which came early in the nineteenth century. Mankind, freed of the chains of inequitable economic and political conditions, was to go forward by leaps and bounds toward the goal of rational and humane institutions and highly developed individual excellence.

It is not surprising that such a philosophy should make a strong appeal in the new land in the western hemisphere which was just coming into national self-consciousness. Here the economic and political influences of frontier freedom had already made themselves felt. Of all lands here was the one which had less of the old to destroy before it could begin to build the new, and what of the new had already developed was showing signs of the excellence which brave minds of Europe aspired to for the older society. Not the least of Dr. Hansen's contributions lies in the fidelity with which he has portrayed the liberal thought of the eighteenth century in the Old World and then shown the reflection of this thought in the American minds which were reacting upon it in full consciousness of the peculiar and, in many respects, more advantageous American conditions.

If eighteenth century liberals had great faith in democracy, they had a no less ideal conception of the rôle to be played by nationality in the prospective improvement of human existence. For them the national form of political organization was taken in a more or less matter-of-fact way as the administrative agency of social reform. Nationality was the existing large pattern of social organization. As such it was the big wheel the function of which was to turn the smaller wheels which were to bring about equity, order, and enlightenment. Their nationalism was not provocative nor competitive, except in good works, nor did it exhibit the prominent factor of emotion which has since come to be associated with the idea. Rather were all nations to be regarded as co-partners in the work of improving the conditions of life for the fostering of individual excellence and happiness.

It is unnecessary in this connection to belabor the point that the actuality of democracy has been arrived at in Western society through a slow and painful process of development and that it is quite a different thing from what the eighteenth century dreamed it would be. Neither has nationalism, as a form of social organization, been altogether faithful to the constructive and beneficent rôle for which it was cast in the expansive thought of that generous era. And yet who shall say that the prophetic eighteenth century vision of a triumphant society—constructive, progressive, creative of all good works—is not the true reality of the democratic national state of which our existing forms are only very poor approximations? As we read this record of eighteenth century thought regarding what men are and how they should live together and what forms of education would serve to hasten the day of a rational and cooperative society, we may discover a renewed faith in the power of education and in the future of mankind.

EDWARD H. REISNER.

Teachers College, Columbia University,
August 17, 1926.

CONTENTS

xiii

CONTENTS

LIBERALISM AND AMERICAN EDUCATION
IN THE EIGHTEENTH CENTURY

LIBERALISM AND AMERICAN EDUCATION IN THE EIGHTEENTH CENTURY

CHAPTER ONE

DOMINANT IDEAS OF THE EIGHTEENTH CENTURY

THE eighteenth century gave birth to and saw in part the fruition of two great movements, the one a movement among the intellectual classes called the Enlightenment, the other a revolutionary movement among the middle classes chiefly and also among the lower classes but involving all human activity—the democratic revolutionary movement led by Rousseau. Common to both of these movements was the revolutionary idea of the indefinite perfectibility of man and of the destructive tendency of fixed institutions of church and state.

Indefinite perfectibility of man and institutions. Near the close of the eighteenth century William Godwin, who summated most adequately [1] the eighteenth century move-

[1] The major reasons for choosing the writings of Godwin as most representative of the eighteenth century philosophy are: First, Godwin's contacts and influence were extensive in England, on the continent, and in America; second, his style has both the raciness and force of the best writers of the Enlightenment and the charm of the more popular writers of the democratic movement; (it was judged best to use quotations from some one eighteenth century source in order that this raciness and force of the writers of that period might be the better felt. One of the purposes of this study has been to provide in brief scope a somewhat adequate source book as well as an exposition of the sources)

ment and whose thought is most significantly representative, said, "There is no characteristic of man, which seems at present at least so eminently to distinguish him, or to be of so much importance in every branch of moral science, as his perfectibility." [1]   To prove this he summarized briefly the evolution of the human mind: "Let us carry back our minds to man in his original state, a being capable of impressions and knowledge to an unbounded extent, but not having as yet received the one or cultivated the other; and let us contrast this being with all that science and genius have effected: and from hence we may form some idea what it is of which human nature is capable." [2]   He went on to show how man had first to progress without "assistance from the communications of his fellows" and without having "had his feeble and crude conceptions assisted by the experience of successive centuries." [2]   Man had in the beginning simply the capacity for progress and had to make his improvement by "untutored efforts."   Each problem had to be solved *de novo*.   The fact that man progressed under such conditions proved that it was the nature of man to progress, to work out new and original solutions.   The essentially progressive nature of man would not be otherwise even though the doctrine were accepted that "man was immediately advanced half way to the end of his career by the interposition of the author of his nature." [2]

third, Godwin most adequately represents the implications of the eighteenth century philosophy for institutional changes and especially the change demanded by it in the content and mode of education.   He conceived of man as creative unless repressed by obsolete and fixed institutions; he believed education to be the only instrument for creating a flexible social organization that would respect the creative genius of man; and he perceived that the mode of education demanded for furthering progress must be creative activity.

[1] Godwin, William, *An Enquiry Concerning Political Justice*, Vol. I, p. 41.   1793.

[2] *Ibid.*, pp. 41-42, 1793.

Accepting, however, the idea of man's evolution from inconsiderable beginnings, the vast achievements that he had made proved to the satisfaction of the eighteenth century philosophers that it was his nature to progress. One of the great achievements that must have taken great time and such effort as no one can imagine was the creation of language. Godwin said that "it is impossible to conceive of an acquisition, that must have been in its origin different from what at present it is found, or that less promised that copiousness and refinement is has since exhibited." [1] If, then, we consider man after he had achieved language in some form, another evidence that would be most enlightening would be to "trace him through all his subsequent improvements, through whatever constitutes the inequality between Newton and the ploughman." [2] Godwin suggested that in order to get an appreciation of the long struggle of man and of his indefinite progress we should "survey the earth covered with the labours of man, houses, inclosures, harvests, manufactures, instruments, machines, together with all the wonders of painting, poetry, eloquence and philosophy." [2] He concluded, "Such was man in his original state, and such is man as we at present behold him. Is it possible for us to contemplate what he has already done, without being impressed with a strong presentiment of the improvements he has yet to accomplish? There is no science that is not capable of additions; there is no art that may not be carried to a still higher perfection" and, he suggested, "If this be true of all other sciences, why not of morals: If this be true of all other arts, why not of social institutions?" He said again that "The very conception of this as possible, is in the highest degree encouraging. If we can still farther

---

[1] Godwin, William, *An Enquiry Concerning Political Justice*, Vol. I, p. 42, 1793.
[2] *Ibid.*, p. 47. 1793.

demonstrate it to be a part of the natural and regular progress of mind, our confidence and our hopes will then be complete." [1]

This conception of man's indefinite perfectibility and of the indefinite perfectibility of institutions had many roots. It was, in part, a result of the Renaissance movement which had brought into fresh view all of the ancient civilizations, and in further part, the stimulation of a high degree of interest in the study of primitive man through the various expeditions into the undeveloped continents.[2] The striking contrasts between the modes of life of primitive tribes and life in the highly developed ancient civilization had raised and accentuated the question of the origin of civilization and of its development. The development of humanity with all of its arts and refinements from the savage state to the most highly civilized could not be denied.[3]

Descartes, Bacon, and Locke had prepared the way for a critical evaluation of institutions in their relation to human progress so that at the beginning of the eighteenth century there was already present a body of doctrines and a conception of method that made it possible to conceive of a directed progress of humanity. They had raised not only the question of the nature of man but they had indicated the need for a science of human development. The utilitarian outlook of these and other writers brought to the foreground the question of how the forces of nature could be utilized for the realization of man's greatest happiness and greatest development. They had broken the authority of sacerdotalism and had caused the intellectuals to believe that there would be a triumph of reason over

[1] Godwin, William, *An Enquiry Concerning Political Justice*, Vol. I, p. 47. 1793.
[2] Tinker, Chauncey Brewster, *Nature's Simple Plan*, pp. 5, 6. 1922.
[3] Levy-Bruhl, Lucien, *History of Modern Philosophy in France*, p. 295. 1899.

ignorance and the unfriendly, obsolete customs. If man, then, were capable of indefinite improvement, that improvement could be furthered through institutions that would be in harmony with his nature.[1]

Man's ability to progress indefinitely in knowledge was the great contribution of Fontenelle. Fontenelle, through the force of an entertaining style and a genius for popularizing the scientific outlook, prepared the way for those who were to stress the perfectibility of man's nature as well as of man's ideas, and also the perfectibility of social institutions.[2] What has been characterized as "Ubiquitous rebellion against tradition" may be said to have been in a large way the inheritance of the eighteenth century. However, it remained for the eighteenth century to give detailed and intelligible form to this rebellion. It is interesting to note, as Bury has pointed out, "The first title he (Descartes) had proposed to give to his *Discourse on Method* was 'The Project of a Universal Science which can elevate our Nature to its highest degree of Perfection.' "[3]

Rousseau became the great apostle of the essential goodness of man and of the principles implied in this theory—principles which came to dominate the revolutionary and democratic movements of the latter part of the eighteenth century.[4] The doctrines of Rousseau became active in the American and French Revolutions. Richard Price and Thomas Paine carried his doctrines largely into America, while Condorcet [5] constantly set forth the idea of the infinite progress of human thinking through the progress of science.[6]

[1] Bury, John B., *The Idea of Progress*, pp. 161-162. 1920.
[2] *Ibid.*, pp. 111-113. 1920.
[3] *Ibid.*, p. 67. 1920.
[4] Levy-Bruhl, Lucien, *History of Modern Philosophy in France*, pp. 242, 244. 1899.
[5] *Ibid.*, p. 293. 1899.
[6] Boucke, O. Fred, *The Development of Economics*, p. 65. 1921.

Man could determine the lines of progress. Perhaps the leading conception of Rousseau's essay, *Le Contrat Social*, was that man, if allowed to do so, could progress indefinitely and could determine the lines of progress. Rousseau said, "In this investigation, I shall endeavor constantly to join the considerations of natural right and public interest, so that justice and utility may never be disunited."[1] His conception was that "Man is born free, and yet is universally enslaved"[2] and that "If there are any slaves, therefore, by nature, it is because they are slaves contrary to nature."[3] The doctrine of unalienable rights implied, according to Rousseau's conception, the right of man to realize himself to the fullest extent. This full self-realization could best come through association and so man was to form a social organization for the achievement of the greatest possible progress.[4] This "transition of a man from a state of nature to a state of society is productive of a very remarkable change in his being, by substituting justice instead of instinct as the rule of his conduct."[5] In this manner, the "Voice of duty succeeds the laws of appetite" and through such association man would be able to direct his endeavors by reason rather than by the caprice of those who were in authority or the caprice of his own appetites.[5]

In referring to the extent of Rousseau's influence, the editor of the Albany edition of *Political Economy and Social Compact* said, "We have good reason to believe that in the present age his (Rousseau's) works have been more generally read and approved of in Europe, than those of any other author. His political works especially, of which these pieces *(Political Economy* and *Social Compact)* are the chief, are repeatedly referred to by eminent writers on gov-

---

[1] Rousseau, *Political Economy and Social Compact*, p. 3.   Albany ed. 1797.   First published 1762; London ed. 1767.

[2] *Ibid.*, p. 4.   1797.   [4] *Ibid.*, p. 11.   1797.

[3] *Ibid.* p. 8.   1797.   [5] *Ibid.*, p. 27.   1797.

ernment, and the framers of numerous constitutions, organized since their publication, appear to have eyed them with deference, copied them in some particulars, and made improvements on them in others." [1]

A mistaken idea of the conceptions of Rousseau has made him seem to be solely an iconoclast. On the contrary, he stated in *Le Contrat Social*, "By entering into the Social Compact, man gives up his natural liberty, or unlimited right to everything which he is desirous of, and can attain. In return, he gains social liberty." Again, "To the preceding also may be added, as the acquisition of the social state, moral liberty; which only renders a man truly master of himself; for to be under the direction of appetite alone, is to be in a state of slavery." [2] From this it will be seen that Rousseau believed that the richest possible living came through society. The unalienable and indivisible sovereignty rested not in the individual but in the whole body of the people. For this reason, "The Social Compact established such an equality among the citizens, that all lay themselves under the same obligations, and ought to enjoy the same privileges." [3] There were decided advantages in the Social Compact. By entering into it, the individuals "only make an advantageous exchange of an uncertain and precarious mode of subsistence, for a more settled and determinate one"; they exchange "their own natural strength, which might be overcome by that of others, for a civil power which the social union renders invincible." In this way men would be "gainers on the whole." [4]

Rousseau believed that man could move most creatively through social organizations. [5] We shall see later how

[1] Rousseau, *Political Economy and Social Compact*, p. 4. Albany edition, 1797.
[2] *Ibid.*, p. 28. 1797.   [3] *Ibid.*, p. 46. 1797.   [4] *Ibid.*, p. 48. 1797.
[5] Levy-Bruhl, Lucien, *History of Modern Philosophy in France*, pp. 261-262. 1899. Barnes, Harry E., "Sociology before Comte," *Amer. Journal of Sociology*, Vol. XXIII, No. 2, pp. 182-183. 1922.

Rousseau saw the relation of education to human progress. The principles of the Social Compact were but an apt expression of the principles involved in a wide and long-continued movement. The control of individual and human welfare was related to the evolution of science as an instrument for the development of natural and human resources. Constructive living involved freedom of the individual to work creatively; the utilization of all resources according to reason and scientific method; and a broad humanitarianism by which the results of man's labours would be shared as widely as possible. Man was to discover as far as passible the laws that governed psychic as well as physical phenomena. Until he had done this, progress would be a matter of accident; the extent to which he would be able to proceed scientifically and coöperatively would determine the degree of his progress. Man could determine the destiny of the race by means of educational and other institutional controls.[1]

This idea of scientific control of all that makes for human progress and welfare was developed by many others, such as Ferguson, Dunbar, and Priestley, and was perhaps an elaboration of Bacon's *Atlantis*.[2] The scheme of Saint-Pierre with all of its extravagances was but a natural outgrowth of the sanguine idealistic philosophy of the eighteenth century.[3] The confidence of Adam Smith in "Those principles of the human constitution, which, wherever they are allowed free scope, not only conduct mankind to happiness, but lay the foundation of a progressive improvement in their distinction and character" was an evidence of his

---

[1] Boucke, O. Fred, *The Development of Economics*, pp. 28-29, 50-52, 52. 1921. Lewinski, Jan St., *The Founders of Political Economy*, pp. 3, 6. 1922.

[2] Bury, John B., *The Idea of Progress*, pp. 221-222. 1920.

[3] *Ibid.*, pp. 144, 145. 1920.

belief in the indefinite perfectibility of man and in the essential goodness of his nature.[1]

Flexible institutions necessary for human progress. The dynamic interpretation of life called for a change in attitude toward institutions.[2] William Godwin said, "Man is not, as has already been shewn, a perfect being, but perfectible. No government, that has yet existed, or is likely presently to exist upon the face of the earth, is faultless. No government ought therefore pertinaciously to resist the change of its own institutions." [3] It should rather be the attitude of government to stimulate researches and not "to restrain the excursions of an inventive mind" for "It is only by giving a free scope to these excursions, that science, philosophy and morals have arrived at their present degree of perfection, or are capable of going on to that still greater perfection, in comparison of which all that has been already done will perhaps appear childish." [4] The doctrine of change had been set forth clearly by Kant and was being set forth by Hegel. This doctrine of development demanded a refashioning of institutions, such a refashioning as would permit life to develop freely. The Encyclopædist movement was an attempt to find a philosophical basis of human action and to secure progress through reason as developed through scientific education. There could be no finality such as had characterized the long-standing institutions of Europe.[5] Such finality enchained rather than liberated man. Institutions could be justified only when they functioned creatively for human development. The doctrine set forth

[1] Smith, Adam, *Essays on Philosophical Subjects,* p. XC. Dugald Stewart. 1795.
[2] Boucke, O. Fred, *The Development of Economics,* pp. 103-104. 1921.
[3] Godwin, William, *Enquiry Concerning Political Justice,* Vol. I, pp. 110-111. 1793.
[4] *Ibid.,* pp. 110-111. 1793.
[5] Levy-Bruhl, Lucien, *History of Modern Philosophy in France,* pp. 234-235. 1899.

in Bacon's *Atlantis,* that society should definitely organize itself for regular periods of readjustment, found expression in the eighteenth century through the writings of Voltaire, Diderot, Saint-Simon and others. That is, institutions should be reconstructed as often as the changes in circumstances demanded and new enlightenment had been gained. Bacon's "idols of the tribe," "of the cave," and "of the forum" were to give way to an energetic, experimental, utilitarian attitude.[1]

The mercantilism that had been perfected in the seventeenth century received its most fatal thrusts from Quesnay, Turgot, Dupont de Nemours, and Smith in the development of the Physiocratic *laissez-faire* theory of social control.[2] The *laissez-faire* theory was made effective largely through the writings of Vanderlint, Mandeville, and other precursors of the Physiocratic movement.[3] The development of the science of economics for social control coupled with a utilitarian philosophy of history as elucidated in the writings of Voltaire, Condillac, Ferguson, Gibbon, Iselin, and Schlozer, made evident the need for institutional reconstruction.[4] Absolutism could not survive the relativism of these virile writers.[5] It was observed by Turgot that each step of progress on the part of the people accelerated the rate of progress.[6] His idea was to trace the development of mankind according to the idea of progress. The commercial

---

[1] Barnes, Harry E., "Sociology before Comte," *Amer. Journal of Sociology,* Vol. XXIII, No. 2, pp. 175, 224. 1917. Tinker, Chauncey Brewster, *Nature's Simple Plan,* p. v. 1922.

[2] Lewinski, Jan St., *The Founders of Political Economy,* pp. 2, 29, 33-34, 35, 39, 100-101. 1922. Boucke, O. Fred, *The Development of Economics,* pp. 105-106, 108-109, 110. 1921.

[3] Palgrave, *Dictionary of Political Economy,* p. 732. 1706-34.

[4] Boucke, O. Fred, *The Development of Economics,* pp. 16-17, 26, 28, 59. 1921. Bastable, Charles Francis, *The Commerce of Nations,* pp. 30-31, 34, 36. 9th ed. 1923. First published 1891.

[5] *Ibid.* pp. 2, 3. 1921.

[6] Bury, John B., *The Idea of Progress,* pp. 153-154, 157, 158. 1920.

revolution with its establishment of ever widening contacts proved to be an irresistible force in the liberation of human thought.[1] The Bourgeoise could not be served by the ancient institutions. The social organization of the eighteenth century was doomed; a new order was inevitable.[2] The political theories that were later to become the basis of the American and French revolutions were vigorously discussed in the parlors and salons of France.[3]

According to Godwin, "Aristocracy in its proper signification implies neither less nor more than a scheme for rendering more permanent and visible by the interference of political institutions the inequality of mankind. Aristocracy, like monarchy, is founded on falsehood, the offspring of art foreign to the real nature of things, and must therefore, like monarchy, be supported by artifice and false pretences. . . . Both depend for their perpetuity upon ignorance." Aristocracy and monarchy could no longer "renew their lease of empire. . . . To make men serfs and villains it is indispensibly necessary to make them brutes. This is a question which has long been canvassed with great eagerness and avidity." [4] Godwin said also, "It is the fortune of the present work to appear before a public that is panic struck, and impressed with the most dreadful apprehensions of such doctrines as are here delivered. All the prejudices of the human mind are in arms against it." [5]

Institutions exist to further progress. Godwin declared that "If science be capable of perpetual improvement, men

[1] Hayes, Carlton J. H., *A Political and Social History of Modern Europe*, Vol I, pp. 62-63, 66, 402. 1919.
[2] *Ibid.*, Vol. I, pp. 208, 393-394, 464, 465. 1919.
[3] Dunning, William Archibald, *A History of Political Theories from Rousseau to Spencer*, pp. 50-51. 1920.
[4] Godwin, William, *An Enquiry Concerning Political Justice*, Vol. 2, pp. 35-36. 1793.
[5] *Ibid.*, Vol. 1, pp. x-xii. 1793.

will also be capable of perpetually advancing in practical wisdom and justice." [1]   The corollary of this position was that institutions that did not function for perpetual improvement were inimical to human welfare.   In the conditions that had existed, "Error is principally indebted for its permanence to social institutions." [2]   Godwin argued, "Once establish the perfectibility of man" and it would not be long until this distortion of the life of man by institutions would be at an end and justice would be "too habitually practiced to be voluntarily counteracted."   In his optimism he declared, "Nor shall we see reason to think upon severe reflection, that this state is so distant as we might at first be inclined to imagine." [2]

Mercantilism had made the mistake of tying up the welfare of mankind with a narrow, selfish, nationalistic conception.[3]   However, while it is true that mercantilism had built up jealousies and rivalries, it had furthered the movement toward the creation of the larger social unit, the nation. In this way it had broken down the old feudal and town prejudices.   The reaction, however, that set in against mercantilism showed clearly that human progress involved the whole of humanity.[4]

The doctrine of the eighteenth century was that "the inner forces of growth and life can be trusted."   Institutions, then, in order to further progress, must be in harmony with these inner forces.   In the eighteenth century the idea dominated that if a scientific evaluation and direction of effort were instituted, it would be possible to realize an indefinite progress of mankind.   Two things were necessary

[1] Godwin, William, *An Enquiry Concerning Political Justice*, Vol. 2, p. 51.   1793.
[2] *Ibid.*, Vol. 2, p. 51.   1793.
[3] Bogardus, Emory S., *A history of Social Thought*, p. 188.   1922.
[4] *Ibid.*, p. 187.   1922.

in order that institutions might function for desirable ends. On the one hand there must be a clear conception of human values, and on the other hand the means for their realization must be scientifically determined and controlled. Through the progress of invention and discovery man had come into a body of materials that might be used for the gaining of incalculably superior materials for the achievement of societal welfare. The liberation that began in the early Renaissance and that had in some phases been increasingly developed was but a small indication of the achievements yet to be made. Science had but barely begun to indicate the possibilities in the development of natural resources and yet it had almost entirely changed the outlook of mankind. Through its method there would ultimately be evolved a basis of rational living. This was the doctrine of Diderot, D'Alembert, and the rest of the Encylopædists.[1] What had been accomplished in the narrow range of smaller social units could be accomplished for humanity at large. The cosmopolitan, humanitarian outlook of the eighteenth century saw in the recognition of and in the determination to erase all narrow class and national distinctions, the possibility of an ultimate synthesis of whatever would be invaluable in human evolution.[2] The task of working out a system that would mean an increase of happiness throughout the world contained sufficient challenge to enlist the energies of all who were interested in the utopia which was ever present in eighteenth century thinking. From either the viewpoint of the mercantilists who believed that they were the productive class, or the viewpoint of the physiocrats who saw the welfare of mankind as largely dependent upon a scientific development of the resources of the earth, there was a

[1] Levy-Bruhl, Lucien, *History of Modern Philosophy in France*, p. 222. 1899.
[2] *Ibid.*, pp. 200-201, 206.   1899.

common desire for amelioration of the conditions that existed.[1]

Whereas man had been a means, he now became the end, and all institutions existed in order to make him free for creative, effective living. But it remained for man to discover the natural laws and to fashion the institutions according to them.[2] Fixed institutions of religion and state were vigorously attacked in the degree in which they failed to aid in human progress. The only way in which they could aid in human progress was for them to be in harmony with the laws of nature.[3] Pascal, Rousseau, Diderot, D'Holbach, Helvetius, and a host of others struggled for the liberation of mankind from the inertia of the past.[4]

John B. Bury, although he is an English writer, says that France and not England gave birth and support to the idea of government for the control of progress.[5] He sets out very clearly how the Encyclopædist movement "supplied the principles for reconstituting society." [6] The humanistic turn of the whole movement in France, with its emphasis upon the ideal of a civilization controlled scientifically and growing more effective in the realization of human happiness, is elaborated at some length in his essay on *The Idea of Progress.*[7]

Education the principal means for progress. Among the means for advancement education was given first place.

[1] Barnes, Harry E., "Sociology before Comte," *Amer. Journal of Sociology,* Vol. XXIII, No. 2, pp. *220, 229-230. 1917.* Lewinski, Jan St., *The Founders of Political Economy,* pp. *30-31, 36-37. 1922.*
[2] Levy-Bruhl, Lucien, *History of Modern Philosophy in France,* pp. 108-109, 202. 1899.
[3] Boucke, O. Fred, *The Development of Economics,* pp. *64-65. 1921.*
[4] Levy-Bruhl, Lucien, *History of Modern Philosophy in France,* pp. 82-83. 1899. Bury, John B., *The Idea of Progress,* pp. 158-159, 226-227. 1920.
[5] Bury, John B., *The Idea of Progress,* p. 218. 1920.
[6] *Ibid.,* pp. 159-160. 1920.
[7] *Ibid.,* pp. 149-150, 109, 127-128. 1920.

Again Godwin may be taken as most ideally representative of the eighteenth century outlook in his conception of education: "Our virtues and vices may be traced to the incidents which make the history of our lives, and if these incidents could be divested of every improper tendency, vice would be extirpated from the world."[1] The new mode of society required a different mode of education, different in content and in method. He declared: "The task of instruction, under such a form of society as that we are contemplating, will be greatly simplified and altered from what it is at present. It will then be thought no more legitimate to make boys slaves, than to make men so."[2] Upon the basis of the essential goodness of the nature of man, education would seek to free the latent possibilities and to give an opportunity for individual initiative: "Mind will be suffered to expand itself in proportion as occasion and impression shall excite it, and not tortured and enervated by being cast in a particular mould."[3]

The child was to be allowed to do and learn the thing that he desired, and whose utilitarian value he recognized. Knowledge was the basis of a happy society. With the introduction of the experimental, scientific procedure, the "lethargy of the soul" would be gone forever. Under such circumstances there would be no "sense of neglect and oppression" but rather a realization of the meaning of further endeavor.[4]

Education and political reform were considered inseparable. Innovation in order to be constructive must be directed and moderated. If the child were allowed to live naturally and to receive his education in connection with real purposeful activities, he would proceed, "With as ardent a passion for innovation as ever"[1] although he would feel "himself more

[1] Godwin, William, *An Enquiry Concerning Political Justice*, Vol. 1, pp. 17-18. 1793.
[2] *Ibid.* Vol. 2, pp. 384-385. 1793.   [3] *Ibid.*, Vol. 2, pp. 284-285. 1793.
[4] *Ibid.*, Vol. 2, pp. 341-342. 1793.

patient and tranquil" because of the habit of experimentation.[1] Education for constructive citizenship should involve
"investigation into the humbler walks of private life" as well
as into "the cause of reform." [2] Education should be an
engine of government but not for the kind of governments
that never changed. "It is the characteristic of the mind
to be capable of improvement. An individual surrenders the
best attribute of man, the moment he resolves to adhere to
certain fixed principles." Under such a system, "He is no
longer a man; he is the ghost of a departed man." [3]

Godwin opposed a national system of education, generally
speaking, because it tended to "perpetuate its institutions"
and for that reason he believed that, as conditions were,
education might better be left to private enterprise.[4] He
did not see the possibility of making education a matter of
scientific, open-minded procedure if it were determined by
a national authority. His advocacy of a system of education
that would be pragmatic and scientific in its method was in
harmony with the eighteenth century movement. He said:
"An incessant recurrence to experiment and actual observation, is . . . the method adopted in the present volume." [5]
He believed that "All education is despotism. It is perhaps
impossible for the young to be conducted without introducing
in many cases the tyranny of implicit obedience." [6] For this
reason he believed that a public system of education would
be better than private tutors because in a public system of
education the pupil would not be under such close surveil-
lance. He would be given freedom of initiative, and greater
personal responsibility for his behavior.[7] Education should

[1] Godwin, William, *The Enquirer,* pp. vii-viii. 1797.
[2] *Ibid.,* pp. vii-viii. 1797.
[3] Godwin, William, *An Enquiry Concerning Political Justice,* Vol. 2,
p. 210. 1793.
[4] *Ibid.,* Vol. 2, pp. 212-213. 1793.
[5] Godwin, William, *The Enquirer,* p. vi. 1797.
[6] *Ibid.,* p. 48. 1797.   [7] *Ibid.,* pp. 45-46, 49, 50. 1797.

consist in allowing the child to evaluate for himself, to direct his own efforts, to learn through activity and real experience, for in this way the child would become the real determiner of his own acts. Godwin urged: "The most desirable mode of education therefore, in all instances where it shall be found sufficiently practicable, is that which is careful that all the acquisitions of the pupil shall be preceded and accompanied by desire. The best motive to learn, is a perception of the value of the thing learned. The worst motive, without deciding whether it be necessary to have recourse to it, may well be affirmed to be constraint and fear."[1] Such learning does not proceed from "intrinsic excellence of the object, but from the accidental attractions which the teacher may have annexed to it."[2]

The teacher must follow the pupil and not the pupil follow the teacher. Godwin said further, "According to the received modes of education, the master goes first, and the pupil follows. According to the method here recommended, it is probable that the pupil should go first, and the master follow. To some persons this expression may be ambiguous. The sort of 'going first' and 'following' here censured may be compared to one person's treading over a portion of ground, and another's coming immediately after, treading in his footsteps." No master, therefore, should direct the pupils in such a way as "to supercede in them the exercise of their own discretion."[3]

Since "Liberty is one of the most desirable of all sublunary advantages, I would willingly therefore communicate knowledge unfringing, or with as little as possible violence to, the volition and individual judgment of the person to be instructed." He added: "Motives are of two sorts, intrinsic and extrinsic. Intrinsic motives are those which

[1] Godwin, William, *The Enquirer*, pp. 62-63. 1797.
[2] *Ibid.*, pp. 63-65. 1797.
[3] *Ibid.*, pp. 63-65. 1797.

arise from the inherent nature of the thing recommended. Extrinsic motives are those which have no constant and unalterable connection with the thing recommended, but are combined with it by accident or at the pleasure of some individual." He continued: "The first of these classes of motives is unquestionably the best. To be governed by such motives is the pure and genuine condition of a rational being." If we are educated in this manner, "It elevates us with a sense of independence." This sense of independence with ability of self-determination was considered essential in the furtherance of progress.[1]

The advantages of the new type of education based on child activity, child initiative, and exploration, were: "First, liberty"; "Secondly, the judgment would be strengthened by continual exercise. Boys would no longer learn their lessons after the manner of parrots"; "Thirdly, to study for ourselves is the true method of acquiring habits of activity." [2] There should be absolute respect for the child. The despotism of masters should be broken. They had exercised their "despotism in security, because its object was unable to resist." [3] Godwin declared that the child "has a claim upon his little sphere of empire and discretion; and he is entitled to his appropriate portion of independence." [3] Godwin saw clearly the relation of enlightenment to institutional change. As long as "falsehood be with mankind at large reduced to a system, recommended by the prudent, commanded by the magistrate, inforced by the moralists, and practiced under a thousand forms, the individual will not always have the simplicity to be sincere, or the courage to be true." He said, "an education, deprived of these errors, seems to present itself as the most

---

[1] Godwin, William, *The Enquirer,* pp. 61-63. 1797.
[2] *Ibid.,* p. 65. 1797. [3] *Ibid.,* p. 71. 1797.

natural exchange, and must necessarily render its subject virtuous." [1]

The reasons for giving at such length this exposition of Godwin's conceptions of education are: first, it is most representative of the scientific, objective method of education; second, it is definitely based upon the eighteenth century conception of the child as a creative being; and third, it shows clearly the relation between the working out of desirable political reforms and the establishment of habits of experimentation and creative activity. The importance of education in the eighteenth century conception of societal advancement may be seen when we find that the Physiocrats with all of their contention for the doctrine of *laissez-faire* believed that the state should institute compulsory education. This attitude may be explained by their fear of the Jesuits. [2]

Condorcet conceived a system of education and proposed it to the French nation, whereby the principles of the French revolution might be diffused and made energetic throughout the nation. The heart of this system was science and experimentation, and an objective philosophical outlook. Condorcet believed that freedom of action lay rather in the type of education than in any mode of external control. To his end he sought to establish a proper public freedom of thought and teaching throughout the educational system of France. In his *Tableau historique des progres de l'esprit humain,* 1793, he elaborated his theory of social progress. [3] In this he gave his dynamic conception of social science through which was to be realized the evolution of freedom through

[1] Godwin, William, *Enquiry Concerning Political Justice,* Vol. 1, pp. 23-26. 1793.

[2] Dunning, William Archibald, *A History of Political Theories from Rousseau to Spencer,* p. 62. 1920. Lewinski, Jan St., *The Founders of Political Economy,* pp. 102-103. 1922.

[3] Barnes, Harry E., "Sociology before Comte," *Amer. Journal of Sociology,* Vol. XXIII, No. 2, p. 223. 1917.

enlightenment.[1] Nothing less than universal education that
would extend to all classes would be adequate for the
achievement of the ends for which the French Revolution
had been fought. The system recommended in his report
may be considered the fruition of the whole of the eighteenth century movement.[2]

The greatest proponent of universal education for law
and order was Rousseau, and his influence was most extensive. He urged that if education were made public and
universal, mankind could in this manner free itself from the
evils that had accumulated through the past generations.[3]
The development of social science should be combined with
a system of education that would liberate the human mind
from tradition and replace the rule of tradition by the rule
of reason.[4] As early as 1740 the idea of general progress
and the relation of education to this progress was a frequent
topic of discussion in the salons of France.[5]

Summary. The doctrine of the indefinite perfectibility of
man and of institutions was defined and its implications elaborated in the eighteenth century. It became the dominant
motif of the Enlightenment and of the revolutionary democratic movements in America and France. The idea that man
was progressive by nature stimulated an analysis of the conditions that govern progress. This led to the conception of
man as a being governed by natural law, the discovery of
which was necessary in order that progress might be scien-

[1] Levy-Bruhl, Lucien, *History of Modern Philosophy in France*, pp.
300-302. 1899.
[2] Bury, John B., *The Idea of Progress*, pp. 206-207, 208, 209, 201-212.
1920.
[3] Levy-Bruhl, Lucien, *History of Modern Philosophy in France*, pp.
237, 238, 239, 245, 265, 266-267, 268. 1899.
[4] *Ibid.*, pp. 8, 13-14, 33, 36-37, 226, 228, 230. 1899; Boucke, O. Fred,
The Development of Economics, pp. 52-53, 75, 77, 82-83, 88-89. 1920;
Bury, John B., *The Idea of Progress*, pp. 164, 165, 227. 1920.
[5] Bury, John B., *The Idea of Progress*, pp. 128, 130-131, 135, 136, 139.
1920.

tifically directed. The institutions that prevailed were in general obsolete and had been the result of chance and superstition. Institutions could alone be justified if they contributed to the advancement and welfare of mankind. In order that mankind might progress maximally, institutions must be flexible, fluid, and evolutionary. The only adequate means for freeing man from the limitations of superstition and archaic institutions would be a system of education that would make inevitable a scientific, objective, experimental attitude that would lead to creative innovation and that would energize reconstruction of everything related to the progress of man. The lines of progress could in this way be scientifically determined.

CHAPTER TWO

PRINCIPLES OF THE AMERICAN REVOLUTION

Separation from England. The separation from England
has been dated from the publication of *Common Sense* by
Thomas Paine,[1] early in 1776. Until that time the principal aim of the colonists had been a modification of the
policy of England toward the American colonies. Some of
the American patriots such as Otis and John Adams had
stood for separation before this, but it took the popular
presentation of this question as it was given in *Common
Sense* to win a sufficient support for a declaration of independence.

Because of his revolutionary principles and his genius for

[1] For the following reasons Thomas Paine has been chosen as typical
of the philosophy, in the main, that forms the basis of the plans set
forth in this study for a national system of education in the United
States : First, Thomas Paine's extraordinary ability to put into the language of the multitude the meaning of the profound principles of the
Declaration of Independence and of the eighteenth century revolt against
fixed institutions, made him the immediate source of much of the American thinking during the period from 1774 to 1800 ; second, the larger
movement toward democracy is also represented by him through his
relation to the liberal or radical thinkers in England and through his
connection with the French Revolution. The wider bearings of the
present study were too complex to be included except by implication,
but it is hoped that other studies may grow out of this that will more
fully set forth the larger movement. Third, again, as with Godwin for
the European phase, Thomas Paine represents the vividness of the as yet
untouched sources of the more radical type of American pamphleteers.
This vividness would be lost unless at least one source were given
somewhat in detail. State papers and reports have smothered these
sources. And, fourth, Paine saw and expressed most clearly the implications of the American Revolution for societal reconstruction—a reconstruction that did not take place in the constitutional conventions.

expressing them, Thomas Paine was brought to America by Benjamin Franklin to be the pamphleteer for the American Revolution. His essays were written by the camp-fires of the Revolutionary army and were read to all of the soldiers by the order of Washington. A sentence in Thomas Paine's *Letter to the People of France* most aptly gives the key to his life work: "Let us punish by instructing rather than by revenge."[1] It was his belief that the abuses of mankind rested ultimately in ignorance and that enlightenment was the sure remedy for oppression. He was made, in fact, the master teacher of the American nation in the principles of democracy.

He did not hesitate to announce immediately that the colonists should seek no course other than that of separation: "This new world hath been the asylum for the persecuted lovers of civil and religious liberty from *every part* of Europe. Hitherto have they fled, not from the tender embraces of the mother, but from the cruelty of the monster."[2] He argued that since the inhabitants of America were from every part of Europe and since England had proved herself to be anything but a mother, there was no more allegiance demanded of the colonists to England than to any other country. The fact was that they had fled to this country for freedom and it would be a mistake to allow the persecutions to pursue them. Hence Paine said, "Wherefore I reprobate the phrase of parent or mother country applied to England only, as being false, selfish, narrow and ungenerous."[3] Thomas Paine gave to the American Revolution from the very beginning the humanitarian motif and cut clean from any allegiance to England. He said, "Examine that connexion and dependence, on principles of nature and

---

[1] Paine's Works, *Letter to the People of France*, p. 362.   1797 ed.
[2] Paine's Works, *Common Sense*, p. 20.   1797 ed.
[3] *Ibid.*, p. 20.   1797 ed.

common sense," [1] and stated further, "In short, independence is the only *bond* that can tie and keep us together." [2]

Thomas Paine announced the doctrine of permanent separation from European quarrels in his publication of *The Crisis,* in 1777, exactly twenty years before Washington's similar declaration. Paine said, "It certainly ought to be a conscientious as well as political consideration with America, not to dip her hands in the bloody work of Europe." He continued: "Our situation affords us a retreat from their cabals, and the present happy union of the states bids fair for extirpating the future use of arms from one quarter of the world." In the same connection he said of the Quakers, "Yet such has been the irreligious politics of the present leaders of the Quakers, that, for the sake of they scarce know what, they would cut off every hope of such a blessing by tying this continent to Britain, like Hector to the chariot-wheel of Achilles, to be dragged through all the miseries of endless European wars." This they did in the name of peace. Here we find, then, the doctrine proclaimed by Washington—that of a complete separation from European affairs. [3]

In 1778 Paine declared for the national character of the United States: "A good opinion of ourselves is exceedingly necessary in private life, but absolutely necessary in public life, and of the utmost importance in supporting national character." [4] Thomas Paine vigorously and constantly set forth this principle throughout his tracts by dwelling upon the vast resources peculiar to America, the strength of American character, the purity of American character as compared with that of lords and ladies, and especially the great courage of the Americans. A much longer list of

---

[1] Paine's Works, *Common Sense,* p. 19.   1797 ed.
[2] *Ibid.,* p. 47.   1797 ed.
[3] Paine's Works, *The Crisis,* p. 83.   1797 ed.
[4] *Ibid.,* p. 171.   1797 ed.

virtues could be added. He also used freely the term, 'United States.' He was on his job every moment for building up the morale of colonies. He declared, "We have equalled the bravest in time of danger, and excelled the wisest in the construction of civil governments." [1] Apropos of the fate of Charleston, he declared, "America, rich in patriotism and produce, can want neither men nor supplies, when a serious necessity calls them forth" [2] and added, "The ravages of the enemy will be short and limited, and like all their former ones will produce a victory over themselves." [3]

In 1782 he wrote as though he considered the intellectual change fairly accomplished. To the Abbe Raynal he wrote, "Our style and manner of thinking have undergone a revolution, more extraordinary than the political revolution of the country." Further, "We can look back upon our prejudices, as if they had been prejudices of other people." He rejoiced in the fact that the Revolution had come violently: "Had America dropped quietly from Britain, no material change, in sentiment, had taken place." [4] He went on, "We are really another people and cannot go back to ignorance and prejudice. The mind once enlightened cannot again become dark." [5] He was convinced that a profound intellectual independence had been established as well as a political independence. He never ceased to urge this national independence and character: "That which must more forcibly strike a thoughtful penetrating mind, and which includes and renders easy all inferior concerns, is the *Union Of The States*. On this, our great national character depends." [6] He concluded, "Our great title is, *Americans—* our inferior one varies with the place." [7]

[1] Paine's Works, *The Crisis*, p. 121. 1797 ed.
[2] *Ibid.*, p. 162. 1797 ed.   [3] *Ibid.*, p. 164. 1797 ed.
[4] Paine's Works, *Letter to Abbe Raynal*, p. 297. 1797 ed.
[5] *Ibid.*, p. 298. 1797 ed.
[6] Paine's Works, *The Crisis* p. 221. 1797 ed.   [7] *Ibid.*, p. 222. 1797 ed.

The natural basis of society. Certain principles were to be characteristic of the new nation. These principles were to be those of nature and not external. The society established here was to be based upon man's natural tendency to associate with his fellows. It is of interest to note that Otis, in his *Speech on Writs of Assistance,* declared that man was naturally a social animal. He said, "If it was inconsistent with the dignity of human nature to say, that men were gregarious animals, like geese, it surely could offend no delicacy to say, they were social animals by nature." He asserted that the rights of life, liberty, and property were "derived only from nature, and the author of nature; and that they were inherent, inalienable, and indefeasible by any Laws, pacts, contracts, covenants, or stipulations, which man could devise." [1] Otis declared further that "every man, merely natural, was an independent sovereign, subject to no law, but the law written on his heart, and revealed to him by his Maker, in the constitution of his nature." This is from President Adams' report from notes he took on the occasion of the delivery of Otis's speech, and he says, "Young as I was, and ignorant as I was, I shuddered at the doctrine he taught." [2] Here we have the full announcement of Rousseau's theory a year before the first publication of *Le Contrat Social.* However, it seems unjustifiable to say that this proves that Rousseau's influence was practically absent from the Revolution. This position is evidently wrong. The political documents and tracts of the period give abundant evidence of Rousseau's influence.

The views of Otis and of Rousseau were also expressed by Thomas Paine. He said that men should not confound society with government, that society was natural and that government was artificial. Government should be in har-

[1] Otis's Speech on Writs of Assistance, *Amer. History Leaflets,* No. 33, p. 19. 1761.
[2] *Ibid.,* No. 33, p. 18. 1761.

mony with the law of nature. In this particular portion
the influence of Rousseau on Thomas Paine seems evident.
The symbolism of nature and the pastoral settings suggest
Rousseau. The clever simplicity and grace with which
Paine indicated the process of society as it evolves and be-
comes more complex is as charming as the style of *Le
Contrat Social.*[1]

In *Common Sense* Paine launches at once into the subject
of the origin of kings and especially the origin of the English
kings. His racy portrayal of this is as follows: "A French
bastard, landing with an armed banditti, and establishing
himself king of England, against the consent of the natives,
is in plain terms a very paltry, rascally original. It certainly
hath no divinity in it." Again, "However, it is needless to
spend much time in exposing the folly of hereditary right;
if there are any so weak as to believe it, let him promiscuously worship the ass and the lion, and welcome." He
argued: "The plain truth is, that the antiquity of English
monarchy will not bear looking into."[2] He went on: "No
truly natural . . . reason can be assigned . . . for the distinction of men into *Kings* and *Subjects.* . . . How impious
is the title of sacred majesty applied to a worm."[3] The idea
of a monarchical government based upon succession was
contrary to natural equality: "All men being originally
equals, no *one* by *birth,* could have a right to set up his own
family, in perpetual preference to all others forever."[4]
Nature had given no assurance that in the next succession
they might not be "under the government of a rogue, or a
fool."[5]

There could be but one basis for a just and permanent
society and that was "the natural constitution of man." This

[1] Paine's Works, *Common Sense,* p. 5. 1797 ed.
[2] *Ibid.,* pp. 14-15. 1797 ed.   [3] *Ibid.,* p. 10. 1797 ed.
[4] *Ibid.,* p. 13, 1797 ed.   [5] *Ibid.,* p. 14. 1797 ed.

"existed prior to government, and would exist if the formality of government was abolished." [1] Man was created by nature for social life. "She has implanted within him a system of social affections." [2] Again, "In short, man is so naturally a creature of society, that it is almost impossible to put him out of it." Since "All the great laws of society are laws of nature" the only sound government is that which recognizes and bases itself upon the nature of man.[3]

The people the source of power. In the *Journal of Proceedings of the Continental Congress* for 1774 we find a resolution *"That* the foundation of English liberty and of all free government, is a right in the people to participate in their legislative council." [4] Richard Price stated the same doctrine when he said, "The question with all liberal inquirers ought to be, not what jurisdiction over them *Precedents, Statutes* and *Charters* give, but what reason and equity, and the rights of humanity give." [5] The Abbe Raynal in his treatise, *The Revolution of America,* said that it was by the "double abuse of credulity and authority that all the absurdities in matters of religion and of policy have been introduced into the world for the harassing and the crushing of the human race." [6] In speaking of the effects upon the individual of England's treatment of the colonies and of similar attempts at absolute control, he said, "The servile disposition which she stamps upon his soul in consequence, extends itself throughout. It makes a duty of resignation as of meanness; and kissing chains of all kinds with respect, trembles to examine either its doctrines or its laws." [7]

---

[1] Paine's Works, *Rights of Man,* p. 348. 1880 ed.
[2] *Ibid.,* p. 349. 1880 ed.
[3] *Ibid.,* p. 350. 1880 ed.
[4] *U. S. Continental Congress, Journal of Proceedings of,* p. 61. 1774.
[5] Price, Richard, *Observations on the Nature of Civil Lberty,* p. 32. 1776.
[6] Abbe Raynal, *The Revolution of America,* p. 15, 1782.
[7] *Ibid.,* p. 15. 1782.

Again he said, "The British ministry violated this dignity of man." [1]   Thomas Paine recognized the same principle, of the people as the source of power, when he said, *"It is only owing to the constitution of the people, and not the constitution of the government,* that the crown is not as oppressive in England as in Turkey." [2]   In his argument for representative government he contended for frequent elections in order that the elected might not form to themselves interests separate from those of the electors.   He argued as did Webster that the only way to keep the legislators from legislating against the interests of the people was through a sufficiently frequent election to establish an identity of interest with the people, since, if their own interests suffered by the laws they passed, they would not be apt to oppress themselves. [3]   John Adams, in this same connection, said, in 1776, "The greatest care should be employed in constituting this Representative Assembly.   It should be in miniature, an exact portrait of the people at large.   It should think, feel, reason and act like them." [4]   Granville Sharp, in *A Declaration of the People's Natural Right to Share in the Legislature, &c.,* said, "Since *all Men are naturally equals,* and *a Man* who submits himself to the Sovereignty or Government of another, does not on that account cease to be *a Man;* neither can the temporal Sovereign himself be released from the *natural* types of *that* relation." [5]   He said further, "To suppose that *The Will of the Prince* is to be allowed *the force of the Law* is the highest absurdity." [6]

The problem of preserving the sovereign right of the

[1] Abbe Raynal, *The Revolution of America,* p. 15.   1782.
[2] Paine's Works, *Common Sense,* p. 9.   1797 ed.
[3] *Ibid.,* p. 7.   1797 ed.
[4] Adams, John, *Thoughts on Government,* p. 9.   1776.
[5] Sharp, Granville, *A Declaration of the People's Natural Right to Share in the Legislature,* etc., p. xiv.   1776.
[6] *Ibid.,* p. xv.   1776.

people and their sovereign power was one of the central issues of the Revolution. It was the disregard of this sovereignty that had driven the colonists from Europe. This was cogently stated by the Continental Congress in 1774:

> "WHEREAS the power but not the justice, the vengeance but not the wisdom of Great-Britain, which of old persecuted, scourged, and excited our fugitive parents from their native shores, now pursues us their guiltless children with unrelenting severity: . . . whereby the unalienable and inestimable inheritance, which we derived from nature, the constitution of Britain, and the privileges warranted to us in the charter of the province, is totally wrecked, annulled, and vacated, posterity will acknowledge that virtue which preserved them free and happy." [1]

The same principle was stated in an *Oration upon the Beauties of Liberty, or, The Essential Rights of the Americans:* "the people are the right and the fountain of power and authority, the original seat of Majesty—the Author of laws, and the creators of officers to execute them." [2] In a work on the *Rights of the People* that ran through a great number of editions it was stated, "In all disputes between power and liberty, power must always be proved, but liberty proves itself; the one being founded upon positive law, the other upon the law of nature." [3] It was said further that "All political societies began from a voluntary union and mutual agreement of men; freely acting in the choice of the governors, and forms of government." [4] The extensive character of this work is indicated by a front page title: "The judgment of whole *Kingdoms* and *nations* concerning the Rights, Power, and Prerogative of *Kings,* and the Rights,

---

[1] *U. S. Continental Congress, Journal of the Proceedings of,* Sept. 5, 1774, p. 31. 1774.

[2] *Oration upon the Beauties of Liberty, or, the Essential Rights of the Americans,* p. v. 1775.

[3] Lord Sommers, *Rights of the People,* p. 31. 12th ed. 1774.

[4] *Ibid.,* p. 26. 12th ed. 1774.

Privileges, & Properties of the *People.*" [1] Following this is a subtitle which shows that the work historically proves that neither man nor God believed in "Absolute *Passive Obedience.*" In the body of the work it is further stated that even God recognized that all government was "to be exercised according to the laws of Nature" and for "the benefit of mankind"; [2] also that every one was master "of his own property and liberty"; and all power was delegated to the ruler by the people. [3] They were the source of power, for "it is by virtue of compacts, stipulations, compromises, and agreements, that all governments have their original and establishment." [4] In his *Defense of the American Constitution* John Adams indicated some of the reasons for the degree of enlightenment that gave rise to the principles of the Revolution:

> "The arts and sciences, in general, during the three or four last centuries, have had a regular course of progressive improvement. The inventions in the mechanic arts, the discoveries in natural philosophy, navigation, and commerce, and the advancement of civilization and humanity, have occasioned changes in the conditions of the world, and the human character, which would have astonished the most refined nations of antiquity." [4]

It is impossible to indicate the many efforts to trace the origin of government in order to demonstrate that the people were the real source of power and had a natural right to alter any government that proved to be unfriendly to their interests. [6]

[1] Lord Sommers, *Rights of the People*, p. i. 12th ed. 1774.
[2] *Ibid.*, p. 9. 12th ed. 1774.
[3] *Ibid.*, p. 12. 12th ed. 1774.   [4] *Ibid.*, p. 14. 12th ed. 1774.
[5] Adams, John, *Defense of the American Constitution*, Vol. I, p. i. 1787.
[6] Priestley, Joseph, *An Essay on the First Principles of Government, and on the Nature of Political, Civil, and Religious Liberty.* 1768; Quincy, Josiah, *Observations on the Act of Parliament Commonly Called the Boston Port-Bill; with Thoughts on Civil Society and Standing*

Inalienable rights of life, liberty and happiness. The doctrine of inalienable rights had many sources. The experience of the colonists as pioneers had caused them to see what would happen if man had the freedom to achieve. The fact that resources were seen to be unlimited and that the development of these resources was conceived to be necessary for the welfare of the community meant that there had been considerable encouragement for the establishment of independent fortunes. Many who had come to America and had had their passage paid, had freed themselves from being "bound out" and had become independent and prosperous. There was also the influence of the liberal movements in France and England during the eighteenth century. The Physiocrats in France had proclaimed the doctrine of *laissez-faire,* which was welcomed by both the rich and poor in America because of the circumstances existing here. The philosophy of Locke had led many English writers to emphasize the social contract as the basis of social control. The sanctions of authority had been largely broken by the most virile writers in England and France.[1]

Armies. Boston. 1774; Wilson, James, *Considerations of the Nature and Extent of the Legislative Authority of the British Parliament.* 1774; *America's Appeal to an Impartial World. Wherein the rights of the Americans, as men, British subjects, and as colonists; the equity of the demand, and the manner in which it is made upon them by Great Britain, are stated and considered.* 1775; Leonard, Daniel, *The Origin of the American Contest with Great Britain, or the Present Political State of the Massachusetts-Bay, in general.* 1775; Sherer, Jean Benoit, *Recherches historiques et heographiques sur le nouveau-monde.* 1777; Russell, William, *The History of America, from its Discovery by Columbus to the Conclusion of the Late War. With an appendix, containing an account of the present unhappy contest between Great Britain and her colonies,* 1778; Linguet, Simon Nicholas Henri, *Political and Philosophical Speculations on the Characteristics of the Present Century with Reflections on the Probable Effects of American Independency.* 1778; Burke, Edmund, *A Vindication of Natural Society; or A View of the Miseries . . . Arising by Mankind from . . . Artificial Society.* 1780; Hilliard, d'Auberteil Michel Rene, *Essais historiques et politiques sur des Anglo-Americaines.* 1781-2.
[1] Sharp, Granville, *Declaration of the People's Natural Right to Share in the Legislature.* 1774; Dickinson, John, *Essay on the Constitutional*

Thomas Paine declared that "Rights are inherently in all the inhabitants; but charters, by annulling those rights in the majority, leave the rights, by exclusion, in the hands of a few." [1] He hated those who lived "in indolence and luxury, on the spoil and labors of the public." [2] Aristocrats did not belong to the producing class in his estimation. He acknowledged himself "a common enemy of sinecure placemen and pensioners." [3]

The volume entitled *English Liberties* contained a documentary history of the progress of liberty in England with

Power of Great Britain over the Colonies in America. 1774; Bollan, William, *The Petitions of Mr. Bollan, an agent for the Council of the Province of Massachusetts Bay, lately presented to the two houses of parliament; with a brief introduction relating to the law of nature, the authority of human rulers, and the subjects common right of defence; with subsequent observations.* 1774; Jefferson, Thomas, *A Summary View of the Rights of British America, set forth in some resolutions intended for the inspection of the people of Virginia, now in convention.* 1774; Almon, John, *A Collection of Interesting Authentic Papers relative to the dispute between Great Britain and America; shewing the causes of that misunderstanding from 1764-1775.* 1775; Regulus, pseud., *A Defence of the Resolutions and Address of the American Congress in reply to taxation no tyranny,* etc. 1775; Toplady, Augustus Montagne, *An Old Fox Tarred and Feathered.* 1775; Demophilus, *The Genuine Principles of the Ancient Saxon, or English Constitution, carefully collected from the best authorities; with some observation on their peculiar fitness for the United colonies in general, and Pennsylvania in particular.* 1776; *Affaires de l'Angleterre et de l'Amerique.* 1776-1669; *Expose des droits des colonies britanniques, pour justifier le projet de leur independence.* 1776; Leacock, John, *The fall of British Tyranny; or, American liberty triumphant. The first campaign, a tragi-comedy of five acts,* as lately planned at the Royal Theatrum Pandemonium at St. James's. The principal place of action in America. 1776; Blacklock, Thomas, *Remarks on the Nature and Extent of Liberty, as Compatible with the Genius of Civil Societies; on the Principles of Government and the Proper Limits of its Power in a Free State.* 1776; Pinto, Isaac de, *Letters on the American Troubles.* Translated from the French. 1776; Pinto, Isaac de, *Reponse de M. J. de Pinto, aux Observations d'un homme impartial, sur la lettre a M. S. B. dans le Jamaique, on sujet des troubles que agitent actuellement toute l'Amerique Septentrionale.* 1776; Dupont de Nemours, *Physiocratie.* 1676; Mercier de la Riviere, *L'ordre naturel et essentiel des sociétés politiques.* 1676.

[1] Paine's Works, *Rights of Man,* p. 400. 1800 ed.
[2] *Ibid.,* p. 304. 1797 ed.
[3] *Ibid.,* p. 306. 1797 ed.

most incisive critical comments.   This ran through several editions in America.[1]

In *Familiar Dialogues between Americus and Britanicus* it was said: "The right of private judgment, continued the animated *Patriot,* the right of private judgment, Sir, is inalienable. . . . It is of heavenly original. . . . The right of private judgment is beyond doubt, Sir, the native right of every peasant in Great-Britain: Why should I say Great Britain?   When I might at once have said, *The Great Globe Itself.*" [2]   A sermon on *The Principles of the Revolution Vindicated* ran through several editions almost as soon as it came off the press.   In this the contention was made that while some disparity might exist "with respect to corporal strength and in intellectual ability", it could not be doubted, "when we compare together the most perfect of our Species with the most imperfect" that there was nothing present in any differences that might be found that could "induce amongst free agents any natural dependence or inequality, any right to dominion on the one hand, or obligation to subjection on the other." [3]   A "System of natural law" prevailed that placed beyond doubt "the natural equality and independence of individuals." [4]

The right of the people to determine the form of government.   The doctrine of natural rights implied the doctrine of revolution.   John I. Johnson in his *Reflections on Political Society* indicated how the revolutionary writers of the eighteenth century had prepared the people for revolution.   He said that "The labours of Montesquieu, of Rousseau, of Vol-

---

[1] Care, Henry, *English Liberties, on the Free-born Subjects' Inheritance, containing Magna Charta, Charta de Foresta, the Statute de Talagio non concedendo, the Habeas Corpus Act, and several other Statutes; with comments on each of them.*   1771.

[2] *Familiar Dialogues between Americus and Britanicus,* p. 12.   1776.

[3] Watson, Richard, *The Principles of the Revolution Vindicated,* pp. 7-8.   1776.

[4] *Ibid.,* p. 10.   1776.

taire, and of Helvetius . . . Hobbes, More, and Machiavel
. . . and the generous Sydney" had been "uniform in their
vindication of freedom of thinking, and freedom of writing"
and it was from such writings that the American and French
Revolutions derived their principles.[1] In the various petitions and proceedings of the legislative bodies there was a
constant reiteration of the basic principles of the Revolution.
Among these was the right to change government by force, if
necessary, in order to secure the natural rights of the people.[2]

Thomas Paine contended both in the American and French
Revolutions for the right of each generation to legislate for
itself. He said, "What have we to do with a thousand years.

[1] Johnson, John I., *Reflections on Political Society*, pp. 14-15. 1797.

[2] Cooper, Myles, *The American querist: or some questions relative to
the present disputes between Great Britain and her colonies.* 1774;
Drayton, William Henry, *A Letter from Freemen of South Carolina, to
the deputies of North America.* 1774; Quincy, Josiah, *Observations on
the Act of Parliament Commonly Called the Boston Port-Bill; with
thoughts on civil society and standing armies.* 1774; Rokeby, Matthew
Robinson, *Considerations on the Measures carrying on with Respect to
the British Colonies in North America.* 1774; Farmer, a Westchester,
pseud., *A View of the Controversy between Great Britain and her
Colonies.* 1774; U. S. Continental Congress, *Journal of the Proceedings
of the Congress.* 1774; *America's Appeal to the Impartial World.
Wherein the Rights of the Americans, as men, British subjects, and
as colonists; the equity of the demand, and the manner in which it is
made upon them by Great Britain, are stated and considered.* 1775;
*Authentic Papers from America: Submitted to the dispassionate con-
sideration of the Public.* 1775; *Declaration (The) by the representatives of the United Colonies of North America, now met in general
Congress in Philadelphia, setting forth the causes and necessity of
taking up arms; the letter of the 12 united colonies by their delegates
in Congress to the inhabitants of Great Britain; their humble petition to
His Majesty and their address to the people of Ireland, collected to-
gether by lovers of peace.* 1775; Leonard, Daniel, *The Origin of the
American Contest with Great Britain.* 1775; Braxton, Carter, *An
Address to the Convention of the colony and ancient Dominion of
Virginia; on the Subject of Government.* 1776; Johnson, Allen, *Readings in Constitutional History, 1776-1786.* 1912; Robinson, Matthew, *A
Further Examination of our Present American measures and of the
Reasons and Principles on which they were founded.* 1776; U. S. Continental Congress, *Journals of the Proceedings of Congress held at Phila-
delphia.* 1776; *Collection of Interesting Authentic Papers, relative to the
disputes between Great Britain and America.* 1777.

Our life time is but a short portion of that period, and if we find the wrong in existence as soon as we begin to live, that is the point of time at which it begins for us; and our right to resist it, is the same as if it had never existed before." [1] The same contention was made by Richard Watson when he said, "No individual can have the right to give his consent for any other; nor any one generation of men, a right to establish any form of Government which their Children will not have an equal right to alter or abolish as they think fit." [2] Rokeby said that unless the doctrine of natural rights obtained, "Here are all mankind at once condemned to a perpetual bondage: 'There remains no right of resistance, no remedy, no redress, no means of recovery for them." [3] "A total, general despotism must by degrees obtain and in the end reign everywhere." [4] The Abbe Raynal declared, "It would be madness to will and to chuse for him who is yet unborn, for him who will not yet exist for ages." [5]

All institutions perfectible, mutable. The right of the people to change the form of government rested upon the doctrine of the mutability of institutions and their perfectibility. Lord Sommers in 1774 made the distinction between positive law and natural law, and argued that "The safety of the people is the supreme law, and what they by common consent have enacted only for the public safety, they may, without any obstacle, alter, when things require it, by the like common consent." [6] Johnson raised the question: "Is

---

[1] Paine, Thomas, *Dissertation on First Principles of Government*, pp. 8, 19, 22, 24, 25, 26, 27. *Third Year of the French Republic.*
[2] Watson, Richard, *The Principles of the Revolution Vindicated*, p. 10. 1776.
[3] Rokeby, Baron, *A Further Examination of our Present American Measures*, p. 79. 1776.
[4] *Ibid.*, p. 79. 1776.
[5] Abbe Raynal, *The Revolution of America*, p. 23. 1782.
[6] Lord Sommers, *Rights of the People*, p. 26. 12th ed. 1774.

there nothing consolatory in the infinitude of mind? Or
has nature prescribed limits to the perfectibility of the human
character?"[1] and he raised the same questions in regard to
institutions: "Is not government an expedient? and as
such, is it not susceptible of indefinite improvement?"[2]
And again, "Is not man essentially progressive?"[3] It is
to be noted that these are rhetorical questions in a treatise
upon the political principles involved in the American and
French Revolutions. The Abbe Raynal saw a direct connection between the American Revolution and the eighteenth
century doctrine of the modifiability of institutions. He
said, "There is no form of government which has the prerogative to be immutable. No political authority, which,
created yesterday, or a thousand years ago, may not be
abrogated in ten years time or tomorrow." He said, more-
over, "Whoever thinks otherwise is a slave. It is to be the
idolator of the work of his own hands." This idolatry he
considered to have been given its death blow in the American Revolution.[4]

Johnson again said, "Science of politics is progressive.
. . . Its perfectible motion is gradually accelerated. . . .
The noblest efforts of the human mind have their imperfections, which time and experience alone can detect. The
labors of the intellect never are to be completed."[5] Again
he said, "With an enlightened people, changes and alterations
may be accomplished." He gloried in the fact that there
was general social upheaval, because "The tranquility of despotism is the tranquility of the grave." He showed at
length how the writers of the eighteenth century had stood
for "reason, toleration, and humanity."[6] Thomas Paine

---

[1] Johnson, John I., *Reflections on Political Society*, p. 10, 1797.
[2] *Ibid.*, p. 11. 1797.   [3] *Ibid.*, p. 16. 1797.
[4] Abbe Raynal, *The Revolution in America*, p. 23. 1782.
[5] Johnson, John I., *Reflections on Political Society*, p. 16. 1797.
[6] *Ibid.*, p. 12. 1797.

held that "Government ought to be as much open to improvement as anything which appertains to man." [1] In *America's
Appeal to the Impartial World* this principle is most aptly
developed and many of its implications are noted, especially
the need of a proper form of education. It is noted, "Some
begin their government with their political existence; it grows
up with them; the great first principles thereof, are never
altered while they continue a people, and become so incorporated with their being, that they have the force of natural,
rather than political institutions. Others after a century or
two have occasion to alter and new-model their old governments, or frame new ones: This is usually attended with
much difficulty and great danger, requires an extensive
knowledge of the genius, tempers, habits, laws and manners
of the people; and great judgment and skill, to adapt new regulations to old usages, so as to form a happy coalition." [2]

The denial of the right to legislate for other generations
implied the right of each generation to refashion all institutions. Paine said, "The fee absolute was not in them
(former generations), it is not in us, it belongs to the
whole family of man, thro' all ages. If we think otherwise
than this, we think either as slaves or as tyrants. As slaves,
if we think that any former generation had a right to bind
us; as tyrants, if we think that we have the authority to
bind the generations that are to follow." [3] Again, "Every
age and generation is and must be (as a matter of right)
as free to act for itself in all cases, as the age and generation
that preceded it. The vanity and presumption of government beyond that of the grave is the most ridiculous and
insolent of all tyrannies." [4] This is almost the same phras-
ing as that used by Noah Webster.

[1] Complete Works of Thomas Paine, *Rights of Man*, p. 389. 1880 ed.
[2] *America's Appeal to the Impartial World*, p. 66. 1775.
[3] Paine, Thomas, *Dissertation on First Principles of Government*, p. 10.
Third Year of the French Republic.
[4] *Ibid.*, p. 12.

The Abbe Raynal expressed the meaning of the Revolution when he said, "There is no society but which has the same right to change as their ancestors had to adopt, their form of government; upon this point, it is with societies as if they were at the first moment of their civilization." [1] He continued, "It is impossible that you Englishmen, who have successfully undergone so many different revolutions in your political constitution, tossed as you have been from monarchy to tyranny, from tyranny to aristocracy, from aristocracy to democracy, and from democracy to anarchy; it is impossible that you, without accusing yourselves of rebellion and of perjury, can think otherwise than I do." [2] Englishmen by the very history of their political struggles were bound to the doctrine of the mutability and perfectibility of institutions.

Nevertheless, the Tory element in America were very active in their attempts to meet the arguments of the revolutionists in regard to the above principles, but with little success. [3] Even afer the close of the Revolution there was a great flood of pamphlets representing all shades of opinion from believers in Utopian democracy who offered schemes for world

[1] Abbe Raynal, *The Revolution in America*, p. 23. 1782.
[2] *Ibid.*, p. 22. 1782.
[3] Johnson, Samuel, *Taxation not Tyranny; an answer to the Resolutions and Address of the American Congress.* 1775; Serle, Ambrose, *Americans against Liberty; or; an essay on the nature and principles of true freedom, shewing that the designs and conduct of the Americans tend only to tyranny and slavery.* 1775; Wesley, John, *Calm Address to our American Colonies.* London, 1775; Shebbeare, John, *An Essay on the Origin, Progress, and Establishment of National Society; in which the principles of government, the definitions of physical, moral, civil, and religious liberty, contained in Dr. ·Price's Observations, &c. are fairly examined and fully refuted.* 1776; Abingdon (4 earl), Willoughby Bertie, *Thoughts on the Letter of Edmund Burke, esq., to the Sheriffs of Bristol, on the Affairs of America.* 1778; Tucker, Hosiah, *The Notions of Mr. Locke and his Followers, that all civil governments whatever, not founded on the personal choice of the governed, are so many usurptions of the unalienable rights of mankind, considered and examined.* 1778; *Case (The) and Claim of the American Loyalists impartially Stated and Considered;* printed by order of their agents. 1783.

peace and individual liberty, to the most enthusiastic supporters of absolute monarchy.[1]

Place of popular education in the Revolution. The bringing of Thomas Paine into the United States, even before the Revolution was well under way, was a recognition of the fact that if it were to be brought to a successful issue, it would have to be by a vigorous course of popular education in the principles of democracy. Thomas Paine was peculiarly fitted for the task and, as we have seen, he effectively brought to the American nation the message it needed for the hour. The philosophy of Paine may be reduced to two principles: "To follow nature" and to objectively "investigate the truth." He brought before the American nation at the critical moment when it was ripe for such a message the humanitarian outlook as the basis of the Revolution and the "control of reason" in the place of "tradition and authority." There was a broader phase of this educational movement which apparently has not yet been set out—the awakening

[1] Perisier, Antoine Marie, *Le destin de l'Amerique; ou, dialogues pittoresque dans lesquels on developpe la cause des evenments actuels, la politique et les interets des puissances de l'Europe relativement a cette guerre, et les suites qu'elle devroit avoir pour le bonheur de l'humanites, traduit fidelement de l'Anglais.* 1780. Not translated from English and published anonymously. Apparently not printed in London. Huntington, Joseph, *A Discourse adapted to the Present Day, on the Health and Happiness, or Misery and Ruin, of the Body Politic.* 1781; Northcote, Thomas, *Observations on the Natural and Civil Rights of Mankind, the Prerogative of Princes, and Powers of Government, in which the Equal and Universal Right of the People to Election and Representation, is Proved by direct and Conclusive Arguments.* 1781; *Indépendance (L') des Anglo-Americains démontrée utile a la Grande-Bretagne.* 1782; *Proposals to Amend and Perfect the Policy of the Government of the U. A. Of America; or, the fulfilling of the prophecies in the latter days, commenced by the independence of America. Containing a new mode of elections; with a method of supporting government without taxing or fining the people.* 1782; Tod. Thomas, *Consolatory Thoughts on American Independence; showing the great advantages that will arise from it to the manufactures, the agricultures, and commercial interest of Great Britain and Ireland.* 1782; *Rudiments of Law and Government, Deduced from the Law of Nature.* 1783; Bell, Robert, *Illuminations for Legislators and for Sentimentalists.* 1784.

of the American nation to the need of making permanent in the educational system a thorough mastery of the principles of democracy. If the power of public opinion were necessary to conduct an organized campaign against tyranny when oppression was evident on every hand, it would be far more necessary for the maintenance of democracy after that crisis was passed. The Abbe Raynal said, "Forget not that the lever of power has no other fulcrum than opinion; that the power of those who govern is in reality but the power of those who suffer government. Remind not the people attentively occupied by their labours, or sleeping in their chains, to lift up their eyes to truths too terrible for you; and whilst they are obeying, bring not to their remembrance their right to command." [1] The logic of this position did not stop with the Revolution.

The position taken in *America's Appeal to the Impartial World* was that "to investigate truth, is the highest achievement of reason; and to follow nature, the perfection of art." [2] If "By nature, every man . . . is his own legislator, judge, and avenger, and absolute lord of his own property", it must follow that if that legislation were to be wise and if it were to preserve his liberties, it must be by a thorough system of education suited to that purpose. [3] The position was further taken that "the strength and spring of every free government, is the virtue of the people; virtue grows on knowledge, and knowledge on education." [4] "Half the sum, employed to diffuse general knowledge; by erecting public seminaries, with masters well furnished to teach children, not only common learning, but to instruct and impress on their young and tender minds, the principles of virtue and rudiments of government, which would grow up with their growth, and derive strength from age; would be more effec-

---

[1] Abbe Raynal, *The Revolution of America*, p. 12. 1782.
[2] *America's Appeal to the Impartial World*, p. 65. 1775.
[3] *Ibid.*, p. 7. 1782.   [4] *Ibid.*, p. 67. 1775.

tual than all the brilliancy of a crown, or fortunes of a rock. This is the only permanent foundation of a free government; this is laying the foundation in a constitution, not without or over, but within the subjects; love not fear will become the spring of their obedience." [1] Thus we find that as early as 1775 the need for a peculiar type of education for democracy was clearly set forth.

Dr. Richard Price stated that the "principle of *Spontaneity, or Self-determination*" is that "which constitutes us *Agents.*" In his *Observations on the Nature of Civil Liberty* he said, "According to these definitions of the different kinds of liberty, there is one general idea, that runs through them all; I mean the idea of *Self-direction, or Self-government.*" [2] He continued, "As fas as, in any instance, the operation of any cause comes in to restrain the power of Self-government, so far Slavery is introduced." [3] Since "All civil government, as far as it can be denominated *free,* is the creature of the people. It originates with them. It is conducted under their direction," the obvious inference was that man should have a "Principle of motion within himself." [4] In the same treatise Dr. Price said that "Laws for the liberal education of youth, especially of the lower class of people, are so extremely wise and useful, that to a humane and generous mind, no expence for this purpose would be thought extravagant." Elsewhere will be noted the further suggestions of Price for a liberal system of education for America. [5] His influence upon thinking in the United States was generously acknowledged by all those who knew him. [6]

[1] *America's Appeal to the Impartial World,* p. 68. 1775.
[2] Price, Richard, D.D., F.R.S., *Observations on the Nature of Civil Liberty,* p. 3. 1776.
[3] *Ibid.,* p. 5. 1776.   [4] *Ibid.,* pp. 6, 16. 1776.
[5] Price, Richard, *Observations on the Importance of the American Revolution,* pp. 2-3, 6, 50, 50-52, 56-57. 1776.
[6] Kippis, Andrew, D.D., F.R.S., A.A., *An Address Delivered at the Internment of the Late Richard Price,* p. 15. 1791; Adams, John, *Defence of the American Constitution,* p. 3. 1786.

Thomas Paine declared that "the moral principle of revolutions is to instruct; not to destroy." [1] A citizen of democracy must be one who "sees the rationale of the whole system, its origin and its operations." [2] John Adams declared that "children should be educated and instructed in the principles of freedom." [3] There are many such expressions in the literature of the period.

Summary. The separation from England was based not so much upon the economic issues that occasioned the protest, as upon an outlook which was the result of pioneer experience and the eighteenth century liberal view of man. The mercantilist policy caused a reaction against its fundamental philosophy. This new outlook was set before the American nation through the writings of Thomas Paine and other pamphleteers, and in the various petitions and proceedings. This outlook involved a recognition of the natural rights of man, the natural basis of society, the mutability and perfectibility of institutions, the utilitarian, creative conception of their functions, and the necessity of a form of education uniquely fitted to further democracy.

[1] Paine, Thomas, *Dissertation on First Principles of Government,* p. 31. *Third Year of the French Republic.*
[2] Paine's Works, *Rights of Man,* p. 327. 1880 ed.
[3] Adams, John, *Defence of the American Constitution,* Vol. III, p. 47. 1786.

CHAPTER THREE

Origin and nature of these plans. The American Revolution was a reaction against mercantilism both in its philosophy and the economic situation that had grown out of a highly developed state control of individual endeavor. Both directly and indirectly the philosophical changes that had taken place in France, particularly during the eighteenth century, were reflected in American conceptions of institutional life and control.

While it is true that in actual practice the break from mercantilism might be considered slight, the undercurrent of thinking which found expression during the Revolution in this country chiefly through Tom Paine, in England through Dr. Price, in France through the Physiocrats, continued to find expression in the more or less ephemeral writings of the period. Perhaps these writings were ephemeral very largely because the machinery of institutional life was of necessity largely that of the old order. Those who controlled the fortunes of the government following the Revolution were more interested in the continuance of a machinery that would guarantee to them a continuance of their social and economic status than in establishing a new order that might jeopardize these. It could not be expected that the aristocracy that had existed before the Revolution would give up its former prestige.

The writings, therefore, represented in this essay are not those that bore any very tangible immediate fruit, but the

44

main principles set forth in these writings have been one of the most potent factors operative in the growth of American democracy.

The principles advocated by Tom Paine and others led many at the close of the Revolution to think that some social instrument must be invented whereby this liberal philosophy could become a permanent part in determining the thought in the new republic and in fashioning institutions in harmony with these principles.

Chief among the means sought was a system of national education that would promote such a national culture as would be an expression of these principles. Many plans were suggested. Here will be attempted a brief delineation of some of these plans.

In a rough way the fundamental thought represented in these plans comprehended two emphases: The one advocated predominantly a rather rigid system of indoctrination in those things that were thought to be peculiarly characteristic of American thinking and life, while the other stressed chiefly the development of an unbiased scientific attitude which was to be openminded to whatever contributions might be made to human progress, regardless of source. The latter was the predominant conception.

Both were nationalistic, the one in a somewhat narrow sense, but none the less nationalistic, because it was conceived that here for the first time in the history of the world had been established a nation whose unique characteristic would be the deliberate creation of an institutional life that would assure a synthesis of values on a humanitarian basis. Hence it was to be a nationalistic culture that would set before the world the possibility of developing society on the basis of fraternity rather than upon the basis of antagonism. This culture, then, would represent the integration of humanity upon humanitarian principles rather than upon the narrow racial and geographical distinctions that had dominated the development of nationalism in Europe and that had built up new antagonisms while it was destroying those that had disrupted Europe under the feudal régime. In both of the solutions offered the American background was essential. This American background meant to the writers on education, in this period, the freeing of the human mind from traditions that had grown out of the circumstances peculiar to the European nations with their narrow national prejudices. They conceived of the whole movement of colonization in America as having as its basis the getting away from whatever might trammel human thought and association, and they also believed that there was a common background in the pioneer experiences of the various orders of thought and institutions represented in the differing outlook of the different social entities on the American continent. In this sense the Virginian and the New Englander had much in common. Hence the northern, the middle, and the southern colonies had, indeed, the basis of an openmindedness, on the one hand, in their common interest in freedom, and a basis of common culture that grew out of their pioneer experiences, on the other.

It is to be expected that all of these attempts at the solution of this problem of unification and of openmindedness would represent variations in the details, but it is striking to find how general was the feeling at this time that nothing should be done that would hinder further progress, that nothing should be created in the way of institutions that would tend to see them as something that should be maintained for themselves. Institutions were to be human agencies, the servants of humanitarian progress, and hence in no way considered of worth in themselves.

Growth was to be the keynote of American education, and the problem of American education would be to establish in the largest way possible means for intercommunication, and intercommunication of such a sort as would lead to continuous modifications of everything that would have to do with human progress. America was to become the one place on the earth where would be realized the eighteenth century principles of progress.

Progress was to be realized by two means: There must be no authoritarian control, and there must be coupled with this freedom from authority adequate means for testing the value of human instruments. These means would undoubtedly be the scientific method wherein hypotheses would be tested and modified according to facts revealed in the line of experimentation. The only means of verification would be the utilitarian results. This pragmatic basis is found to be universal in the plans presented.

For various reasons, the more or less arbitrary date of 1800 has been set as the limitation of this investigation. There is an historical basis for this, perhaps, in the reaction that set in at this period, a reaction largely due to the excesses of the French Revolution, which excesses checked the progress of the democratic principles in this country as well as in Europe. There is, of course, a further and more mechanical reason for setting such a limit, the abundance of material to be considered.

In former chapters has been developed the eighteenth century background out of which the Revolution grew, and also to some extent the political as well as the educational bearing of the principles at the basis of the Revolution. There remains, then, to be set forth some of the plans presented for giving permanence to these principles.

It will be found that in all of the plans a strong emphasis is placed upon a mind free from prejudice and one that comprehends the real meaning of objective scientific procedure. For this reason the classification suggested is in no sense an absolute one, but it does indicate that some were more strongly in favor of rather specific indoctrination than others. For instance, Benjamin Rush contended that American youth should be made to have "a SUPREME REGARD TO THEIR COUNTRY," [1] that "The principle of patriotism stands in need of the reinforcement of *prejudice*" [2] and that the youth should be converted into "republican machines." [3]   On the other hand, he rejoiced that while in Europe political science was chained, "The chains which have bound this science . . . are happily unloosed in America. *Here* it is open to investigation and improvement." [4] He stressed in many passages the element of human progress as opposed to the establishment of narrow prejudices.

Benjamin Rush's Plan for a National System of Education

During the very troubled times in 1786, Benjamin Rush of Philadelphia [5] produced a plan of education that he hoped

[1] Rush, Benjamin, *Thoughts upon the Mode of Education proper in a Republic*, p. 20.   1786.
[2] *Ibid.*, p. 14.   1786.
[3] *Ibid.*, p. 27.   1786.
[4] *Ibid.*, p. 22.   1786.
[5] Benjamin Rush, 1746-1813, was one of the leaders in the Revolutionary movement.   He graduated from Princeton in 1760 and from Edinburgh in 1768 and was a professor in the College of Philadelphia when the Revolution broke out.   He was one of the leaders in the movement for the Declaration of Independence, and moved the Declaration.   During the Revolution he was part-time surgeon general of the American army.   He wrote extensively upon methods of protecting the health of the Revolutionary soldiers.   He was also a writer in chemistry and composed various medical treatises.   As a part of his political activities, he was a member of the Pennsylvania Constitutional Assembly and worked for the ratification of the Federal constitution.   He was one of the founders of Dickinson College, and wrote and spoke upon educational topics frequently.   He was interested in social reforms of various sorts, as may be seen by consulting his writings.   His chief contention, perhaps, along this line was for a reform of American education in harmony with American needs, and conducive to the promotion of the principles of democracy.   He was a most active member of the American Philosophical Society, and also of the Society for Promoting Political Enquiries.

might meet the needs of democracy. He along with Adams, Madison, and others, saw the possibility of the United States going upon the rocks, and he believed that the only ultimate security of any republic lay in a proper form of education. Hence he wrote this treatise entitled "THOUGHTS upon the MODE of EDUCATION proper in a REPUBLIC." [1]

Education must take place within the United States. In the interest of homogeneity some general, uniform system of education should be established that would be adequate for all the essential purposes of citizenship. As long as we sent our youth to foreign countries for their education we could expect the divergencies of those countries to be echoed here. The youth would there gain prejudices inimical to democracy. It should be recognized that "The principle of patriotism stands in need of the reinforcement of *prejudice,* and it is well known that our strongest prejudices in favor of our country are formed in the first one and twenty years of our lives." [2] Since this is true, we should establish such a system as would make education in our own country "to be preferred to an education in a foreign country." [3] When this is accomplished, "Our schools of learning, by producing a general, and more uniform system of education, will render the mass of the people more homogeneous." [4]

Nothing, perhaps, would promote unity of feeling as much as the forming of friendships and earlier associations in common schools, and in common occupations. These strong ties of sympathy could not be neglected without leading to undesirable results and perhaps to the ultimate destruction of the union.

Supreme regard for country. Among the various motives that dominated life might be enumerated: the love

---

[1] Rush, Benjamin, *Thoughts upon the Mode of Education proper in a Republic,* p. 13.   1786.
[2] *Ibid.,* p. 14.   1786.   [3] *Ibid.,* p. 14.   1786.   [4] *Ibid.,* p. 14.   1786.

of life itself, the love of popularity, regard for family honor, loyalty to parties, and love of all fellow creatures. These are of necessity strong motives in life, but, above all, even above the love of life itself, must be established a supreme regard for country. Hence Rush said: "I wish to see a SUPREME REGARD TO THEIR COUNTRY, inculcated upon them." [1] This is reasonable, for "Our country includes family, friends and property, and should be preferred to them all." [2] For this reason it would be necessary to establish a public system of education that would, by its character, inculcate this regard, rather than the motives that dominated private schools.

Duty must be coupled with "republican principles"; with progressive development. The love of country should not be instilled in such a way as to create a blind adherence. It should be coupled with enlightenment in the meaning of democracy, for, "While we inculcate these republican duties upon our pupil, we must not neglect, at the same time, to inspire him with republican principles." [3] One of the basic factors in the new nation was that the nation was established for the progress of mankind. It would be a mistake to train up the youth of the nation in such a manner that they would simply continue the institutions that had been established. These institutions were to function progressively, and hence must be modified constantly. For these reasons the pupil "must be taught that there can be no durable liberty but in a republic, and that government, like all other sciences, is of a progressive nature." [2] Benjamin Rush saw that no final solution of social control had been reached. One of the proper duties of American education, then, would be to stimulate this attitude of improvement, for

---

[1] Rush, Benjamin, *Thoughts upon the Mode of Education proper in a Republic*, p. 20. 1786.
[2] *Ibid.*, p. 20. 1786. [3] *Ibid.*, p. 22. 1786.

"The chains which have bound this science in Europe are happily unloosed in America. *Here* it is open to investigation and improvement." [1]

He showed how natural philosophy had advanced while government had failed to do so. Education was the sole instrument whereby this evil could be remedied, and change promoted. He further showed how even republican governments had persisted in obsolete forms. This would have to be obviated here as far as possible if real progress were to be achieved.

Amusements may educate for democracy. The reconstruction of education should not stop simply with a reformation of the formal school procedure. It should permeate also the amusements of youth, for there are "Amusements that are proper for young people in a republic." [2] All amusements which had a tendency to establish habits contrary to the spirit of democracy should be discouraged and others take their place which would be in harmony with the system of morals peculiar to our form of government.

A new type of education required for new type of duties and new social control. To any one who had seen the chaos following the Revolution, it was evident that "The business of education" had "acquired a new complexion by the independence of our country." [3] Two things were clear. One was that the form of government that had been assumed had "created a new classs of duties to every American." [4] The other was that the force of former controls had largely disappeared. Hence Rush concluded: "It becomes us, therefore, to examine our former habits upon this subject, and in laying the foundations for nurseries of wise and

[1] Rush, Benjamin, *Thoughts upon the Mode of Education proper in a Republic*, p. 22. 1786.
[2] *Ibid.*, pp. 25-26. 1786.   [3] *Ibid.*, p. 13. 1786.
[4] *Ibid.*, p. 13. 1786.

good men, to adapt our modes of teaching to the peculiar form of our government." [1] The business of life had become very different, and required a system of education that would secure the new values of freedom through a training that would make each citizen comprehend all of the problems of democracy and that would enlist him in the solution of its problems.

Latin and Greek not suited to American education. Besides the demand made for a new type of education, politically, the economic conditions peculiar to American life demanded certain changes in education. The traditional curriculum that stressed Latin and Greek must be replaced by one that would function immediately.

In the *Museum Magazine* Rush published an essay entitled: "OBSERVATIONS UPON THE STUDY OF THE LATIN AND GREEK LANGUAGES, AS A BRANCH OF LIBERAL EDUCATION, WITH HINTS OF A PLAN OF LIBERAL INSTRUCTION, WITHOUT THEM, ACCOMODATED TO THE PRESENT STATE OF SOCIETY, MANNERS, AND GOVERNMENT IN THE UNITED STATES. [2] He recognized that what he was about to advocate was so revolutionary a conception that "It requires the recollection of escape from a lion and a bear, to encounter the strong and universal prejudice, in favor of the Latin and Greek languages, as a necessary branch of liberal instruction." [3] There were definite reasons why the Latin and Greek languages were not proper in democratic education. Rush said, "The study of the Latin and Greek languages is improper in the present state of society and government in United States," for, "While Greek and Latin are the only avenues to science, education will always be

---

[1] Rush, Benjamin, *Thoughts upon the Mode of Education proper in a Republic,* p. 13. 1786.

[2] Rush, Benjamin, *Essays. Observations upon the Study of Latin and Greek,* etc., p. 21. 1798.

[3] *Ibid.,* p. 21. 1798.

confined to a few people." [1]   At the basis of democracy must
be universal education: "It is only by rendering knowledge
universal, that a republican form of government can be pre-
served in our country." [2]   There were still "other reasons
why the study of these languages is improper in a peculiar
manner in the United States." [1]

Education and the development of national resources.   In
a country where "opportunities of acquiring knowledge and
of advancing private and public interest are so numèrous,
and the rewards of genius are so certain," it would be a mistake if "a particle of time should be misspent or lost." [2]
Where a people were occupying a new country, their "principal business should be to explore and apply its resources"
and education should be so modified as to carry forward
these explorations and developments with "enterprize and
haste." [2]   "Under these circumstances, to spend four or five
years in learning two dead languages, is to turn our backs
upon a gold mine, in order to amuse ourselves catching but-
terflies." [2]

*Effect of devoting to science the time then spent upon
the study of Greek and Latin.*   The prosperity of the United
States depended chiefly upon the advancement of science, and
"The rejection of the Latin and Greek languages from our
schools, would produce a revolution in science, and in human
affairs." [3]   There were two reasons for this: First, those
who studied Latin and Greek gained certain habits and
biases that were prejudicial to the study of science; and,
second, there was not sufficient time in our economic situation to gain a mastery of both the languages and science.
We were so situated in this country that there were sufficient motives to cause us to "shake off the fetters of those

---

[1] Rush, Benjamin, *Essays. Observations upon the Study of Latin and
Greek,* etc., p. 25. 1798.
[2] *Ibid.,* p. 39. 1798.   [3] *Ibid.,* p. 43. 1798.

ancient languages" and Rush said that the "nation which shall first shake off the fetters of those ancient languages, will advance further in knowledge, and in happiness, in twenty years, than any nation in Europe has done in a hundred.[1]

Elimination of prejudices against higher education. If science were substituted for the Latin and Greek studies, it would have a "tendency to destroy the prejudices of the common people against schools and colleges."[1] In the traditional college prejudices were established against those activities that had to do with everyday life. Such a change in the curriculum would have to take place as would establish a direct connection between the higher schools and life. If such a change were brought about, "It would greatly increase the number of students in our colleges, and thereby extend the benefits of education through every part of our country."[2] If the college were seen to function directly, "The excellency of knowledge would then be obvious to everybody, because it would be constantly applicable to some of the necessary and useful purposes of life, and particularly to the security and order of wise and just government."[2] It will be remembered that Rush was a member of the Society for Promoting Political Enquiries, and also of the American Philosophical Society, the first standing chiefly for a spread of intelligence in regard to principles of democracy and social control, and the other predominantly for the furtherance of scientific development.

Curriculum suitable for American democracy. What, then, should be the curriculum that would function in political and economic life? One can see quite clearly in the nature of this curriculum the similarity to the notions of education

[1] Rush, Benjamin, *Essays. Observations upon the Study of Latin and Greek,* etc., p. 43. 1798.
[2] *Ibid.* p. 44. 1798.

held by Benjamin Franklin.[1] The utilitarian character of this curriculum also suggests that perhaps it was through the influence of Rush that the prize was later offered by the American Philosophical Society for an essay on American education. He outlined the following curriculum: "Let the first eight years of a boy's time be employed in learning to speak, spell, read and write the English language."[2] "Arithmetic and some of the more simple branches of the mathematics should be acquired between the twelfth and fourteenth years of his life";[3] and since "Natural history . . . is the foundation of all useful and practical knowledge in agriculture, manufactures and commerce, as well as in philosophy, chemistry, and medicine, this subject should find a prominent place."[4] It might be introduced early because "This study is simple and truly delightful. Animals of all kinds are often the subjects of conversation and disputes among boys in their walks and diversions."[4] The study of geography could also begin early: "Geography is a simple science, and accommodated to the capacity of a boy under twelve years of age. It may be perfectly understood by means of cards—globes—and maps; for each of these modes of conveying instruction, seizes upon the senses and imagination."[5] In place of the ancient languages should come the "French and German languages" for "These will be equally necessary, whether commerce—physic—law or divinity is the pursuit of a young man,"[6] and he suggested that "They should be

---

[1] Smyth, *The Life and Writings of Benjamin Franklin.* 10 vols. Macmillan Co., 1906 ed. Vol. II, pp. 386-396. "Proposals Relating to the Education of Youth in Pennsylvania. Philadelphia: Printed in the year, MDCCXLIX." Vol. X, pp. 9-31. "Observations Relative to the intentions of the Original Founders of the Academy in Philadelphia, June, 1789."

[2] Rush, Benjamin, *Essays. Observations upon the Study of Latin and Greek,* etc., p. 45. 1798.

[3] *Ibid.,* p. 49. 1798.   [4] *Ibid.,* p. 47. 1798.

[5] *Ibid.,* p. 48. 1798.   [6] *Ibid.,* p. 49. 1798.

acquired only by the ear." [1] While Rush held that English,
should not be learned through grammar [2] he said that "Be
tween his fourteenth and eighteenth years, he (the pupil)
should be instructed in grammar—oratory—criticism—the
higher branches of mathematics—philosophy—chemistry—
logic—metaphysics—chronology—history—government—the
principles of agriculture, and manufactures—and in every
thing else that is necessary to qualify him for public useful-
ness or private happiness." [1] In the place of "what is called
Moral Philosophy," there should be given to the youth, "a
course of lectures . . . upon the evidences, doctrines and
precepts of the Christian religion." [1] He believed that the
tendency of the courses in *"Moral Philosophy"* was to teach
anti-Christian and pagan morals, which he held to be inconsistent since we were essentially a Christian nation, and
hence instruction should be Christian in character.

Special emphasis upon history for nationalistic culture.
For the achievement of the nationalistic ends indicated,
"Above all, let our youth be instructed in the history of the
ancient republics, and the progress of liberty and tyranny
in the different states of Europe." [3] For constructive citizenship, men must know the laws that govern human progress; they must know those factors that tend to repress
and those that tend to liberate. Such knowledge could best
be gained through a careful analysis of the movements of
humanity toward gerater enlightenment and toward "PRAC-
TICAL LEGISLATION." [4] Hence instruction must be given
not alone in theory of government but also in the way
in which history could be brought to function practically

---

[1] Rush, Benjamin, *Essays. Observations upon the Study of Latin and
Greek,* etc., p. 49. 1798.

[2] *Ibid.,* p. 45. 1798.

[3] Rush, Benjamin, *Thoughts upon the Mode of Education proper in a
Republic,* p. 29. 1786.

[4] *Ibid.,* p. 30. 1786.

in human affairs. It would be necessary to make all "acquainted with all the prerogatives of the federal government." [1] Such prerogatives could alone be understood in viewing their tendencies historically. The American youth should also be made familiar with the history of the development of institutions in America, especially the history of recent years.

Young men made by education into "republican machines." Organized life as well as the life of the individual is largely a matter of habit. It could not be doubted that if a "republic is sophisticated with monarchy or aristocracy" it would not "revolve upon the wills of the people." [2] To avoid a repetition of the experiences through which the colonists had been passing, "the wills of the people . . . must be fixed to each other by means of education" for only in this manner could they "be made to produce regularity and unison of government." [2] Rush said then: "From the observations that have been made, it is plain, that I consider as possible to convert men into republican machines." [2] There is no uncertainty here for the need of a new type of education that would make a new national culture possible. It should be an education that would give a thorough grounding in democratic principles and that, at the same time, would make for whatever modification of instruments of society that would be necessary for progress toward greater freedom. In comprehension of these principles and in the establishment of habits of thinking and action in accord with them would unity be made possible.

Education of women in citizenship; their peculiar duties in a republic. The author apologizes "for having delayed so long, to say anything of the separate and peculiar mode

[1] Rush, Benjamin, *Thoughts upon the Mode of Education proper in a Republic*, p. 32. 1786.
[2] *Ibid.*, p. 27. 1786.

of education proper for *Women* in a republic." [1] Any system of education that would render the laws of a democracy effective, must provide adequate training for women, and must give them also a grasp of the principles involved in a democracy, for "they must concur in all our plans of education for young men." [1] A broader training than any that had yet been offered must be given. It must be recognized that "To qualify our women for this purpose, they should not only be instructed in the usual branches of female education, but they should be instructed in the principles of liberty and government; and the obligations of patriotism, should be inculcated upon them." [1] This is a noteworthy conception when we remember that this essay was written in 1786.

Utilitarian character of female education. What must have seemed a vulgar utilitarianism to those who were addicted to aristocracy was considered by Rush as the only basis for female education suited to the United States. In an address delivered to the "Young Ladies Academy in Philadelphia, 28th July, 1787, at the close of the quarterly examination," [2] he said that "the education of young ladies in this country, should be conducted upon principles very different from what it is in Great Britain, and in some respects, different from what it was when we were part of a monarchical empire." [3] It is significant to remember that this address was delivered in 1787. The date of the publication of the volume of essays is given below for convenience of reference. In many ways a "peculiar mode of education" was required in the United States. [4]

---

[1] Rush, Benjamin, *Thoughts upon the Mode of Education proper in a Republic*, p. 33. 1786.

[2] Rush, Benjamin, *Essays. Thoughts upon Female Education, Accommodated to the Present State of Society, Manners, and Government, in the United States of America*, p. 75, 1798.

[3] *Ibid.* p. 74. 1798.   [4] *Ibid.*, p. 75. 1798.

Peculiar duties of American womanhood. It seemed that due to certain economic reasons there had developed a tendency for very early marriages of women in the American colonies. This meant that their opportunities for education were decidedly "contracted" and hence it would be best "to confine it chiefly to the more useful branches of literature."[1] A further change in the status of woman through economic pressure was the part she must play in the material advancement. This material advancement could not be realized "without the assistance of the female members of the community."[1] "They must be the stewards and guardians of their husbands' property."[1] Again, upon woman devolved "a principal share of the instruction of children" and they must be prepared "by a suitable education, for the discharge of this most important duty of mothers."[1] Perhaps the most crucial part of education was that pertaining to instruction and habituation in the life of a democracy. This would "make it necessary that our ladies should be qualified to a certain degree by a peculiar and suitable education, to concur in instructing their sons in the principles of liberty and government."[2] A further problem that "should have great influence upon the nature and extent of female education in America" was the lack of well trained servants. Woman must be, along with her duties as related to the economic and political phases of her life, in a large way the manager of her home.[3]

Kind of education required. In order to discharge these various obligations, the principal part of woman's education should consist of a mastery of the English language, ability to read and write well;[3] "knowledge of figures and bookkeep-

---

[1] Rush, Benjamin, *Essays. Thoughts upon Female Education, Accommodated to the Present State of Society, Manners, and Government, in the United States of America,* p. 75. 1798.
[2] *Ibid.,* pp. 76-77. 1798.   [3] *Ibid.,* p. 77. 1798.

ing is absolutely necessary"; [1] "an acquaintance with geography and some instruction in chronology"; [1] "vocal music should never be neglected"; [2] dancing is by nó means an improper branch of education for an American lady"; [3] "the attention of our young ladies should be directed, as soon as they are prepared for it, to the reading of history—travels—poetry—and moral essays" [3] and to these were to be added "regular instruction in the christian religion." [4] Instrumental musical instruction Rush considered practically ruled out of American life because both instruments and instruction were so expensive and the immediate demands were such that a sufficient amount of time could not be given to the required practice. [5] He said: "Rousseau has aserted that the secret of education consists in 'wasting the time of children profitably," [6] and he would not have any educational regimen that would be destructive of health.

If woman were thus educated she would play no mean rôle in the material and intellectual development of the United States, and a most important part of the service that she could thus render would be the influence she would have in making the youth of the land the real guardians of democracy. Some feminist enthusiast may some day set forth the rôle played by woman in the development of the western continent.

Indigenous manners and institutions. There had been developing for a considerable time a keen sense of the incongruities of the transplanted manners, customs and institutions, with American life. These must become indigenous in character in order to assist rather than retard American

---

[1] Rush, Benjamin, *Essays. Thoughts upon Female Education, Accommodated to the Present State of Society, Manners, and Government, in the United States of America*, p. 79. 1798.

[2] *Ibid.*, p. 80. 1798   [3] *Ibid.* p. 81. 1798.
[4] *Ibid.*, p. 82. 1798.   [5] *Ibid.*, pp. 84-85. 1798.
[6] *Ibid.*, pp. 82-83. 1798.

progress. The sentiments of the following are echoed widely throughout the literature of this period:

"It should not surprize us that British customs with respect to female education, have been transplanted into our American schools and families. We see marks of the same incongruity, of time and place, in many other things. We behold our houses accommodated to the climate of Great Britain, by eastern and western directions. We behold our ladies panting in a heat of ninety degrees, under a hat and cushion, which were calculated for the temperature of a British summer. We behold our citizens condemned and punished by a criminal law, which was copied from a country, where maturity in corruption renders public executions a part of the amusements of the nation. It is high time to awake from this servility—to study our own character—to examine the age of our country—and to adopt manners in every thing, that shall be accommodated to our state of society, and to the forms of our government." [1]

Schools to teach forgetting. Rush was so convinced of the error of copying European institutions that he facetiously suggested the need of the establishment of special schools to develop the skill of forgetting:

"We suffer so much from traditional error of various kinds, in education, morals, and government, that I have been led to wish, that it were possible for us to have schools established, in the United States, for teaching *the art of forgetting.* I think three-fourths of all our school-masters, divines, and legislators would profit very much, by spending two or three years in such useful institutions." [2]

Liberation of thought and life; Society for Promoting Political Enquiries. There is room for an extensive research setting forth the instruments created prior to the Revolution,

[1] Rush, Benjamin, *Essays. Thoughts upon Female Education, Accommodated to the Present State of Society, Manners, and Government, in the United States of America,* p. 87. 1798.
[2] Rush, Benjamin, *Essays. Thoughts upon the Amusements and Punishments which are Proper for Schools,* pp. 71-72. 1798.

as well as during and following the Revolution, that had as
the chief motive the liberation of human thought and life.
In the Preface to the Laws of the Society for Promoting
Political Enquiries, we have this motive declared to be the
reason for its organization:

> "Accustomed to look up to those nations from whom we have
> derived our origin, for our laws, our opinions, and our manners;
> we have retained, with undistinguishing reverence, their errors,
> with their improvements; have blended, with our public institutions
> the policy of dissimilar countries; and have grafted, on an infant
> commonwealth, the manners of ancient and corrupted monar-
> chies." [1]

Benjamin Franklin and other members of this organization labored for the freeing of American thought and for the
creation of institutions that would tend to free the thought
and life of mankind. The scientific attitude and method
was thought to be the only means of accomplishing this end.
This Society believed that proper education was at the root
of any effective democracy.

Liberal national support for education—trained teachers.
To carry any such system of education into effect, the nation
should provide schools and colleges adequately equipped for
national purposes and should provide in these schools and
colleges teachers well qualified for their task. A fair notion
of how Rush would carry out such a national system as has
been suggested may be gained from the plan he suggested
for Pennsylvania. There should be one state university, four
colleges, and free schools in every township. He said, "By
this plan the whole state will be tied together by one system
of education." [2]

The schools and teachers should be so liberally supported

[1] Rush, Benjamin, *Essays. An Enquiry into the Effects of Public
Punishments upon Criminals and upon Society,* p. 136. 1798.
[2] Rush, Benjamin, *Essays. Plan for Establishing Public Schools in
Pennsylvania,* pp. 1-4. 1798.

that the best talent would be attracted into the teaching profession.[1]   Until we were ready to pay adequate salaries no adequate talent could be enlisted.   A very clever contention was made that the cost of the maintenance of such a system would not be a burden, since there would result such an advancement of agriculture and manufacture, and such a defense "from hasty and expensive experiment in government" that "these institutions will *lessen* our taxes." [2]

Summary.   The system of education, then, for American youth, advocated by Benjamin Rush, demanded training for both sexes for the understanding of the principles of democracy, for understanding the machinery whereby democracy might be made effective, and for creating a seriously purposeful attitude for the maintenance of democratic institutions. The youth were to be so trained that they would have the experimental attitude and see that the science of government demanded constant improvement and readjustment according to the exigencies that might arise.   These schools were to be supported liberally, and provided with well trained teachers.

Robert Coram's "Plan for the General Establishment of Schools throughout the United States"

Purpose of the plan.   In 1791 Robert Coram [3] of Wilmington, Delaware, brought out a plan for the general estab-

---

[1] Rush, Benjamin, *Thoughts upon the Mode of Education proper in a Republic*, p. 32. 1786.

[2] Rush, Benjamin, *Essays.   Plan for Establishing Public Schools in Pennsylvania*, p. 4.   1798.

[3] Robert Coram was the author of several articles in the Delaware Gazette, under the signature of Brutus.   He was a student of Indian life and customs, and of the French and Colonial policies.   Some of the writers comprehended in his criticisms were Blackstone, Gouget, Barbyrac, Titius, Locke, Grotius, Puffendorf, Priestley, Turneaux, Beccaria, Raynall, Fielding, Goldsmith, Macaulay, Swift, Addison, Gee, Rapin, Vanderbilt, Garth, and Dupaty.   Coram understood the problems involved in making governments stable and, at the same time, pro-

lishment of schools throughout the United States. He had a very definite philosophy of life and of democracy and saw the relation between education and the furtherance of democratic principles. The complete title of the work is: "Political Inquiries: To which is added a PLAN for the general establishment of SCHOOLS throughout the United States," but, in fact, according to the writer's own statement, the purpose was not the discussion of political theory but rather of the relation of political theory to education.[1] That the principles for which the revolution was fought were still valid, but few doubted. The chaos due to bad currency and worse sectionalism and class interests called for the establishment of some means of preserving the revolutionary principles intact. The contention for a national system of education upon a nationalistic basis was not a movement away from those principles, but rather a sensing that the problems of their preservation had changed. In the revolution monarchical control had been broken, and for the lack of something to take its place there had been developed a destructive individualism. Now this absolute individualism threatened the happiness and freedom of man. The "pronounced differences in the tendency of political thought" were not differences in viewpoint but a difference of means needed for the accomplishment of the same ends.

Mode of education must be adapted to democracy. If substantial progress were to take place, the principles of

gressive, and he believed that a most essential principle was that of the harmony of government with the nature of man. This harmony he thought was represented best in democracy because it was favorable to progress.

In reality the scheme presented by Coram in this treatise belongs to the same period as the one by Benjamin Rush, for Coram stated that he had had in mind to write this before Webster's essays appeared in the American Magazine. Coram, Robert, *PLAN for the general establishment of SCHOOLS throughout the United States*, p. 76. 1791.

[1] Coram, Robert, *Plan for the general establishment of Schools throughout the United States*, Preface. 1791.

democracy must be respected, for these had their basis in the nature of man and society. These principles are developed in the earlier part of the treatise, but it is stated that the "Work is intended merely to introduce a better Mode of Education . . . throughout the United States."[1] We shall find later what is meant by a "better Mode of Education."

Status of the public schools (1791). In viewing the status of the public schools of the period, one thing was obvious: Educational opportunity was very unequal in the country and in the city. Thus Coram devotes one chapter to the "Wretched State of the Country Schools, through the United States; and the absolute Necessity of a Reformation."[2] The author's description of the conditions as they existed at that time is so apt that it may be given at some length:

"The country schools, through most of the United States, whether we consider the buildings, the teachers, or the regulations, are in every respect completely despicable, wretched and contemptible. The buildings are in general sorry hovels, neither wind tight nor water tight; a few stools serving in capacity of bench and desk, and the old leaves of copy books making a miserable substitute for glass windows. The teachers are generally foreigners, shamefully deficient in every qualification necessary to convey instruction to youth, and not seldom addicted to gross vices. Absolute in his opinion, and proud of what he calls his European method, one calls the first letter of the alphabet *aw*. The school is modified upon this plan, and the children who are advanced, are beat and cuffed to forget the former mode they have been taught, which irritates their minds, and retards their progress. The first quarter being finished, the children remain idle until another master offers, few remaining in one place more than a quarter. When the next schoolmaster is introduced, he calls the

[1] Coram, Robert, *Plan for the general establishment of Schools throughout the United States,* Preface. 1791.
[2] *Ibid.,* p. 94. 1791.

first letter *a* as in *mat*—the school undergoes another reform, and
is equally vexed and retarded. At his removal, a third is introduced who calls the first letter *hay*. All these blockheads are absolute in their reforms, and will by no means suffer the children
to pronounce the letter as they were first taught, but every three
months the school goes through a reform—error succeeds error—
and dunce the second reigns like dunce the first." [1]

That Coram had given long and careful consideration to
the problem which he discusses in this treatise is very evident. He had made himself acquainted with practically all
of the writings on education and he knew the social and
economic conditions that existed at that time.

Purpose of education—means for independence. The
nature of the school system depended upon the purposes to
be achieved. The conclusion had been accepted that "to
make men happy, the first step is to make them independent.
For if they are dependent, they can neither manage their
private concerns properly, retain their own dignity, or vote
impartially for their country; they can be but tools at
best." [2] By making men independent Coram meant that a
different type of control must prevail, one not dependent upon external pressure. He concluded that the
system recommended by Mr. Webster would be required. [3] As a necessary part of his scheme for making
men independent we shall find that he stressed the economic
factor.

Schools to be adapted to American needs. A further consideration of making men independent was that it was "high
time to check that blind adherence to transatlantic policy,
which has so generally prevailed." [4] The transplanting of

[1] Coram, Robert, *Plan for the general establishment of Schools throughout the United States,* Preface. pp. 94-95. 1791.
[2] *Ibid.,* pp. 104-105. 1791.   [3] *Ibid.,* pp. 104-105. 1791.
[4] *Ibid.,* pp. 88-89. 1791.

European institutions to America could in no sense meet the demands of the situation here. Schools must be "better adapted to the present circumstances in America." [1] As long as we followed blindly the customs of Europeans we could expect to suffer the miseries of Europeans. If we cherished the form of government that we had established it was up to us to preserve that form of government, which meant that we must provide educational means for its preservation. Upon this point there could be no doubt. The common experience as pioneers furnished what amounted to a tradition, but it was a tradition that had freedom and open-avenues-ahead as its essence. This is the trend of all of the plans suggested during this period.

Education in relation to civilization. The general conclusion had been reached that "In the savage state, education is perfect," while "In the civilized state, education is the most imperfect part of the whole scheme of government, or civilization; or rather, it is not immediately connected with either." [2] For this reason failure on the part of civilized society to use the most potent means for its development should be remedied, and the only way in which this could be done would be by education being "incorporated with the government, or regulated by it." [2] The failure on the part of the government to use education effectively grew out of the fact that education failed to progress with the development of society. Where mankind was ruled by an autocratic government, obsolete systems of education might exist without the government being destroyed, but the peculiar experiment being made in the United States demanded that this condition should be remedied, that government must be

---

[1] Coram, Robert, *Plan for the general establishment of Schools throughout the United States, Preface,* pp. 88-89. 1791.
[2] *Ibid.,* p. vi. 1791.

directly related to education, and that education must be made an instrument of government.

Social and economic basis of education—conditions in the eighteenth century. The Abbe Raynal is quoted as saying that throughout Europe

> " 'In our provinces, the vassal, or free mercenary, digs and ploughs the whole year round, lands that do not belong to him; and he is even happy, if his labor procures him a share of the crops he has sown and reaped. Observed and harassed, by a hard and restless landlord, who grudges him the very straw on which he rests his weary limbs; the wretch is daily exposed to diseases, which, joined to his poverty, make him wish for death, rather than for an expensive cure, followed by infirmities and toil. Whether tenant or subject, he is doubly a slave; if he has acres, his lord comes and gathers them where he has not sown; if he has but a yoke of oxen, or a pair of horses, he must employ them in a public service; if he has nothing but his person, the prince takes him for a slave. Everywhere he meets masters, and always with oppression.' " [1]

Coram observed that under such circumstances man was but a machine controlled by his master and hence it was not surprising that education should be of a very limited sort and for the few, and scarcely at all fitted to promote progress.[1]

Here a very great percent were economically independent. They planned the development of their own resources. They were responsible for the utilization of all of the means that were available.   Also here every man had political as well as economic responsibilities. He was a determiner of the government under which he lived. Very directly it would

---

[1] Coram, Robert, *Plan for the general establishment of Schools throughout the United States,* Preface, p. 11. 1791.

be he who could make possible the realization of that freedom which had just been purchased at so great a cost. Hence the immediate connection between the social and economic phases of life with education was very direct, and consequently education must be fashioned to meet the political and economic needs of democracy.

Equality—artificial versus natural origin of government. Issue was taken with the Abbe Raynal on the question of the origin of government. The Abbe believed that government had its origin in primitive inequality and was created for the lessening of these inequalities, but Coram believed that "the primitive equality" was "disturbed and broken by an external force, not by members of the same society opposed to each other, but by the conquest of one society by another." [1] Education, then, for the purpose of equalizing opportunity was not contrary to nature but was in accord with it. It would be but the means of bringing men again into the state of this primitive freedom. Without education no equality in government could exist.

Relation of education to right of property. The general distribution of property in this country was at the basis of a successful working out of democratic principles. Economic slavery could be quite as harassing and hampering as political slavery. This principle was recognized very generally, as may be seen in the fight to do away with primogeniture. The writer felt that certain exponents of law in the eighteenth century were quite unable to readjust themselves to the demand that property should be divided generally and not concentrated in large estates. The author criticized Blackstone because he failed to show the injustice of the

---

[1] Coram, Robert, *Plan for the general establishment of Schools throughout the United States,* Preface, p. 92. 1791.

system that prevailed in Europe,[1] and Coram showed that a part of man's education in this country should be of such a sort as to overcome these conditions which kept man in slavery throughout Europe. He must be here educated to recognize that the earth was a gift "common to the whole race" and that a man "when lying on his death bed, and no longer to maintain possession, should (not) be entitled to tell the rest of the world, which of them should enjoy it after him."[2] This was a revolution in the conception of education in relation to the right of property.

Traditional basis of property a source of evil. The principle of "meum & teum, which principally receives existence with civil society, is but little known in the rude stages of natural liberty; . . . where all property is common."[3] In departing from this principle civilized man had brought practically all the miseries and vices to man, and Coram continued: "We have also demonstrated, that the civilized man has been unjustly deprived of his right to the bounties of Providence, and that he has been rendered, as much as human laws could do it, an abortive creature."[3] In order that the society newly formed in America would not continue the evils of this system, he said: "We will now inquire the best mode of alleviating his miseries."[3] It is not held that man should go back to the primitive state, in which there was not private ownership of property, but it would be necessary that man should be educated to recognize property as chiefly of social value, to be considered as a social trust to be used for the betterment of mankind and not for personal aggrandizement nor for the gaining of advantage over one's fellow men.[3] Hence the state must so regulate and control

---

[1] Coram, Robert, *Plan for the general establishment of Schools throughout the United States,* Preface, p. 27. 1791.
[2] *Ibid.,* p. 23. 1791.   [3] *Ibid.,* p. 55. 1791.

education that man will become an agent literally subservient to social welfare.

Education a state function—both lower and higher must be universal and equal. There could be no other way out of the difficulties than that "Society should then furnish the people with means of subsistence, and those means should be an inherent quality in the nature of government, universal, permanent and uniform, because their natural means were so." [1] The only effective way for the realization of this general diffusion of opportunity and possibility of happiness would be through the state controlling education so that man might gain knowledge of the arts and sciences necessary for complete living, "that is, the education of children should be provided for in the constitution of every state. By education, I mean, instruction in arts as well as sciences. Education then ought to be secured by government to every class of citizen, to every child in the state. The citizens should be instructed in the sciences by public schools; and in arts, by laws enacted for that purpose. . . . Education should not be left to the caprice, or negligence of parents, to chance, or confined to the children of wealthy parents." [1] With a considerable degree of feeling the author declared: "It is a shame, a scandal to civilized society, that part only of the citizens should be sent to colleges and universities to learn to cheat the rest of their liberties." [1] Through a universal and equal education, both lower and higher, this evil could be remedied, and man be rendered truly free. Coram believed that the ideas of reform presented by Becarria would offer "a foundation whereon to erect a system, which like the sun in the universe, will trans-

[1] Coram, Robert, *Plan for the general establishment of Schools throughout the United States,* Preface, pp. 56-57.   1791.

mit light, life and harmony to all under its influence—I mean—A SYSTEM OF EQUAL EDUCATION." [1]

Education for social integration and intelligent control. National education must solve the problem of social integration and control, for without universal education of the kind suggested, "What is the bond of society, but a rope of sand, incapable of supporting its own weight? A heterogeneous jumble of contradiction and absurdity, from which the subject knows not how to extricate himself." [2] Through education suited to the demands of democracy man would gain a knowledge of democratic principles, and loyalty to them would be established. National integration demands then, intelligent national control, and intelligent national control in a democracy depends upon the education of all, since all are the determiners of government. The duty of a government is to make all men better. This obligation could not be neglected without the ultimate destruction of the very principles for which democracy stands. This duty implies a nation-wide obligation for educating its youth. [3]

Education in order to know obligations to the government. How else could a democracy continue unless by an education that would make each citizen aware of his responsibilities? "An education is . . . necessary, in order that the subject may know the obligation he is under to government." [4] How far education in the three R's comes from being adequate is shown by an analysis and a realistic description of social conditions in England and on the Continent, and an analysis of the relation of these to inequalities in educational opportunities. He said:

---

[1] Coram, Robert, *Plan for the general establishment of Schools throughout the United States,* Preface, p. 54. 1791.
[2] *Ibid.,* p. 57. 1791.   [3] *Ibid.,* p. 79. 1791.   [4] *Ibid.,* p. 65. 1791.

"Mr. Noah Webster is the only American author, indeed the only author of any nation, if we except perhaps Montesquieu, who has taken up the subject of education, upon that liberal and equitable scale which it justly deserves. I had the present work in idea, sometime before Mr. Webster's essays made their appearance; and was not a little pleased to think that he had anticipated my idea."[1]

After quoting Webster at some length and after showing how it would be necessary for us to change our system of education both as to its nature and its extent, he quoted Webster further:

"It is observed by the great Montesquieu, that the laws of education ought to be relative to the principles of government. In despotic governments the people should have little or no education except what tends to inspire them with a servile fear. Information is fatal to despotism—in monarchies education should be partial and adapted to each class of citizens. But 'in a republican government,' says the same writer, 'the whole power of education is required.' Here every class of people should know and love the laws. This knowledge should be diffused by means of schools and newspapers; that an attachment to the laws may be formed by early impressions on the mind.—Two regulations are essential to the continuance of republican governments. 'First. Such a distribution of lands, and principles of descent and alienation as shall give every citizen the power of acquiring what his industry merits. Secondly. Such a system of education, as gives every citizen an opportunity of acquiring knowledge, and fitting himself for places of trust. These are fundamental articles, the *sine qua non* of the existence of American republics.

"'Hence the absurdity of copying the manners and adapting the institutions of monarchies.'"[2]

To overcome these inequalities of educational opportunity it would be necessary to have a national system

[1] Coram, Robert, *Plan for the general establishment of Schools throughout the United States,* Preface, p. 76. 1791.
[2] *Ibid.,* p. 77. 1791.

of education that would provide equal educational opportunity for all, including the necessary economic provision for support of those who did not have sufficient means.[1]

That Coram had selected from Webster the passages that dealt most directly with nationalistic motif as the basis of education shows that he was in hearty accord with him. The system of government which he thought to be "a most glaring solecism in government" was the one in which "The constitutions are republican, and the laws of education are monarchial." [1] He continued to quote Webster as showing that "Of such consequence is it to society, that the people who make the laws, should be well informed, that I can conceive no legislature can be justified in neglecting proper establishments for this purpose. Such a general system of education is neither impracticable nor difficult: and excepting the formation of a federal government, that shall be efficient and permanent, it demands first attention of American patriots. Until such a system be adapted and pursued; until the statesman and divine shall unite in their efforts in forming the human mind," no permanence could be assured to the American experiment.[1] In hearty accord with other writers of the period, he again said:

> " 'America affords the fairest opportunities, for making the experiments, and opens the most encouraging prospects of success.' . . . There is but one way to effect this important purpose—which is by incorporating education with government—*This is the rock upon which you must build your political salvation!*" [2]

Equal representation demands equal educational opportunity. The principle was generally acknowledged that "An

---

[1] Coram, Robert, *Plan for the general establishment of Schools throughout the United States, Preface*, p. 78. 1791.
[2] *Ibid.*, p. 79. 1791.

equal representation is absolutely necessary to the preservation of liberty." [1]   Coram saw that there can never be equal representation until there is an "equal mode of education for all citizens." [1]   So long as the economic inequalities existed, for instance, between the farmer and the merchant or the professional man, such as the lawyer, there could be no equality of representation in the government, for the sons of the farmer could not get the necessary preparation which would bring them into the positions of leadership in the nation, and hence the farmer would remain unrepresented in the councils of the government. We would still remain in the hands of class legislators who would continue the inequalities so characteristic of Europe. Even though the farmer might succeed in getting himself elected to the legislature, unless he had the necessary education to "speak with propriety in the legislature" his presence there would be but a deception of the people into a belief that they were being represented in government. The only remedy for this was that "education . . . should be brought home to every man's door." Equal educational opportunity was at the root of equal representation in government, the principle for which the Revolution was fought.[1]

Equal opportunity in country and in town. To any fair-minded person "The necessity of a reformation in the country schools, is too obvious to be insisted on." [2]   The evidences were so patent that "he that runs may read."[3] Whether or not the author was justified in feeling that the nation at that time was controlled entirely by the merchants, he certainly was right in saying that "the country should have as good schools as seaport towns." [3]   The conclusion was well

---

[1] Coram, Robert, *Plan for the general establishment of Schools throughout the United States,* Preface, p. 93. 1791.
[2] *Ibid.,* p. 97. 1791.   [3] *Ibid.,* p. 96. 1791.

founded that "If education is necessary for one man, my religion tells me it is equally necessary for another." [1] He could see no reason for discrimination and disrespect. Democracy demanded an equality of opportunities in country and town. These could not be assured without equal representation in governmental affairs. This equal representation demanded equal educational opportunity.

Nature of the curriculum. What should be the nature of the curriculum in such a system of schools? It must be of a broad and liberal character and obviously, "No modes of faith, systems of manners, or foreign or dead languages should be taught in those schools." [2] The curriculum must be adapted to American needs. We were not concerned with the existence of a certain faith or a certain mode of living, but we were concerned with an attitude of progress on a scientific basis. While American youth should be assured an education in democratic principles, it would be necessary to avoid the establishment of another system equally hampering to human thought as the systems of Europe. [3]

General tax for support of schools. There could be no general opportunity for a democratic education of this character unless schools were provided for by a general tax throughout the United States. At the root of any successful plan for the general establishment of schools in the United States there lay the question of general support. The objection that one man had to pay for the education of another's children was not valid because there was a solidarity of

---

[1] Coram, Robert, *Plan for the general establishment of Schools throughout the United States,* Preface, p. 96.　1791.

[2] *Ibid.,* p. 101.　1791.　　　　　[3] *Ibid.,* pp. 88-89.　1791.

interests that made each person dependent upon every other person. Every citizen must suffer more or less for the failure of any one to meet the demands of democracy in this respect.[1]

Practicability of a national school system—estimated cost compared with the cost of private schools. A rough estimate is given of the cost of initiating such a system, and it is demonstrated that even with heavy expense at the beginning the cost would be less than one-half as much per pupil as was the cost in private schools. This was demonstrated in detail as follows:

"To demonstrate the practicability of establishing public schools, throughout the United States, let us suppose the states to be divided into districts according to population, and let every district support one school, by a tax on the acre, on all lands within the district. Let us suppose for argument's sake, six miles square, which will be 36 square miles—sufficient for a district for the mean population of the United States. The school house should be built of brick, and in the center of the district; it would be three miles from the school-house door to the boundary of the district. The building might be two stories, with a large hall on the lower floor, for the school room; the rest of the house should be for the master's family, and might consist of two rooms on the lower floor, and three or four in the second story, with perhaps an acre of ground adjoining. We will suppose the ground to cost £10, the building £800, the master's salary £150 per annum, and £50 for an assistant, with £50 for mathematical instruments; in all £1,060, of which £800 is for building the school-house; and as people enough will be willing to contract for building the house, to wait a year for half the money, we will suppose £400 to be paid the first year. Now in 36 square miles, are 23,040 acres, which is better than 4d. per acre; the next year's payment will be £660, which will be about 7d. more than the succeeding years, there will be the teacher's salary, £150, the assistant £50 & £50 for

[1] Coram, Robert, *Plan for the general establishment of Schools throughout the United States,* Preface, p. 98. 1791.

contingent expenses, books, etc., will be £250 per annum, which will not amount to 3d. per acre. Consider that such a trifling tax, by being applied to this best of purposes, may be productive of consequences amazingly glorious, can any man make a serious objection against public schools? . . . The common rate at present is 8s. 4d. per quarter, which is 33s. 4d. per year, which for 4 children is £6 13 4. Now if you hold 300 acres of land, you will pay toward the support of decent public schools, at 3d. per acre, 900d. or £3 15 per annum." [1]

Summary. Analyses of conditions convinced Coram that there was a need for reformation in education. He did not feel that the principles of democracy had failed, but he was keenly conscious of the necessity of making conscious provision for their fruitful operation. If democracy failed it would be because no provision had been made for education that would train for democracy. Schools were not so run as to produce intelligent citizenship. Both the private and public interests of persons in a democracy called for education peculiar to that form of social control. He believed that the system recommended by Noah Webster—a system that would insure control from within the individual—was altogether essential. Education must be incorporated as a part of the government. Hitherto, education had not been fitted to promote progress, but rather the very opposite. As long as educational opportunity was solely for the few, so long would these get higher education in order that they might exploit the many. Opportunity must be universal. Through education also must society be integrated. This problem of social integration and maximal individual achievement demanded a new type of education. The very nature of a representative government demanded equalization of educa-

[1] Coram, Robert, *Plan for the general establishment of Schools throughout the United States, Preface,* pp. 99-101. 1791.

tional opportunity.   Hence, there should be a tax-supported
national system of education, available to all alike.

James Sullivan's Plan for a National System of Education

The conditions that led to the constitutional convention
caused many to think that a fundamental reconstruction of
education was necessary.   If disintegration were to be
checked, they felt that it must be checked through some
force other than external constitutional control.

The many forces that were at work for disrupting the
nation were given by James Sullivan [1] in 1791 as still operat-

[1] James Sullivan, 1744-1808, was one of the few really great leaders
of the Revolutionary period who has been quite thoroughly neglected.
Throughout the whole Revolutionary period he was a very prolific pub-
licist.   During the same period he was lawyer and judge on the supreme
bench.   For seventeen years he was attorney general of the state of
Massachusetts.   After 1806 he became governor of the state.   His political
activities were of a high order and were constant.   He collaborated with
Hancock, Adams, Warren, Hawlet and others in the preparation of
many appeals to his own countrymen and also to the people of Europe
throughout the Revolutionary period.   He was selected to prepare the
response of Massachusetts to the Declaration of Independence, and was
collaborator with Adams in the Address to the People on the Adoption
of the State Constitution of Massachusetts.   He was a writer upon every
phase of the American struggle for independence, and later was a defender of the Revolution in France.   The fortunes of the French Revolution in no way affected his faith in the principles for which the Revolution had been fought, but did make him feel more profoundly the necessity of a proper universal education in order that democratic institutions
might be made permanent.   He numbered many worthy Frenchmen
among his friends.   During the period previous to the adoption of the
American constitution he was one of the chief advocates of liberal
principles and at the same time contended for a strong federal government, although he was an anti-federalist.   Throughout his whole life
he was a writer upon law.   He contended for the development of our
own common law rather than for continued dependence upon the English
common law for precedent.   He believed that we must develop a system of law in accord with the very different social conditions that
existed in America.   He exerted his energies constantly for the development of whatever was peculiarly American.   He was thoroughly versed
in Grotius, Valen, Puffendorf, Vattel, Burlamaqué, Turgot, Price, Hume,
De Lolme, etc.   Hardly a writer in the field of social and political science

ing even after the constitution had been formed and the federal government established. In these untoward elements he saw the need for a more effective social control. He summarized these elements as follows:

> "The dreadful apprehension of a disunion of, and controversy among the states; the mortification of our national pride, upon seeing that we must soon lose all confidence and credit with other nations; the destruction of our commerce, for want of a general, systematical regulation; the distress of public creditors, who had parted with their property to aid their country in the day of her danger; the injustice which had arisen from paper money and tender acts; and the alarms arising from insurrections, urged all to adopt some measure to secure them against such insupportable calamities."[1]

At the root of all of these difficulties was the failure of the citizens to discern their responsibilities peculiar in a democracy. This was the main reason for Sullivan's writing his treatise entitled "Observations upon the Government of the United States of America." Since these difficulties continued in a large way after the establishment of the national government, there was revealed the necessity of a more sure means of national integration. Such a means was to be found in a system of education that would stress the principles of democracy and that would thus create intelligent citizens.

National outlook and character; national objects of pursuit. James Sullivan was a leader in political activities fol-

had escaped his attention. As governor of Massachusetts he was noted for his free interpretation of American law and yet for his loyalty to the principles of democracy. In 1780 he was one of the originators of the American Academy of Arts and Sciences and remained an active member of the organization throughout his life. As first president of the Massachusetts Historical Society, 1791-1806, he was active in the preservation of historical documents. No topic that received his attention was more frequent than that of an education peculiarly fitted to secure the permanency of the democracy that had been established.

[1] Sullivan, James, *Observations upon the Government of the United States of America*, p. 29. 1791.

lowing the Revolution, and his position as Attorney General of Massachusetts gave him an intimate knowledge of governmental and economic problems; but with all this awareness of the disrupting forces at work, he had a certain faith in the power of his country to "set up objects to pursue, and habits to establish . . . by which to effect great national purposes," for he believed that a nation as well as individuals might set up objects and pursue them, and so, while some might think him "fanciful in the extreme," he would set up a few such objects that might in the end make the American nation a great force in the advancement of mankind, and cause it to develop its own unique character.[1]

The first thing necessary, however, if we were to have a character of our own was to free ourselves from slavish adherence to European ways of thinking, for we had become "so habituated to their fashions and opinions, that we have scarcely dared to wear our coats, if not cut in their modes, though they should change with every moon; or even to think, but in the trammels, which they had forged for us;— it is now full time, that we should assume a national character, and opinions of our own; and convince the world, that we have some true philosophy on this side of the globe."[2] We were happily situated for setting before the world new conceptions of life. We were isolated from European quarrels. We were practically independent of their physical resources. A continuous constructive program would not be interfered with by frequent convulsions, and hence if this country would set itself to the task of realizing in its institutional and individual activities the full meaning of the principles announced in the eighteenth century, we could set before the world an example that would challenge it to a new

[1] Sullivan, James, *Thoughts upon the Political Situation of the United States of America*, p. 18.   1788.
[2] *Ibid.*, p. 21.   1788.

mode of living. We were morally obligated to live up to the ideals of which we were aware and to use the resources at our command for their realization.

Education and government. No other object could be of greater importance in a republican government than "to form the morals of the people to the genius of the government." [1] Ultimately, the nature of education determines the character of any people, so "for this purpose it is necessary to pay great attention to the education of youth." [1]

The greatest resource at the command of the nation for carrying out its avowed democratic program for the liberation of mankind was the youth of the nation. Prejudices and habits, long established, would of necessity make the present generation incapable of realizing that progress which they undoubtedly desired. The greatest service that they could render would be to train the next generation in the principles of government and of democratic industrial life so that that generation might come into possession of the philosophical outlook characteristic of democracy, and the habits of life that would naturally further democratic institutions. The government then stood obligated to launch in support of the democracy that had been established a national system of education that would "set up" these objects and "pursue them." [2]

Freedom of thinking and acting. Fortunately, in this country, "The freedom of thinking, with which our ancestors began to cultivate society . . . grew with their growth." [3] Again, we had an advantage because "the more enlightened view of society, which for the last century and a half has been opening among them (Europeans)" had been studied by the pioneers on this side, who had "kept equal pace, per-

[1] Sullivan, James, *Thoughts upon the Political Situation of the United States of America*, p. 27. 1788.
[2] *Ibid.*, pp. 13, 27. 1788.
[3] *Ibid.*, p. 13. 1788.

haps, with Europeans" in following these movements and who had certainly gone further in the realization of the principles involved because of their freer environment in which to act.[1] Hence eighteenth century thought had been less hampered in America in its developments, for it had been perhaps equally comprehended by the Colonials.

The circumstances under which Colonial life developed were propitious for the evolution of the ideals of the Enlightenment and of the democratic movement characteristic of the eighteenth century. The unfriendly factors of long-established feudal customs and religious regulations, that prevented the development of freedom in Europe, were in a large way absent from the American environment. Here we were able to think freely and to act freely. This was the *sine qua non* of democracy. It was this experience of freedom for one hundred and fifty years before the Revolution that made it possible to survive the period between the Revolution and the formation of the federal constitution; but it would be a mistake to think that the formation of a federal union through a convention would adequately solve the problem of national unity and progress. Through a proper system of education, could control be united to freedom, but not through written instruments.[1] There was freedom in colonial life for embodying the eighteenth century thought in its practice.

Researches into the basis of happiness. Provision should be made in education for the making of researches into the basis of happiness. No ultimate solution of the problem of how to guarantee the greatest degree of human happiness had yet been reached and might never be reached, but no mean function of the government would be that of making possible a growing solution of this problem. Unfriendly

[1] Sullivan, James, *Thoughts upon the Political Situation of the United States of America*, p. 13. 1788.

forces would always be at work against the achievement of the purposes for which the republic had been established. Also, it was to be expected that in the years to come there would be a greater clarity of understanding of the rights and privileges of human beings. This could be achieved more generally and more scientifically if promoted by the national government, through its support and control of education. This would mean, then, a clearer comprehension of the dangers to democracy, as well as of the instruments for its preservation and development.

Being aware of the tendencies toward anarchy, on the one hand, and toward monarchy on the other, Sullivan said: "I wish to excite some of my younger countrymen . . . to bend their attention, and endeavor to make deep researches into what constitutes man's happiness individually, and in society." [1]

That there should be great interest in human welfare was a natural consequence of the Revolution and of earlier American history. Considering this history in the large sense, it had been a movement for freeing man economically, religiously and politically. The evolution of the principles that came to dominate the Revolution was gradual, but Sullivan continued: "Some native American may break forth upon their and our posterity, with some system of politicks, or morals, or both, which shall surprise and charm the world; and in Lord Bacon's words, shall come home to men's business and bosoms—being founded upon more good sense and experience than any which has preceded it." [2]

The general attitude was that only a beginning had been made. Sullivan felt that "In the science of increasing man's happiness Europe has yet much to learn." [3] While great

[1] Sullivan, James, *Thoughts upon the Political Situation of the United States of America,* p. 95. 1788.
[2] *Ibid.,* p. 96. 1788.   [3] *Ibid.,* p. 97. 1788.

progress had been made during the seventeenth and eighteenth centuries, and while he was sensitive to this, he believed that it was only the beginning of what might prove to be a continuous and more fruitful evolution of human happiness through superior social control.

Specialists to gather and interpret data pertinent to effective political control. Sullivan thought with Washington and others that through governmental control of higher national education a superior political economy might be developed through careful historical and statistical study of certain trends. In this way, men of superior talents might be designated and "scattered through the states, whose whole attention should be paid to a science, which among moderns has obtained the name of political arithmetick." [1] Such a body of men would be able "to collect the extent of settlements, numbers and strength of inhabitants, their occupations and longevity, and every other particular of calculation, which can conduce to public utility." [1] Until the nation should, through such a system of education founded upon nationalistic principles of the broadest character, with all the institutions free and open to all, seek to control its destiny, no guarantee could be had that the chief "objects of pursuit" in the nation would be accomplished.[2] A body of specialists was to be at the head of the national system of education whose function would be to gather and interpret data pertinent to effective human control.

Specialists to gather and interpret data pertinent to industrial control and development. The happiness of the nation involved many factors, the political being only one of such. If the nation were to progress, "all works of human industry" must be "brought to their utmost perfection." [3] Hence,

[1] Sullivan, James, *Thoughts upon the Political Situation of the United States of America*, p. 154.   1788.
[2] *Ibid.*, p. 18.   1788.   [3] *Ibid.*, p. 155.   1788.

"another set of men might be usefully occupied at public expense, to be investigating upon the true principles of reason and common sense, the ends and purposes for which men should wish to associate with each other in society; also the limits which nature, detached from custom and preconceived opinion, has assigned them in their social intercourse." [1]

Since "division of labor is the great modern expedient for bringing all works of human industry to their utmost perfection," such a body of specialists "after removing the prejudices which all of us, more or less, have imbibed from our educations" could "point out the real improvements which society might arrive to, after being previously prepared for it." [1] No one would deny that a nation with such unlimited resources must be carefully guarded against false ambitions by a system of education that would cause its citizens to see in these resources means for human development. With the adoption of the principles of democracy it became the duty of the nation as a whole to scientifically develop all of its possibilities, and to use them wisely, in order that society might the more rapidly arrive at the utmost of improvement. [2]

"Education forms the man." *Relativity of right and wrong.* Sullivan declared that "Those things which are most laudable in one country, are most detestable in another. [3] Viewing the contrasts of morals and customs in the various countries, he was assured that "Education forms the man." [4] He cited many instances illustrating this point. The power of education was shown when, "In America any kind of exposure of woman, in company of men, is disgraceful in

---

[1] Sullivan, James, *Thoughts upon the Political Situation of the United States of America*, p. 155. 1788.

[2] *Ibid.*, pp. 95, 96, 97, 154, 155. 1788.

[3] Sullivan, James, *A Review of the Causes and Principles of the French Revolution*, p. 21. 1798.

[4] *Ibid.*, p. 21. 1798.

the extreme," while, "In Russia, the women and men occupy the warm baths promiscuously, without a charge of indecency, or a temptation to incontinency."[1] Again, "In America polygamy is severely punished; when in Turkey, it is disreputable to have but one wife."[1] He developed many other illustrations, such as suicide, religious customs, etc., and concluded that "Prejudices in politics insert themselves into the human mind, in the same manner as they are seen in matters of religion and morals."[1]

Since this was true, the office of education was clear. "To form a nation, there must be a public opinion."[2] "Upon the rectitude and permanence of that opinion depends essentially the stability and prosperity of it (the nation)."[2] This was the conviction of practically all of the leaders of thought in America immediately following the American Revolution. Education appeared to them as well as to many of the eighteenth century philosophers to be an almost omnipotent instrument for determining human conduct.

In America far more than in European countries opinion was the controlling element, and hence a unique type of opinion must be created through education. The "stability and prosperity" of American institutions rested not upon ignorance and its accompaniment, blind adherence, but upon the ideal of individual responsibility for social progress. For this reason, American education must be as comprehensive as life and must provide an insight into all of the forces that make for or against human happiness.[3]

Freedom from religious and political dominance. Because they were founded upon fear, governments had generally

[1] Sullivan, James, *A Review of the Causes and Principles of the French Revolution*, p. 21. 1798.
[2] *Ibid.*, p. 22. 1798.
[3] *Ibid.*, pp. 21, 22. 1798; *Thoughts upon the Political Situation of the United States of America*, pp. 18, 21. 1788. See Samuel Harrison Smith on effects of such a system on the individual, the United States, and the world, p. 161.

been agencies for keeping people in ignorance. "When the mass of people are ignorant, poor and miserable, there is no public opinion excepting what is the offspring of fear."[1]

In such governments, *"ignorance is the mother of devotion."*[1] This was "The religious maxim in France, for eight hundred years together."[1] There, for instance, "The political tenet adopted· and established" was "that a passive obedience to the will of the sovereign is meritous and proper; but that an inquiry into the origin of civil authority, or an examination of the rectitude of its administration, is an heinous offence."[1] There, "The civil authority guarded the church as infallible, and holy, and the church anathemized all who did not confess, that the powers which *be are ordained of God."*[1] Under such regimen, ignorance must be at a premium, and the union of church and state made possible the continuance of ignorance for the furtherance of their purposes. Here we had substituted the rule of reason for the rule of superstition and fear. Here it was in reality a crime not to inquire into the origin of civil authority and not to examine into the rectitude of its administration. Passive obedience in the United States was a crime and not a virtue. This position made it absolutely essential that the government should provide the means of intelligent criticism of all civil institutions.

Summary. The general disturbances following the Revolution were ascribed by Sullivan to a lack of preparation for democracy. The logical conclusion was that there must be a national system of education to meet the unique demands of popular social control. This education must be of such a character as would result in a broad national outlook, and such as would assure loyalty to democratic principles. He believed that a nation might set up definite objects related to

[1] Sullivan, James, *A Review of the Causes and Principles of the French Revolution*, p. 22. 1798.

the happiness and welfare of man, and that it was the duty of the United States to set up such objects and achieve them through education. We were morally obligated to create whatever instruments might be necessary for the realization of democratic ideals. The national government should provide universal opportunity for education, and it should stimulate researches into the basis of happiness. This it could do through an education that would encourage progress and seek revision of customs and institutions. That "Education forms the man" was considered beyond dispute.

Nathaniel Chipman's Plan for a National System of Education

Function of government based on man's nature—instrument for man's progress. Among the many writers of the period who sought a way out of the difficulties in the way of national unity on the one hand and in the way of human progress on the other, was Nathaniel Chipman,[1] federal judge

[1] Nathaniel Chipman (1752-1843) came of New England stock that dated back to John Howland of the *Mayflower* and to John Chipman of the expedition of 1630. Very early Nathaniel Chipman became interested in methods of study, and criticized education because it failed to direct this important educational effort. He graduated from Yale in 1778, but the degree was granted in his absence because he became a revolutionary officer. He was admitted to the bar in Connecticut in 1779 and was made a member of the Vermont legislature in 1785. In 1788 he was elected assistant judge of the supreme court. In the same year he was chosen to correspond with Alexander Hamilton about Vermont's ratification of the national constitution. In the Vermont convention he urged its ratification and was appointed to negotiate with Congress for the admission of Vermont into the union. He was appointed federal judge for the District of Vermont in 1791 and made chief justice of the supreme court in 1796. He was elected to the United States senate in 1797. In line with his democratic principles he contended in the senate, as elsewhere, that all who held office were but the "agents" of the people whom they served. He believed in natural laws as the source of justice; he was not a legalist. His political experience was in one of the stormiest centers during the post-revolutionary period and he

of the district of Vermont. Through his extensive contact with the prevailing conditions in the fulfillment of his duties as judge, he became aware of two urgent needs: first, the need of developing some form of social control that would stimulate progress; and second, the need of some means whereby the activities of the nation might be integrated. Through his analysis of the situation he believed that the reason for revolution lay in a lack of harmony between the government and man's social nature and also the general status of man's progress. Hence he proposed "to analyze the social nature of man" in order to "derive the principles, which ought to be pursued in civil institutions." [1] So long as governments were "merely arbitrary" that harmony could never exist which is necessary if governmental control is to be favorable to man's progress. He said that he believed it would "be readily perceived, that this is the only certain ground of investigation, the only mode, in which any general, consistent, practicable principles in the science of government can be established." [1] Hence he said: "This mode of investigation has been attempted in the following sketches." [1] It was his intention to carry on this investigation of natural principles as nearly as possible "uninfluenced by the weight of authority on the one hand, or a spirit of opposition on the other." [1]

As is often the case at this time, this does not turn out to be a treatise simply on principles of government but rather on the principle of societal welfare, based most directly upon the kind of education provided, and in this case an education suited to the democratic principles at the basis of our national government. Chipman held that "the civil

knew the difficulties of forming and continuing a union. His general philosophical outlook united with his long experience in law and political service caused him to look to education as the only real solution of democracy.

[1] Chipman, Nathaniel, *Principles of Government*, preface, p. iii. 1793.

and political institutions of these United States differ in principles and construction very essentially from all that have preceded them." [1]

Influence of Rousseau; statement of the positions of Rousseau and the Abbe Raynal. Nathaniel Chipman was a scholar in the field of political science. He seems to have had a well thought out reaction to practically all of the great writers in the field from the time of Plato down to the last of the eighteenth century philosophers. He believed that he differed from Rousseau and Abbe Raynal, in that he believed that man is by nature fitted for civilization as much as the savage is fitted for his state of life. He did not believe that "what are generally called social improvements, serve only to deprave" but that with a proper form of education social improvements meant added means for happiness.[2] He said, further, that "some political writers, of great eminence, —Locke, Beccaria, and many others—have admitted that man was originally designed for civil government, and that he is under a certain necessity of nature to adopt it." [3]

That man, then, is constituted by nature for progressive development is the basis of his treatise, and the problem that arises therefrom is how institutions may be created that will be in harmony with "natural liberty, and natural rights . . . those rights to which man is entitled by the law of his nature." [4]

Man a social being capable of improvement. The conclusion is reached that "man is by the laws of his common nature, as constituted by the author of his being, fitted for a state of society and of social improvements." [1] It is because this is the law of his nature that he revolts when

---

[1] Chipman, Daniel, *The Life of the Honourable Nathaniel Chipman*, p. 205. 1846.
[2] Chipman, Nathaniel, *Principles of Government*, p. 13. 1793.
[3] *Ibid.*, p. 14. 1793.   [4] *Ibid.*, p. 15. 1793.   [5] *Ibid.*, p. 50. 1793

institutions fail to serve his needs. It is because he is social by nature rather than because he is individual that revolutions take place. "He was not made for independence, but for mutual connexion, mutual dependence, and to this, everything in his nature is, more or less relative." [1]

The fact is that "Men have a relish for society" rather than being opposed to it, for "It is the scene of their improvements, and the great force of their happiness." [2] It is only through society that the greatest improvement can take place, and since "The nature of man points him to improvement" he will be social unless the influences brought to bear upon him are of such a character as to distort his very nature. Man is essentially good, or if not good, he has capacities for good. [3]

Man's progress does not take place in any mythical fashion: "His progress is in particulars." [4] When man meets a difficulty he invents a way out, or when he strikes something novel the very novelty challenges him. Man should be educated according to the principle that "Objects, in the progress, arising singly, and surprising by their novelty, have a powerful effect upon an unimproved mind." [4] The necessity of education lies in the fact that society can in this way most economically further this progress by providing the "particulars."

If a government is to be good, it must have within itself the capacity for growing better. The author optimistically concluded that "Man is, by nature, capable of improvements, which may render an amelioration in government as easy and familiar as in any science." [5]

The evidence of the history of man shows that "Man desires to associate with man, and feels a pleasure at the

[1] Chipman, Nathaniel, *Principles of Government,* p. 82.   1793.
[2] *Ibid.,* p. 92.   1793.   [3] *Ibid.,* p. 99.   1793.
[4] *Ibid.,* p. 100.   1793.   [5] *Ibid.,* p. 282.   1793.

approach of his mind.   The appetite is so universally preva-
lent, that it cannot well be denied to be the work of nature." [1]
Certainly there is no appetite "which terminates in itself,
not one which stands opposed to society." [2]   If man, then,
were to provide institutions as the means of advancement
according to his nature, there would be continual "instructive
harmony." [3]   The struggle of man with man has been based
very largely upon failure to provide a rational basis of
education, but there was hope, for "Within little more
than a century, experimental reasonings have banished almost
innumerable absurdities." [4]   The newly established democracy could create a means for accelerating the destruction
of superstitious absurdities and for the development of a
rational basis of life.

Government must possess "capacity of growing better."
The foregoing could not be taken for granted, however,
unless special provision were made, for no matter what
form of government might exist, if it did not consciously set
up instruments whereby it would develop a "capacity of
growing better" it would degenerate "into a species of despotism." [5]   Social betterment depended upon an education
that would enable man to "trace the laws of human actions
. . . with no inconsiderable degree of certainty. . . . This
is, indeed, the only solid foundation for political science." [6]
If such a progressive institutional spirit should prevail,
"Knowledge equal to this task is the result, only of accumulated experience." [7]   This "accumulated experience" could
alone take place through civil institutions and civil institutions that respect the present, for, "Men have commonly
regarded only some of the most obvious, the most predominant, existing relations, with little knowledge of the change

[1] Chipman, Nathaniel, *Principles of Government*, pp. 33-34.   1793.
[2] *Ibid.*, p. 35.   1793.   [3] *Ibid.*, p. 38.   1793.
[4] *Ibid.* p. 283.   1793.   [5] *Ibid.*, p. 281.   1793.
[6] *Ibid.*, p. 285.   1793.   [7] *Ibid.*, pp. 285-286.   1793.

in the present relations, or of the future improvement of the species." [1]

Improvement of nature of man and society. We see, then, that this is really a treatise upon the principles of "social improvement," such a social improvement as shall be "the result of his (man's) whole nature," rather than a formal treatise on the principles of government.[2] It is a conception of government which states that government is, or should be, an instrument for human progress. The establishment of social institutions of whatever character should have progress as the determining principle.

Forces against change or improvement in institutions. The difficulty of creating institutions for promoting change rather than for hindering it was very great. Vested interests were always active in preserving "the present order of things" and were responsible for hindering progress until revolution became necessary.[3] Also, "an habitual veneration for ancient establishments, and a dread of encouraging a spirit of innovation," operated to the same end.[4] These "have occurred to prevent any regular plan of fundamental reformation." [5] All of these forces combined "to continue as unalterably perfect, those institutions, which were adapted only to the weakness, ignorance, and barbarous manners of an infant people." [4] Furthermore, "By the force of habit, and inveterate national prejudices, abuses are rendered sacred," and this to the extent that "those institutions which were the offspring of chance or violence," had come "to be extolled as the most perfect productions of reason, founded in the original and unalterable principles of nature." [5] The author was sure that such was the case with the British, for: "The greater part of the nation

---

[1] Chipman, Nathaniel, *Principles of Government*, pp. 285-286. 1793.
[2] *Ibid.*, p. 15. 1793.
[3] *Ibid.*, p. 287. 1793.
[4] *Ibid.*, p. 286. 1793.
[5] *Ibid.*, p. 287. 1793.

appear fully persuaded, that all further improvements are impracticable, and that because their government was once the best, perhaps, which existed in the world, it must through all the progressive advances in knowledge, in morals, and in manners, continue the best, a pattern of unchanging perfection, though in its principles, it is much too limited for the present state." [1]

If one viewed history in the large, he might "learn to account for the constant superiority, in most nations, of private to political morality, as practiced by the same individuals." [2] Hence the great problem was how to make institutions keep pace "with the general improvements of the people." [3] As an example of survival he cited the custom of foot-binding in China.[3] His argument was that Americans would become as blind in a smugness of their own, as were the English or the Chinese unless they deliberately set up agencies that would insure progress through an attitude of experimentation in all things.

Fluid institutional provision needed. A kind of education was needed that would break the despotism of tradition. The task of creating institutions that would be fluid enough to keep abreast of progress and to further it, was very difficult and complex, for, "Indeed could every individual in society, have an intuitive prescience of the changes, as they were to arise, in their order, it would still, perhaps, be impossible to form any human institution, which would accommodate itself to every situation in the progress." [4]

Public opinion the basis of government in the United States. "In the United States of America, political opinions, though considered as merely theoretical, cannot be wholly inconsequential." [5] Here there must be generally diffused

---

[1] Chipman, Nathaniel, *Principles of Government,* p. 287. 1793.
[2] *Ibid.,* p. 288. 1793.   [3] *Ibid.,* p. 289. 1793.
[4] *Ibid.,* p. 286. 1793.   [5] *Ibid.,* p. 16. 1793.

the conception "of government, of the necessity of laws, of the end to be attained by them and the means of attaining that end," for the influences and sentiments of the people will at least "in some measure, form the features of the government, and give a complexion to its laws."[1] We were in the position here to be peculiarly free to establish the right kind of opinion. The implications of popular government could not but be evident. No system of education that had been created during a monarchical régime could function constructively in a democracy.[2]

Montesquieu's principles analyzed and criticized. After analyzing the treatise of Montesquieu, Chipman showed that Montesquieu was substantially right in saying that fear is the principle of despotic government,[3] honor the principle of a monarchy, but that "The principle of a Republic, or rather a Democratic Republic," which "he calls virtue," is understood only when it is seen that in a republic the religious and state institutions are not for limiting knowledge but for furthering it, for the priest and the church have always aided despotism and monarchies.[4] Here we were fortunately free from this alliance so destructive of human freedom.

Principles of a Democratic Republic. Knowledge should be of a very special and thorough character in a Republic, for "In a democratic republic, the law is, or ought to be, an expression of the will of the society, being the aggregate of the individual wills."[5] It was not alone necessary that there should be "a general approbation of the result," of government; there must be the ability on the part of the community to see the "general good of the community," and there should be also "an attachment to the general

[1] Chipman, Nathaniel, *Principles of Government*, p. 16. 1793.
[2] *Ibid.*, pp. 16, 19, 20, 21. 1793.   [3] *Ibid.*, p. 19. 1793.
[4] *Ibid.*, p. 20. 1793.   [5] *Ibid.*, p. 21. 1793.

good of the community." [1]   Until we should see that "In this kind of government, no force can be applied, in the execution of the laws, but what depends on this principle" we were in no real sense a democracy.[1]

Pre-revolutionary basis for nationalism.   The condition was not hopeless, however, because of several factors that lay at the basis of common sentiments and a common outlook. There had been the long and vigorous wars against the Indians coupled with the wars against the French on the frontiers. These common enemies had made the colonists conscious of their mutual interests.   The struggle with Great Britain for a respect for their common welfare had also made their relations with the mother country more tenuous and had bound the colonies by their common interests.   Not least among these unifying forces was the pioneer struggle in establishing themselves in a new country.   These common experiences had made it possible for them to get together in the time of crisis.   "This was the germ of that general union of counsels and sentiments, which produced the American." And then it was not to be forgotten that they were descended from common stock.   These were some of the most outstanding factors that kept the union from being completely demoralized during the earlier years by the strain which they all felt, and which made them realize that no external control could solve the problem adequately.[2]

National unity threatened—demoralization.   The reason for this emphasis upon nationalism as the basis of government lay in the fact that after the conclusion of the war the nation was threatened with disruption and anarchy. Something had to be done to give "any degree of nationality to the Union." [3]   How severe was the strain was known

---

[1] Chipman, Nathaniel, *Principles of Government,* p. 21.   1793.
[2] *Ibid.* pp. 241-247.   1793.   [3] *Ibid.,* p. 247.   1793.

by Nathaniel Chipman because of his immediate contact with conditions. He said:

> "A want of public credit, and its concomitant evil, a depreciating paper currency, had nearly ruined their morals, their industry, and their commerce as well as private credit. Many other causes, not necessary here to enumerate, concurred to heighten the evil. Dangerous insurrections actually existed in some of the states, and others trembled in expectation of the like event. Many began to suppose that the liberty, for which they had risked so much blood and treasure, was but a phantom of the imagination." [1]

In the midst of these conditions it was natural that an analysis should be made of the forces that would insure permanency.

Civil and natural rights. It was not to be concluded that because man is social by nature that the position taken by Thomas Paine and Locke and others was correct. Man does receive certain privileges from society, but the fact is that "Society grants him nothing." [2] It simply protects him in his existence and keeps him from becoming a prey of unfavorable elements. Man does not exist for society; society exists for man. "Nature has pointed out civil government as a means not an end." [3] The United States should be considered as an attempt to establish a government on the basis of natural rights and of progress. Legislation from this standpoint did not come from without, for if it did, it would do violence to the nature of man, because "If society and civil government be founded in natural principles, the laws, which naturally and certainly result from such a state, are the laws of nature." [4] Man is by

---

[1] Chipman, Nathaniel, *Principles of Government,* pp. 246-247.   1793.
[2] *Ibid.,* p. 108.   1793.
[3] *Ibid.,* p. 111.   1793.
[4] *Ibid.,* p. 225.   1793.

nature progressive. Hence, to be an intelligent citizen and especially to be an intelligent lawmaker, implied a knowledge of the nature of man and of the elements that made for progress.

Modern conception of history—social development. There was great need for a more thorough investigation of the laws that determined the development of nations. Historians in the past had largely been captivated by "battles and sieges only, the intrigues of statesmen, and the revolution of empires." [1] History had not been permitted; thus, to make its contribution to the welfare of mankind. Man could not progress intelligently as long as history was written in this vein. "Had they attended to the science of human nature, the development of the human mind, the powers, faculties, passions, and appetites of man; . . . the history of man in society, the natural history of the human mind, they would" have discovered the psychological and sociological basis of society, and Chipman reflected that "This science, so important to man, has till very lately, been hardly attempted by any writer." [2]

It was time, then, that the development of society should be on scientific principles. Why should not scientific methods be applied to social control? The experiment being carried on here offered the best opportunity yet provided to institute new social controls congenial to man's progress and happiness. Success beyond the expectations of the most sanguine had attended the efforts up to this time. [3]

History of the elements of progress. As soon as we would have this new history, it would not be true as it had been in the past when "One half of the progress has generally passed unnoticed." [4] Historians had been "hurried away by the more splendid events of history," and had

---

[1] Chipman, Nathaniel, *Principles of Government*, pp. 31-32. 1793.
[2] *Ibid.*, pp. 31-32.   [3] *Ibid.*, pp. 239-240. 1793.   [4] *Ibid.*, p. 32. 1793.

"mostly neglected those facts, which serve to make the progressive improvement of the mind." [1]

The creation of institutions for the development of man must be preceded by a different kind of history of civilization than had heretofore been written—a history of the social and economic forces operative and a scientific history of the development of the nature of man. This type of history would throw much light on the problem of social control for maximal development or progress. It is certain that "With man a state of improvement is not opposed to a state of nature.[2] Man is endowed by nature with all those qualities that tend toward progress. However, institutions must be made so fluid that they will be modified constantly and will become the instruments of man's forward-movement rather than hindrances to be broken by revolution, as they had been in the past.

The author's definition of man is suggestive: "Perhaps as good a definition as any, which has been given of man, in this view, is, that he is a being capable of improvement, in a progression, of which he knows not the limits." [2] The chapter title is also illuminating: *"Of the Appetite for society."* [2] It is through the perfecting of society that man is to develop and not by its destruction.

Education for democracy. The conclusion that there must be education for democracy is obvious: "The government of the several American states, as well as that of the Union, are of the democratic republican kind. We ought to know their principles, to study well their tendency, and to be able both in theory and practice, to exclude all foreign principles." [3] Unless such a system of education should be installed, the incongruities that were present everywhere would continue and these incongruities meant retardation.

---

[1] Chipman, Nathaniel, *Principles of Government* p. 32. 1793.
[2] *Ibid.*, p. 33. 1793.   [3] *Ibid.*, p. 236. 1793.

There could be little doubt, that "The student should carefully learn to distinguish those principles, which are peculiar to that government, or governments of a similar constitution; to distinguish the reasonings, which are accommodated to those principles, or solely dictated by them. He ought to know that they are not universal; that in a democratic republic, they are wholly inadmissable." [1]

While this would seem to be a great advance, it is evident that "This is not enough. He should be led through a system of laws applicable to our governments, and a train of reasoning congenial to their principles. Such a system (of education) we yet want. Can none be found equal to the arduous, the important task? Perhaps we are not fully ripe yet for the undertaking." But even though this undertaking require great talent, "Surely genius is not wanting in America." [1] The only way out of this dilemma would be through an education that would give to the citizens a philosophical, rational, and genuinely patriotic outlook upon life.[2]

Education and democratic government. From these considerations, the most vital problem in a democracy was how "To render the public sentiment a more rational, and a more powerful check upon every department of government." To effect this desirable end, "it is most essential, that there be, in the constitution of every free state, an effectual provision for the dissemination of useful knowledge. . . . To this end, common schools, as well as public seminaries, should be considered as an important object of legislative attention." [3]

The real permanency of the nation depended upon some system of education that would create a calm philosophical outlook together with a "persevering zeal of patriotism,"

---

[1] Chipman, Nathaniel, *Principles of Government*, pp. 237-238. 1793.
[2] *Ibid.*, pp. 291-292. 1793.   [3] *Ibid.*, p. 152. 1793.

that would seek the "improvement of its principles" through impressing "indelibly, on the minds of the rising generation, the sentiments of liberal virtue and genuine patriotism."[1] From the context, it is plain that "genuine patriotism" is here opposed to chauvinism and is based upon a rational appreciation of values rather than upon sentimentality; it is, in effect, a spirit of improvement and of progress.

Education in its relation to national opportunity and dignity. In a speech before the Vermont convention in which Chipman was urging the ratification of the federal constitution, he argued, "Again, we may take another view of the subject, as it relates to the promotion of learning and liberal science." He contended that if a state should isolate its endeavors, such an isolation would fail to stimulate genius "for want of great occasions and great objects to expand the powers of the mind." A state system of education would become as contracted as those interests, "commensurate with the exigencies of the state, and the narrow limits of our government." This would be unfortunate, for "In proportion as the views are more confined, more limited, and more local, the more is the mind contracted by local prejudices." Whereas, if the state of Vermont were to unite her educational endeavors with the rest of the states by being "received into the bosom of the union," her citizens would "become brethren and fellow-citizens with more than three millions of people. Instead of being confined to the narrow limits of Vermont," they would "become citizens of an extensive empire." Such national educational endeavor would "expand the social feelings," and "the necessity and facility of mutual intercourse will tend to eradicate local prejudices; the channels of information will become wide and far extended; the spirit of learning will be called forth

[1] Chipman, Nathaniel, *Principles of Government*, p. 152. 1793.

by every motive of interest and laudable ambition, and exalted by the magnitude of the objects presented." By these means, "Genius will soar to the heights of science," while if they remained independent they "might ever continue little, and, I had almost said, contemptible." By coming into the union their educational outlook would be as broad "as those of the union." Such a broad conception of their educational activities would, when carried out, give their local interests due weight in the national councils. "From the encouragement given to arts and manufactures, as an inland country, we shall reap more than a proportional advantage." Furthermore, "National safety, national pride, and national resentment,—not the petulance of a tribe, but great as the nation offended,—will all conspire in our defence." [1]

National education the only means of promoting broad culture and genuine patriotism. All citizens who were interested in perpetuating the American democracy could alone do so adequately through the establishment of a national system of education. The author concluded his work with the following sentence; "To an ardent wish for its perpetual duration, let us add the only means of securing it. Let us endeavor to diffuse, extensively, the principles of useful knowledge, and to impress, indelibly, on the minds of the rising generation, the sentiments of liberal virtue, and genuine patriotism." [2]

Summary. Out of Nathaniel Chipman's belief that revolution arose because of a lack of harmony between the nature of man and the institutions that sought to control him, and out of his wide contact with the reactionaries and the liberals during the anarchic period following the Revolution, grew

---

[1] Chipman, Daniel, *The Life of the Honourable Nathaniel Chipman,* pp. 87-88. 1846.
[2] Chipman, Nathaniel, *Principles of Government,* pp. 291-292. 1793.

his plan of a national system of education that would make possible straight thinking. He believed that social control could be scientific, that is, in harmony with the nature of man and conditions. To live fruitfully man must live not according to arbitrary laws, but according to the laws of nature which were as universal as existing things. He held that man is a social being capable of indefinite improvement, and that it is the office of the state to aid man in making the greatest improvement possible. This progress would not take place in a mythical fashion, but must be scientifically provided for in a very particular way. Education could be the means of banishing the innumerable absurdities that tended to retard man's development. America was the one place on earth where there were no powerful vested interests and where the church had lost its power to dominate dogmatically men's minds, and where we were remarkably free from "habitual veneration" and could construct a system of education on a scientific basis. We did not have "unalterably perfect" institutions. By the nation providing universally a scientific system of education, the experimental progressive attitude could be made permanent and a fluid institutional life could be developed in harmony with the principle of progress in man's nature. Here public opinion was the basis of government, and that opinion could be made democratic, responsive to the growing needs and knowledge of man. Happily we had here a long experience in self-determined social control while we were colonies. The history of that experience and the history of all that had aided human progress, if embodied in education, would make it possible to create institutions for "the progressive improvement of the mind." A national system of education was necessary, one that would lead to the broadest conception of citizenship.

CHAPTER FOUR

ACTIVITIES OF THE AMERICAN PHILOSOPHICAL SOCIETY IN
BEHALF OF A NATIONAL SYSTEM OF EDUCATION

Origin and purpose of the American Philosophical Society. The American Philosophical Society grew out of a union in 1769 of the Junto formed in 1727 with the American Philosophical Society formed in 1743, both of which were organized by Benjamin Franklin and others. The members of the Junto felt the necessity of mutual encouragement in those things that would make for a more unified scientific development of colonial interests. To accomplish this on the broadest possible scale, in 1769 the Junto was merged into the more comprehensive organization called the American Philosophical Society for Promoting Useful Knowledge. Franklin was elected president in 1769 and was annually reelected to that office until he died in 1790. He was succeeded by David Rittenhouse, and upon the death of Rittenhouse in 1796, Jefferson was elected to the presidency, which he held for nineteen years. The avowed purpose of this organization was to communicate with the North and the South and as far as possible to establish connections with societies of similar character all over the world. To carry forward this communication of "all philosophical experiments that let light into the nature of things, tend to increase the power of man over matter, and multiply the conveniences or pleasures of life," [1] a

[1] *Proceedings of the American Philosophical Society,* Vol. III, p. 9. 1843.

committee of seven members was at first organized in Philadelphia. These were to be "a physician, a mathematician, a chemist, a mechanician, a geographer, a general natural philosopher, besides a president, a treasurer, and secretary." [1] These members were to meet once a month or oftener, "to communicate to each other their observations and experiments; to receive, read, and consider such letters, communications, or queries as shall be sent from distant members; to direct the dispersing of the copies of such communications as are valuable, to other distant members, in order to secure their sentiments thereupon." [1]

The lines of activity. Everything that had to do with the furtherance of human happiness was considered an interest of this organization. The members discussed questions and published material in the fields of "natural philosophy, natural history, moral science, history, politics." [2] They conducted "investigations in botany; in medicine; in mineralogy and mining; in mathematics; in chemistry; in mechanics; in arts, trades, and manufactures; in geography and topography; in agriculture." [3] They frequently discussed political questions, and it is worthy of note that during the colonial period they discussed such questions as: "What form of government contributes most to the public weal? Which was the first that prevailed among mankind? Can any one suit mankind?" [3] "Is it consistent with the prerogatives of the crown, and the security of the people's privileges, that the executive powers of government over any territory should be made hereditary, and transferable in the family of any subject?" [2] They also discussed such questions as the education of children at public expense; the establishment of public baths; and how to supply the poor

[1] *Proceedings of the American Philosophical Society,* Vol. III, p. 9. 1843.
[2] *Ibid.,* Vol. III, p. 15.   1843.   [3] *Ibid.,* Vol. III, p. 9.   1843.

with fire-wood at a moderate cost. In the first circular it was stated: "The spirit of inquiry is awake, and nothing seems wanting but a public Society, such as the American Society is now proposed to be, formed on a plan to encourage and direct inquiries and experiments, collect and digest discoveries and inventions made, and unite the labours of many to attain one grand end, namely, the advancement of useful knowledge and improvement of our country." [1] To attain this end more effectually they sought to "enlarge the plan" of their society in order that they might call to their "assistance men of learning and ingenuity from every quarter." [1] Before 1800 over six hundred and fifty of the greatest minds of America and Europe had become members.

Cosmopolitan character of its membership. Men of every creed and interest were elected to its membership. Even during the French Revolution the royal French refugees were elected, apparently without prejudice. This is the more remarkable since it was at this time that the Hamiltonian struggle for the establishment of a monarchy was taking place in this country. Under such circumstances it would have seemed that the "liberal" members of the organization would not have permitted the royal refugees of France to come into it.

French members of the American Philosophical Society before. 1800. This organization became one of the greatest channels of French influence in America. As early as 1768 Buffon was elected. In the same year Du Simitiere was elected; he was very diligent in his attendance upon its meetings and active in adding to its collections. Linnæus was elected in 1769. In 1772 Le Roux of the Academy of Sciences in Paris became a member and "in 1775 Franklin,

---

[1] *Proceedings of the American Philosophical Society*, Vol. III. p. 18. 1843.

president in the chair, presented books by several French authors, Decquemare, Dennis, Rozier, Condorcet, Daubenton, Dubourg, Le Roux, Lavoisier, and they were elected." [1] Thus we find that the French influence found here before the opening of the Revolution a most ready instrument for modifying American thought. At the conclusion of the Revolution, "Girard de Rayneval, the first French minister sent here was elected, and a bound volume of the *Transactions* was presented to him and received with expression of his intention to forward the interests of the Society in France. He attended the meetings and agreed to forward thanks to Buffon for the gift of his works." [1] This became a precedent which caused the other ministers from France to become active members of the Society. Ternant, Luzerne, Adet, Otto, Genet, Fauchet, Hyde de Neuville and Poussin all became members. Lafayette, Chastelleux, Barbe de Marbois, Vergennes, Guichen, Cabanis, Cadet de Naux, and Le Veillard, all of whom were friends of Franklin during his stay in Paris, were elected. St. Jean Crevecoeur, who resided in this country, was an active member in propagating the interests of the Society in France. Brissot de Warville while a refugee here from the French Revolution, along with Moreau de St. Mery, a refugee from the French West Indies, was elected. Moreau de St. Mery opened a book store in the United States and secured many exchanges of documents with French scientific societies. Lerebours and Talleyrand and Volney, all of whom were exiled from France, became members. Charles Rochefoucault, Du Ponceau, and Rochefoucault de Liancourt were also elected to membership. "In 1789 Quesnay de Beauregard, who had served in the Revolutionary war, presented his elaborate Plan of the Academy of Sciences and Belles Lettres, estab-

[1] Rosengarten, J. C., *Early French Members of the American Philosophical Society*, pp. 87-88. 1907.

lished by him in Richmond, Va.; it was a very broad scheme for a sort of exchange bureau and clearing house of scientific and literary intelligence between the United States and France and other European countries."[1]   He was a grandson of Quesnay, the founder of the Physiocratic movement in France. Most of the exiles from France, who were men of note, became members and some of them rose to positions of prominence in the organization, such as Du Ponceau, who was its president for a number of years. In this way was brought to America both the liberal philosophy of the eighteenth century in France and also the reactionary philosophy of royalty.

Among the exiles was Du Pont de Nemours who was a leader in French political life before and during the Revolution. While his sympathies with royalty caused him to be exiled, he was a leader in the Physiocratic school in France and brought here the French liberal attitude rather than the reactionary. Through the influence of Jefferson he presented his plan for a national system of education that would comprehend the primary, secondary, and higher schools, colleges and universities. Two of the plans here indicated came from the leaders in French politics and education.[2] The source of American thought and institutions has not yet been adequately traced. There can be no doubt that the American Philosophical Society was one of the instruments that helped to give America the philosophy of the Revolution.

The American Philosophical Society an instrument for creating national consciousness. A study of the American membership of the Society makes evident the fact that American genius from the north to the south found here a

---

[1] Rosengarten, J. C., *Early French Members of the American Philosophical Society,* pp. 89-90. 1907.
[2] *Cf.* p. 168.

means of thinking together. From Charleston to Boston the leaders of American thought and science were elected to its membership. The distribution of members in this country as well as in Europe was of sufficient significance for some of the representative members to be given here.[1]

Interest of the American Philosophical Society in American education. It is not surprising to find that the American Philosophical Society, when the Revolution was over, began to interest itself in the peculiar problems which had arisen through the change wrought by the Revolution. They immediately set themselves to the task of aiding and furthering the purposes of the national government. It was in line with this view of its relation to the new government that there was offered by the Society a prize for "the best system of liberal Education and literary instruction, adapted to the genius of the Government of the United States; comprehending also a plan for instituting and conducting public schools in this country, on principles of the most extensive utility." [2] Many essays were received in answer to this, but the premium was divided between the two best, that of Samuel Knox, and that of Samuel Harrison Smith. Unfortunately these two are the only plans that now exist of the great number that were presented.

Samuel Knox's Plan for a System of National Education "Adapted to the Genius of the Government of the United States"

The title of Samuel Knox's [3] essay was that suggested by the Society, and in its published form it had "prefixed an

[1] Tom Paine, Hamilton, Rush, Jefferson, Madison, Washington, Franklin, Bowdoin, Smith, Adams, and Pickering are but a few of the American members who found here their inspiration in thinking through the problems of national development.

[2] Knox, Samuel, *Essay on Education*, p. 45. 1797.

[3] Samuel Knox, 1755 or 6-1832, was a physician, educator, and minister. At the time of the writing of the essay he was president of

Address to the Legislature of Maryland on the Subject." [1] Like the essay offered by Samuel Harrison Smith it comprehended two phases: First, it was to be a "liberal education"; and second, it was to be "Adapted to the Genius of the Government of the United States." [2] In other words, it was to be nationalistic and at the same time humanitarian or "humanistic."

"It should be not merely an "Eutopian idea" but it should be one that could be maintained in peace or war. Such a national system of education ought to be favorably considered by the democracy that had been established. "No country, surely, ought to despair of seeing the existence of such a national spirit." [2] However, Knox was somewhat pessimistic because of "the manner in which the subject of instituting a *National University* passed through the great legislative council of the nation." [2] But little attention had been paid to the contention that Washington had made for the necessity of such an institution. Knox continued:

> "Is it to the honour of the freest country on earth—of the vindicators of that national independence which never could have originated, much less existed, but from the enlightened independence of the public mind, that the wisdom, philanthropy and patriotism of that man, *'who unites all hearts,'* has never been treated even with the appearance of disrespect, save in his liberal endeavors to cherish into maturity and perfection the all important object of an uniform national education?" [2]

Since this recommendation made by Washington had

---

the Frederick Academy in Fredericktown, Maryland. He was a Latin, Greek and Hebrew scholar. He was a student of various treatises upon education by Quintillian, Cicero, Morhof, Sturm, and Locke. He was familiar with the writings of Price, Priestley, Webster, and others. He was an admirer of the work of Dr. Rush and of Rittenhouse. He became a member of the American Philosophical Society. For his treatise on education there were over two hundred and fifty subscribers, Washington being among the number.

[1] Knox, Samuel, *Essay on Education*. Title page. 1799.
[2] *Ibid.*, pp. 31-32. 1799.

met with such indifference, Knox believed that if the state of Maryland would immediately institute such a state system, it might aid rather than hinder the establishment of a national system.

Function of the school. The function of the school was to be intimately related to the function of the state. No state could be efficient as a democracy without "The most effectual provision for diffusing the blessings of general knowledge or scientific improvement throughout the *State.*" [1]

The government established here was begun as an institution that would make possible the greatest liberty for individual and institutional development, "In proportion, then, as our government is superior in its nature and constitution; in its principles and practice, to the systems of those which have been instituted for enslaving the minds, as well as the bodies, of their ignorant vassals, so should the most general means of diffusing and promoting knowledge, be adopted, be patronized, and supported in this and every other portion of the union." [2] An adequate provision for public education comprehended all of the schools from the primary to the university. This provision should be made in such a way that it would be alike for all.

Elementary education and public opinion. Whatever might be done by enlightened monarchs in enforcing systems of education, we were here dependent upon enlightened public opinion. The recurrent emphasis upon the inappropriateness of a system of education developed prior to the Revolution undoubtedly caused the American Philosophical Society to offer the prize for the best plan suited to democracy. There was a large portion of the public opinion that was still monarchical in character, and a great number were indifferent. Those who were aware of the essential change that

[1] Knox, Samuel, *Essays on Education*, p. 6. 1799.
[2] *Ibid.*, p. 8. 1799.

had recently been made were anxious to create a public opinion that would support education as the chief means whereby the principles of the Revolution could be sustained. No great progress could be made until such opinion were created. It was at least certain that "In order to conduct Education on the best plan, it is necessary that the community be so convinced of its importance, as cheerfully to furnish every accomodation." [1]

Organization and method in the primary school. Knox thought that there was not alone the necessity of making further provision in establishing schools, but that the schools that existed needed to be reorganized and conducted upon more efficient methods. It is rather curious to find him advocating that "children will make much more progress by first teaching them to read, and after having read their lesson to spell words out of it suited to their capacity, than by confining their attention to long dry lists or arrangements of words and syllables, however skilfully digested." [2] He suggested that "Soon as the pupils can read with tolerable ease and readiness, Webster's Institute might be properly introduced." They should be led early to see that reading was not something mechanical but was an instrument for gaining ideas. In order that this might be accomplished, "Initiating books for children should abound with easy reading lessons." [2] By learning to read in this fashion they would be thinking beings and would approach their work intelligently.

Reading: prose and poetry. There was a great lack of properly prepared textbooks. Something was being done to remedy this but much more must be done before instruction could be efficient. It was not alone necessary to prepare better books for beginners but also "For the most advanced

---

[1] Knox, Samuel, *Essay on Education*, p. 95. 1799.
[2] *Ibid.*, p. 99. 1799.

reading classes proper books should be prepared." [1] Knox believed that "The first of such collections would be best without any verse pieces," and ought to consist "entirely of fragments from the best historians, and papers from the Rambler, Guardian and Spectator." These should be arranged so "that the easiest should come first, proceeding from the simple through all the various species of style." After they had been thus introduced to prose and made proficient in it, "The latter part of the collection should consist entirely of poetry, both rhyme and blank verse. The first pieces might be all of the pastoral kind; the second elegiac; the third didactic, and the last heroic or epic; the nature of these several pieces should be carefully explained by the teacher." [1] Education should thus be made liberal, comprehending both prose and poetry of a varied character.

Grammar, writing, arithmetic. It is true that Knox did not see as clearly as Smith the implications of democracy for education. He was much more conventional in his conceptions. He suggested:

> "Soon as the pupils were capable of reading with tolerable accuracy, English grammar should be introduced, and writing; and after considerable progress in these, arithmetic." [2]

Knox also held that:

> "In acquiring a proper knowledge of English grammar, let the scholar, after having committed the rules to memory, write exercises, and parse in the same manner as is practiced in learning Latin." [2]

Here is betrayed the origin of the study of English grammar. As long as English grammar took its pattern from Latin grammar, it was a study of language form that was

[1] Knox, Samuel, *Essay on Education*, p. 100. 1799.
[2] *Ibid.*, p. 101. 1799.

not native to English. Webster was aware of this inconsistency, but it appears that Knox was not. Hence we will find that Webster contended for the creation of grammar that would be true to the spirit of the American language. (Cf. p. 244.)

Educational objectives. Liberal education on a nationalistic basis would at least have "two great leading objects to which it should be adapted, *the improvement of the mind, and, the attainment of those arts on which the welfare, prosperity, and happiness* of society depend." [1] For the most adequate national development, "Education ought to comprehend every science or branch of knowledge." [1] If an adequate system for the United States were to be provided, it must have due regard for two elements: the development of the natural resources, for they were basic to human welfare, and, along with the scientific education of this character, "the exertion of that refined and sublime knowledge on which the improvement of genius, science and taste, rather than worldly circumstances, chiefly depends." And again: "It is certainly laudable to pay due regard to those sciences that tend to enlarge the sphere of worldly interest, and without which the various and complicated business of human life cannot be transacted." [2] In this manner, "The course of education, instituted in the public seminaries, should be adapted to youth in general, whether they be intended for civil or commercial life, or for the learned professions." [3]

This view of education, then, would mean that "To confine it to a system that comprises only the knowledge of mechanical, commercial or lucrative arts; or even a knowledge of the world, as far as it can be attained by literary accomplishments, would be to view its advantages in a very

[1] Knox, Samuel, *Essay on Education*, p. 73. 1799.
[2] *Ibid.*, p. 74. 1799.   [3] *Ibid.*, p. 77. 1799.

narrow and illiberal light." [1] If we were to achieve the ideals for which we had thus far struggled, it could be accomplished only through a system of education that would set up the universal values of mankind, and would make possible their realization through making man efficient in his daily tasks. We could not have a divided system of education in this country, based upon class distinctions. There could be no real equality without equality of educational opportunities.

Double function of the elementary and secondary schools: preparation for college and for life. Knox did not free himself sufficiently to get a consistent view of the meaning of universal opportunity in education; or it may be that he saw the dualism of his own system but felt that the exigencies of the situation called for a recognition of the fact that some had wealth and others did not. In any case he said:

> "Of the inhabitants of a country so wide and extensive as this, but few, comparatively speaking, can ever attend colleges or a university; and hence the importance of paying due attention to the parish and county schools, both as nurseries for the colleges and university; and also the instruction of such as cannot extend their education to a more advanced stage of the system." [2]

He seems here to have fallen short of his ideal and to have supported the dualism that still exists.

Education as growth. Man was superior to other animals in his capacity for growth, and the mind of man was "formed for a progressive course of improvement." [3] By nature he was constituted for the "most ardent researches." [3] For this reason, "Education is the training up of the human mind by the acquisition of sciences calculated to extend its knowledge and promote its improvement." [4] While it is true that we have "a structure of body and soul superior to

[1] Knox, Samuel, *Essay on Education,* p. 73. 1799.
[2] *Ibid.* p. 85. 1799.   [3] *Ibid.,* p. 51. 1799.   [4] *Ibid.,* p. 49. 1799.

all other animals; yet experience evidently manifests that, without the aid of education, communicated by some means or other, mankind, instead of improving their mental faculties, too soon degenerate to a state of deplorable ignorance." [1] Knox did not have the faith of some of the eighteenth century philosophers in France that man was doomed to progress. He believed that unless provision were made for progress, man would degenerate.

Growth and indefinite perfectibility. Since man had been formed "for a progressive course of improvement" [2] and since he had shown himself capable of progress under untoward circumstances when provision had been made for such progress, "Such education or discipline as may be most conducive to this effect should be most highly esteemed and diligently cultivated." [3] "It is then the design of a liberal education to call forth all the latent powers of the human mind, to give exertion to natural genius, to direct the powers of taste and criticism, and to refine and polish, as well as to exercise, strengthen and direct, the whole economy of the mental system." [3] When such educational provision were made, no human being could know the limits of man's accomplishments.

Respect for personality. Any system of education that failed to regard the varying genius of man undoubtedly failed to develop the finest resources of the nation. When "highly distinguished genius" was confined to formal and traditional regimen, it frequently rose "superior to that more restricting discipline which may be absolutely necessary for those of weaker endowments." [4] While this might tend to prove "that a general system of education ought rather to be adapted to those whose parts may be more properly assigned to mediocrity, than to excellence," it certainly did

---

[1] Knox, Samuel, *Essay on Education*, pp. 49-50. 1799.
[2] *Ibid.*, p. 51. 1799. [3] *Ibid.*, p. 52. 1799. [4] *Ibid.*, p. 20. 1799.

not prove that provision for genius should be neglected.[1] He would have studies tried in order to test the capacities of the child. He would have a period of exploration for general culture, not too highly specialized, in order that genius might discover itself, and concluded that "A general national system of instruction ought therefore to be well accomodated to every different genius."[2] There should be respect for personality.

Leadership and genius. We were facing a condition in this country that demanded leadership. The incidents following the war, and also the vast possibilities of development if the nation could be properly led, demanded a type of education that would put a premium upon the creation of leadership. We should no longer foster such an education as that which sought "a smattering in French, and the accomplishments preparatory for the compting-room" or that which "initiated in the science of a smart or graceful air; and all the little arcana of social pertness and confidence."[3] American education must be, if anything, substantial and solid and of such a sort as to invite the youth of America to lead in the development of the nation's possibilities. "From these considerations it would certainly appear most proper, in establishing, or extensively patronizing, a liberal system of education, that it should be generally adapted to the various natural endowments and genius of those who are to be trained up by its discipline."[4]

But, in any event, it would also be necessary to remember, "While such a system, instead of imposing restraint, should tend to encourage the ardour of extraordinary genius and application, it should, at the same time, provide for the most suitable nurture of those of slower growth; yet equally rising to some maturity in improvement and knowledge."[4]

---

[1] Knox, Samuel, *Essay on Education*, p. 20. 1799.
[2] *Ibid.*, p. 172. 1799. [3] *Ibid.*, p. 17. 1799. [4] *Ibid.*, p. 20. 1799.

By such a system we would have a competent leadership and an intelligent following.

Private versus public education. Would not this matter of education for leadership be best taken care of by private schools? The leaders of the past had in most cases been educated in them. There were certain objections to this provision: First, it did not offer equal opportunity, and genius is in no sense confined to those who have means. The nation would lose a great deal in this way. Second, private schools tended to isolate those who were educated in them and to establish double standards. Leadership must grow out of understanding and sympathetic relationship. A system of public schools afforded the best advantages for stimulating friendships, friendships of a nobler character, that were above the distinction of class. Third, as had been seen so often, private schools stood for luxury and immorality to such an extent that they presented a great danger of moral corruption. Some would say that the "Abuse of an institution is no argument against its excellence," but when the abuse becomes characteristic, then it is certainly an argument against its excellence.[1] Fourth, private schools tended to make education the concern of the few. "One conclusive argument, however, in favour of public education, arises from its becoming an object of national patronage and encouragement on some uniform and approved plan or institution."[1] Fifth, private schools had a tendency to divide rather than to unite. In fact, the different private schools had different standards in themselves and so in this way promoted division even among the higher classes. Sixth, public schools would stimulate emulation and "It is hence too that the best means would be furnished for distinguishing literary genius and merit; and consequently pointing out to public view such talents as are best fitted to fill the various

---

[1] Knox, Samuel, *Essay on Education*, p. 65. 1799.

stations and offices which the different exigencies of the state, and the many departments of society require." [1] In this way the public school would become a place for the discovery of genius, and its most adequate preparation for public service. And, seventh, if the nation were to make this universal provision, "In such institutions, also, the means and apparatus for acquiring a competent knowledge of the arts and sciences, may be supposed to be more liberal and extensive." [2]

Public education a necessity. If the public but realized it, "their interest, their character, their freedom and their happiness depend on the state of education of their youth." [3] If the public could be brought to see this, "surely we should witness no patriotic exertions more zealously or generously called forth; or more munificently supported, than a well-digested systems of *public education.*" [3] Nothing less than "An entire, general, uniform national plan" would meet the demand. [4]

There is no more "convincing proof" of Washington's "regard for civil liberty; and its lasting and immortal existence among his fellow citizens, than his uniform patronage and liberal encouragement of public education." [5] More will be said later about Washington's plan for national education.

Separation of church and state. A very happy circumstance obtained here in that we were free from the force that had proved itself to be the supporter of ignorance throughout history—the union of church and state:

"Perhaps there is no circumstance that can be brought to view, in the history of scientific improvement, that has more retarded its progress, or tended to enslave the human mind, than that of admitting any combination to exist between the interests of academical instruction; and the, too often, partial interests of par-

[1] Knox, Samuel, *Essay on Education*, p. 66. 1799.
[2] *Ibid.*, p. 60. 1799.   [3] *Ibid.*, p. 26. 1799.
[4] *Ibid.*, p. 48. 1799.   [5] *Ibid.*, p. 29. 1799.

ticular religious bodies. On its dissolution the cause of *genuine Federalism,* as much as the cause of science, ultimately depends."[1]

Here we could fashion, on humanitarian principles, a national system of education that would give a new light to the world.

Until recently this separation of church and state had not existed and, until it did exist, no general system of education could be introduced which would not be prejudicial to progress. "It is a happy circumstance peculiarly favorable to an uniform plan of public education, that this country hath excluded ecclesiastical from civil policy, and emancipated the human mind from the tyranny of church authority; and church establishments."[2] Now we could institute a "solid and extensive" system "of education which would deserve the patronage of this country."[3] By doing this, "Instead of circumscribing the power of genius of improvement it ought to lay open the widest as well as the fairest field for still higher and higher degrees of future progress and exertion."[3]

Curriculum of the primary, secondary and higher schools. What should be the curriculum for the realization of these objectives? It must be such as would create citizens who would discharge the humanitarian obligations resting upon them. These obligations included the most intelligent development and use of the nation's resources. It must combine the creation of high moral sense and practical efficiency.

Function and curriculum of the primary school. The primary school should give instruction in fundamentals with a slight extension of the curriculum and a modification in the method of teaching that would make the fundamentals of immediate use to the pupil. "The English language; writing,

---

[1] Knox, Samuel, *Essay on Education,* p. 12. 1799.
[2] *Ibid.,* p. 78. 1799.   [3] *Ibid.,* p. 81. 1799.

arithmetic and practical mathematics, compleated by some approved compend of history and geography" constituted the substance of the curriculum of the primary schools.[1] Knox seemed to think that by not criticizing the curriculum of the primary schools too much, the movement for a national system of education would be the better approved. The material, however, was to be graded more carefully, and "to assign to each stage its own particular parts" would "tend to support a due encouragement to the whole."[2] Considerable attention was given to the various details of how to teach the alphabet, how to use books most advantageously, the best sort of print for books, and the quality of paper. The conditions were such that a clearer notion of, and a forced control of this matter were rendered necessary. Pretentious school-masters and teachers claimed to teach anything to any one. To break up this vicious tendency would require the best efforts of the nation in creating schools adapted to the immediate needs.

Arithmetic was to be made more practical. Some attention should be given to natural science, and the method should be such as "to habituate them to call forth their own exertions."[3] The teacher must be careful, however, in introducing this method, to do it "in such a manner as not to discourage, or check the ardour of their pursuit. To cherish and keep up this ardour constitutes no small share of the merit of the good teacher."[3] It is remarkable to see the number of times that this change in method was advocated. Pupils were to learn to do, to initiate, to execute, on their own responsibility. In geography and history considerable attention was to be given to modern as opposed to ancient, with due emphasis upon the geography and history of the United States.

[1] Knox, Samuel, *Essay on Education,* p. 97. 1799.
[2] *Ibid.,* p. 98. 1799.   [3] *Ibid.,* p. 103. 1799.

Function and curriculum of the county academies. A clean sweep was made when it came to the matter of academies or secondary schools. It was said, "As these Academies, agreeably to the plan laid down, are to accommodate all the youth in the country, . . . it is consequently necessary that in every respect they should be founded and conducted on a more extensive Scale." [1] Pupils were to enter the academies at the age of thirteen, and a completion of the primary courses was to be made a requisite of entrance. This was to be ascertained by strict examination. Thus they would be prepared to go on for "A classical and thorough mathematical education." [2]

Language, history, geography, mathematics, goals for academies. There was to be a considerable extension of the curriculum beyond that of the primary schools. The students were to have "a tolerable knowledge of the Latin and Greek languages, so as to translate with propriety and ease either prose or verse, to be able to write Latin, if not classically, at least grammatically; a like knowledge of the French language; a tolerable acquaintance with ancient and modern history, geography, with such a knowledge of prosody, Greek and Roman antiquities, rhetoricks, criticism and composition, as is necessary to read the classicks with propriety and taste." [3]

"In addition to the rudiments of mathematics previously acquired, they should by this time have also attained a thorough knowledge of Euclid's elements, at least of the first six, and the eleventh and twelfth books; Conic sections, Algebra with its applications to Geometry, and plain and spheric Trigonometry." Such students as were to be prepared for immediate business, and, as already suggested, not intended for the State college, might receive a less scien-

[1] Knox, Samuel, *Essay on Education* p. 112. 1799.
[2] *Ibid.*, p. 114. 1799.　　　　[3] *Ibid.*, p. 130. 1799.

tific course of mathematics, so that they could devote more of their studies to the useful or practical branches. It might be necessary that such continue a year longer at the County Academy.[1]

The emphasis here was upon general scholarship, not upon specialization, although a certain degree of specialization was to be allowed. The addition of another year for those who were to graduate into life rather than into college shows the degree of emphasis upon this phase. Hence, "Through the whole of the term allotted to this seminary, it would be proper, occasionally, to give the students a view of what constituted the compleat scholar and man of science." [1]

We have seen before that the secondary schools were to begin to take account of the problem of graduating into life and also were to furnish a background for those who were to go into the learned professions. This more complete summary is given:

> "Under this view, it would comprehend a classical knowledge of the English, French, Latin and Greek languages, Greek and Roman antiquities, ancient and modern Geography, Universal Grammar, Belles Lettres, Rhetoric and Composition, Chronology and history; The Principles of Ethics, Law, and Government; the various branches of the Mathematics, and the Sciences founded on them; Astronomy; Natural and Experimental Philosophy; to which of course ought to be added the ornamental accomplishments, Drawing, Painting, Fencing and Musick." [2]

Amusements and manners. Since many would graduate from the academies into life, and since all of those who went on to college would there be introduced more or less into social circles, "it would be a great acquisition to a place of public instruction, could such tutors be procured, as would

[1] Knox, Samuel, *Essay on Education,* p. 130. 1799.
[2] *Ibid.,* p. 77. 1799.

teach dancing, a polished address in conversation, and also the proper attitudes, gestures and actions in elocution." [1] Another accomplishment was that of music, which should be given at the second or third sessions. In this last session was to be added fencing. Looking toward possible military service and also as a matter of health regimen, the "Manual of military exercise" should be in all County Academies. This would also tend to strengthen the national spirit.[2]

Physical education and recreation—spontaneity. Physical education should be given considerable attention. It should be the duty of the careful tutor "to point out to youth from time to time as they advance in years, the proper diversions, exercises and amusements suited to those of their years, and views in life." [3] Their amusements should conform to the principles of democracy. "Their recreations, however, should be laid under no restraint" because unless they were spontaneous they would not be beneficial.[4] "Exercise and temperance are necessary both for the vigor of body and mind." [4]

Purpose of the curriculum: appreciation and progress. The teachers ought to assist the pupils in learning to appreciate the meaning of "various forms of government, manners, and customs" in order that they might intelligently act as citizens and be free from the prejudices that forced upon each generation the obsolete practices proper under other times and circumstances.[5] Again, they were to be helped to appreciate "the causes of the arts or sciences flourishing under one system, and being lost under another; as also how to estimate whatever is most conducive to the improvement and happiness of man." [5] For purposes of appreciation of the religious force in life, they might be given

[1] Knox, Samuel, *Essay on Education*, p. 146.   1799.
[2] *Ibid.*, p. 135.   1799.   [3] *Ibid.*, p. 133.   1799.
[4] *Ibid.*, p. 134.   1799.   [5] *Ibid.*, p. 105.   1799.

some understanding of the history of natural religion and morals. In this way they would be enabled to contribute to the progress of the nation.

Function and curriculum of the state colleges. The system recommended by Knox comprehended a uniform plan of education for state colleges, "under the direction of a Literary Board." [1] If such general higher education were made possible, there might be equalization of opportunity throughout the United States. Equal opportunity could be provided only through the same facilities being provided for all. [2] Uniform qualification for the members of the faculty, uniform entrance requirements, uniform administrational facilities, such as buildings, equipment, etc., and, as far as possible, a uniform curriculum, were basic in carrying out the national program.

College entrance. If the work in the colleges were to be of a college grade, this must be by the establishment of strict entrance requirements. The following were suggested:

"They (the students) ought to be admitted only on the following considerations:—

"*First,* That they should have previously gone through the course of education prescribed by the Primary school and County academy, or if instructed by private tuition, that their progress should be equal to, and on the same plan with, such as were taught at those seminaries.

"*Secondly,* That none, educated either publicly or privately, should be admitted, but such as on public examination should give satisfaction both in their classical and mathematical proficiency.

"*Thirdly,* From the close of the 15th till the expiration of the 18th year of their age." [3]

This comprehended to what amounted to state supervision over primary and secondary private education, for the

[1] Knox, Samuel, *Essay on Education,* p. 136. 1799.
[2] *Ibid.,* p. 137. 1799.   [3] *Ibid.,* p. 138. 1799.

setting of these examinations by the national Literary Board
would mean in the end that the national institutions would
set the standards for private schools. It is true that there
was here the conventional emphasis upon the classics and
mathematics. Knox did not, in this respect, take the same
stand as Smith, Webster, and others.

Course of study in the state college. The first year of the
college was to be devoted to "Exercises of classical criticism" one-half time. This was to be supplemented by "A
course of lectures on the history of Literature; the names
and customs of the Greeks and Romans; and toward the
end of the sesssion, on taste, criticism, and composition." [1]
Knox believed that "It is essentially necessary in order to
impress literary, and especially mathematical subjects, on the
minds of youth with lasting advantage, that their memories
should be frequently exercised in the repetition of what they
have already attained." [2]

The school was not, however, to be separated from life
as much as it had been in the past. Arrangements should
be made so that "the students in the State Colleges should
have time to mix a little in society, see their friends and
know something of the world as well as books." One provision that might help toward this end would be to extend
the vacation between each session. Something must be done
to overcome the disconnection between school experience and
life experience. [2]

During the second year the course in lectures should be
continued. Further work should be done in "classical reading and criticism." The students were also to "be introduced to a concise view of rhetoric, logic, and moral philosophy." Mathematics should be completely mastered, and
"geography by the use of the globes; the laws of motion, the

[1] Knox, Samuel, *Essay on Education,* p. 139. 1799.
[2] *Ibid.,* p. 141. 1799.

mechanical powers, and principles of astronomy." Attention should be given to the philosophy of Locke and Bacon, especially to "Locke's Essay on the Human Understanding and Bacon's Novum Organum." [1] These would give the basis for understanding the operations of the human mind, and the principles of experimentation which were necessary if progress were to be made. He also believed that *"A thorough knowledge of Euclid's Elements* is preferable to the best system of Logic that ever was taught." [2]

In order that they might become intelligent citizens and comprehend the principles involved in democracy, they should be given a thorough knowledge of "Moral Philosophy, under the several views of Natural Theology, Œconomicks and Jurisprudence." Because of the demand that would be made upon them to contribute constantly to the discussions of politics and national problems "The students should be required to write and produce essays." Their knowledge should not be of an idle sort.[2]

In the third year they were to give "Chief attention to Natural Philosophy" and all its branches, especially in its applications to the immediate problems of developments.[3]

Differentiation of courses. Just as in the secondary schools there would be two classes, one graduating into life and the other graduating into college, so it would be in the colleges. Some would go on to the national university, while others would not be able to do so. Those who were to go on into the national university should give more attention to the classics, especially by the double translation method, and should make a more thorough study of classical grammar.[4] Those who were "not intended for the University, might begin French" and devote more time to the study of "Latin and mathematics." [5] These should early in their course

[1] Knox, Samuel, *Essay on Education*, p. 142. 1799.
[2] *Ibid.*, p. 143. 1799. [3] *Ibid.*, p. 144. 1799.
[4] *Ibid.*, p. 118. 1799. [5] *Ibid.*, p. 120. 1799.

read "Rollin's Ancient History and Goldsmith's abridgement of the History of the Grecian and Roman republicks." [1] On the other hand those who were to go on to the university would give less attention to modern languages, and more to the ancient.[2]

Languages. Much attention was to be given to languages throughout the secondary schools, state colleges, and the University. It was thought that "the Latin and Greek languages" could not be excluded "from a system of liberal and polite education," [3] for "From this view then it is not merely the language that is to be taken into account; but also the various information the mind receives; and the refinement of our powers of taste and criticism in every species of composition." [4] Besides, according to the psychology prevailing at that time, the languages were deemed the best instruments for developing the faculties.

Function and curriculum of the National University. It seemed almost axiomatic that a government which was based upon popular intelligence, both for initiating and executing legislation, could not be too munificent "in founding, endowing and supporting a suitable seat of national improvement." [5] To make a national scheme of education effective there must be "placed at the head" of such a scheme a "National University . . . connected with every branch or seminary of the general system." This would also "confer upon it that national dignity and importance, which such a combination of public patronage and interest would justly expect and merit." Such an institution "would continue to be the fountain head of science, that centre to which all literary genius of the commonwealth would tend, and from which, when matured by its instructive influence, would diffuse

[1] Knox, Samuel, *Essay on Education,* p. 120.   1799.
[2] *Ibid.,* p. 122.   1799.   [3] *Ibid.,* p. 65.   1799.
[4] *Ibid.,* p. 57.   1799.   [5] *Ibid.,* p. 147.   1799.

the rays of knowledge and science to the remotest situations of the united government." [1]

Aims of the National University: Flexibility to meet changing conditions. Such an institution as the National University recommended here was not at any time to become fixed in its organization and curriculum. "It should comprehend every description of situation and circumstance, uncircumscribed by partial endowments, local prejudices, or personal attachments." It should be left absolutely free to accommodate itself to whatever exigency might arise. "In this view of the subject, as well as in many others, appears the great importance of *an incorporated Board of Presidents of Education.* Their abilities, literary knowledge, extensive information, and correspondence with the learned world, would enable them occasionally to enrich such a plan as the foregoing with whatever might best tend to promote its success." [2] Under no circumstances was it to be a fixed institution. It could not be inflexible if it were to meet the demands of a nation whose future would undoubtedly be very different from its present. Hence what seems to be very rigid in the requirements of the classics and mathematics undoubtedly was but tentatively so in the mind of the author, for "Indeed it is only just to allow such an ample field for progressive improvement, as it would be illiberal to have circumscribed it by any fixed or exclusive system." The aim, then, of the University, as well as of any other parts of the system, was to be: "Proper instruction of youth in every circumstance of life and also for any particular business or profession." The end to be kept in mind always was "The highest possible improvement in the Arts and Sciences." [3]

Organization and administration. Equal provision was to

---

[1] Knox, Samuel, *Essay on Education*, p. 149. 1799.
[2] *Ibid.*, p. 166. 1799.   [3] *Ibid.*, p. 165. 1799.

be made for all stages of education because "In a liberal course of public education, no one stage of it ought to be better provided for than another." [1] This vision of a democratic provision for education is still prophetic.

It was argued that if a universal system of justice could be established that would be democratic, a universal system of education would no more endanger democracy. Hence no one should be troubled if it were necessary "In order to found, lay out and carry into effect, the several seminaries." *"A board of education"* must be incorporated, "under the sanction of the united authority of the states. These gentlemen should be nominated and appointed in every state, either by the united government, or by the respective state assemblies; one or two in each state might be sufficient." To give force to the plan, "Their office should not only be to preside over the general interests of literary instruction, to digest, direct, and arrange an uniform system in all its parts; . . . but more especially, in their individual capacity, to preside with regard to it in those states in which they were resident." [2]

Such a board could perform many useful services: "One leading department of this office should be to ascertain, by the best possible information, the annual state of all the primary or parish schools, county academies, and also the college, in that state in which he presided, in order to lay it before the board at their stated time of meeting.[3] Under the direction of these state presiding officers of education there should also be county officers "to assist in procuring proper tutors; to visit every school in the respective counties and, at least twice a year, to make a just report of their state and proficiency." These county officers "should also attend quarterly and public examinations of the primary schools." To

[1] Knox, Samuel, *Essay on Education*, p. 84.   1799.
[2] *Ibid.*, p. 85.   1799.   [3] *Ibid.*, p. 87.   1799.

them the master of each school was to make a report on each pupil, and in this report was to be indicated "such as discovered any extraordinary genius, or even attention." These were to be suggested as material for the national university. No mean conception was held of these county officers: "In order faithfully to discharge this office, it is obvious it would require a gentleman of the first erudition, who would devote the whole of his attention, and consequently should have a liberal salary paid by the county." [1]

The chief difficulty in establishing such a system as that suggested was the lack of well-qualified tutors and the lack of men qualified for directorial positions, whether in the county, the state, or the nation. More will be said of this later, in the discussion of the possibility of securing the best through offering higher salaries.

Faculty of the National University. It would be necessary to attract into the national University men of superior qualifications, men who could justify to the nation, by their researches, the support of such an institution, and who could train the best youth of the nation for positions of leadership. In order that the work might be free from prejudice and from pecuniary limitations, "All these different professors should have fixed salaries, so that their support should not depend on the precarious attendance of many or few students in the respective sciences or arts." [2] In this way a just balance of interest would be established. To begin with: "There ought to be a Professor of classical learning or belles lettres and composition; a professor of Latin and Roman antiquities; a professor of Hebrew and Oriental languages; a professor of rhetoric, logic and moral philosophy; a professor and assistant professor of natural philosophy; a professor of mathematicks; a professor of

---

[1] Knox, Samuel, *Essay on Education*, p. 87. 1799.
[2] *Ibid.*, p. 158. 1799.

astronomy; a professor of history and chronology; a professor of law and the principles of government, and a professor of elocution and oratory. Besides these the various professors in the medical department, and also the professors of the ornamental arts, would compose that respectable faculty to whom the important charge of this seminary should be entrusted under the direction of the Literary Board." [1] With such direction the education of American youth and the greatest possible national improvement might take place.

Expert supervision and direction—efficient administration. Knox argued that if this "Essay is to lay, in the first place, some claim to the public attention, as in that respect superior to any system of instruction known to the writer of this Essay" it must be through "the introduction of such a learned body for the purposes already specified." [2] The circumstances that would also assure its success would be the uniformity of this plan of public instruction. Such a system of education "might also, in no small degree, be productive of, not only harmony of sentiments, unity of taste and manners, but also, the patriotic principles of genuine Federalism amongst the scattered and variegated citizens of this extensive republick." [2]

The name of the body that was to be at the head of instruction throughout the nation might be "Presidents of Literary instruction and Members of the board of National education." [3] Through the establishment of such a system there would be reports each year to the state presidents, which reports in turn would be digested and interpreted by these presidents to the National council of education located at the seat of government.

[1] Knox, Samuel, *Essay on Education*, p. 157. 1799.
[2] *Ibid.*, pp. 166-167. 1799.   [3] *Ibid.*, p. 85. 1799.

Uniform textbooks. One chapter of the Essay is *"On the Advantage of Introducing the Same Uniform System of School-Books into a Plan of Public Education."* [1] A rather deplorable condition existed throughout the nation in that "Every teacher has his favorite system, and consequently the books best adapted to it are those he recommends." [2] How far it might be advisable to adopt a uniform system of school books did not seem clear, but that something should be done to raise the quality both of the matter and of the construction of school books was certain. Perhaps, "There ought to be a Printer in each State, for the express purpose of supplying the various seminaries, in their respective states, with such school-books and other literary publications, as should be recommended or directed by the Board of Education." In this way, "Throughout the United States, the same uniform system of the most approved school-books would be established." Certainly, "Nothing would come under the direction of the Literary Board of greater importance than the selection of the best school-books for each department of science." [2] Because of the defective workmanship, the public printers should be made to follow the uniform type, binding, and construction of texts. This uniformity of text-books would apply to the colleges, academies, and primary schools, but could not apply to the national university, for its office was to further improvements, and for this reason it must be left free in this respect.

Equal support for all grades of education; equal opportunity to enjoy all grades of education. There were two principles that were inseparable if education were to be established throughout the nation. Equal support must be given to all its stages, and all grades must be equally open to the youth of the nation. "From the elementary or gram-

[1] Knox, Samuel, *Essay on Education,* p. 90. 1799.
[2] *Ibid.,* p. 91. 1799.

mar school up to the university, though in various situations and different departments, it should be considered, supported, and encouraged as constituting one entire system." Everything should be done that might "best contribute to its success."[1]

Teacher supply. If a universal provision of education were to prove effective, well qualified teachers would be necessary. Some provision must be made whereby those who had special abilities might be encouraged to be "educated for the purpose of becoming teachers." At first undoubtedly there would be a shortage of such, but if proper inducements were given, "This in the course of a few years would train up a proper supply of tutors, both masters and assistants for the different seminaries."[2] The chief item of encouragement would be that of offering adequate salaries. Perhaps this ought to take precedence over "providing buildings and accommodations."[3] If the legislature would liberally provide for such who had proved themselves persevering in the profession, and certified only such as were qualified, this would tend to raise the standard of teachers.

Importance of a system of national education. That it should be necessary to labor at such length to gain support for a national system of education was no less than an anachronism. "To have dwelt upon the national advantages of national education, in the present enlightened age of the world, would appear like an eulogium on the benefits of the light of the sun to the solar system." Governments had been active in the establishment of various kinds of institutions for the general benefit, but in the midst of all this: "it would appear, in some degree, unaccountable that little hath been done in promoting some general plan of education equally suitable and salutary to the various citi-

---

[1] Knox, Samuel, *Essay on Education*, p. 82. 1799.
[2] *Ibid.*, p. 111. 1799.   [3] *Ibid.*, p. 33. 1799.

zens of the same state or community." [1] Where national provision had been made for education it was largely in preparing for military service, "either for self-defence, or for butchering the human species, than seminaries suited to literary acquisition; the conduct of life; or the improvement of the human mind." [2] France was excepted from this indictment because of her more recent attempts at making education an institution for the furtherance of the interests of peace. Due to many influences no general provision had been made in the United States; the wide dispersion of the citizens in the United States was a chief factor. "In undertakings, however, of the first national importance, difficulties ought not to discourage. It does not appear more impracticable to establish an universal system of education, than a system of legislation or civil government: provided such a system could be digested as might justly merit, and meet with general approbation." [3] But little had been done; much was yet to be done. If we set about this task as thoroughly as we had that of establishing a system of justice, the end undoubtedly could be gained, and the results were no less desirable.

Advantages of a national system of education. Universally "Diversity of modes of education" tend to "obstruct the operations of government and improvement" and lead to many "disagreeable consequences." [3] There was a necessity here for removing social barriers and for overcoming disintegrative factions. We were suffering practices that might prove fatal to the continuance of our republic because there had been no adequate agent for the establishment of common bonds, common interests and a common outlook. "But were an approved system of national education to be established, all these imperfections of its present state, would,

---

[1] Knox, Samuel, *Essay on Education*, p. 66. 1799.
[2] *Ibid.*, p. 67. 1799.   [3] *Ibid.*, p. 69. 1799.

in a great measure, be remedied, and at the same time accompanied with many peculiar advantages." [1] Such a system would further "the polished enjoyments of social intercourse." [2] No one could calculate the veils arising from insufficient and diverse provisions for education. "Great, surely, must be the difference between two communities, in the one of which, good laws are executed only in some particular situations, while in others they are almost totally neglected; and in the other are universally established with equal and impartial authority. Such, surely, must be the difference between the effects of education when abandoned to the precarious uncertainty of casual, partial or local encouragement; and of that which has been established uniformly and generally by the united wisdom and exertions of a whole nation." [1] Conditions existed here which made it imperative to establish such a uniform and general system for, "In a country circumscribed and situated as the United States of America, a considerable local diversity in improvement, whether with respect to morals and literature, must be the consequence of such a wide extent of territory, inhabited by citizens blending together almost all the various manners and customs of every country in Europe. Nothing, then, surely, might be supposed to have a better effect towards harmonizing the whole in these important views than an uniform system of national education." [3] Dr. Price was referred to as having set forth "the evidences of a future period of improvement in the state of mankind," and he had contended for one thing above all else: "an improvement of the state of education." [4] It was further noted that he "believes there may remain a secret in it to be discovered which will contribute more than anything to the amendment of mankind: and adds, that he who would advance one step

---

[1] Knox, Samuel, *Essay no Education*, p. 70. 1799.
[2] *Ibid.*, p. 69. 1799. [3] *Ibid.*, p. 71. 1799. [4] *Ibid.*, p. 72. 1799.

toward making this discovery would deserve better of the world than all the learned scholars and professors who have hitherto existed." We had the opportunity to show that "National exertions directed to this important object could not fail to have the happiest effects on society." [1]

Summary. In response to the offer of a premium of the American Philosophical Society for the best essay on a national system of education, Knox presented his comprehensive plan of a system adapted to the genius of democracy. He conceived of the function of the school as intimately related to the function of the state, and maintained that the superiority of American principles of social control demanded a new kind of education, an education that would mean universal enlightenment and progress. The welfare of society demanded an education based upon science instead of superstition and prejudice. Man was by nature "formed for a progressive state of improvement," and it was the business of the state to provide universally every opportunity for man to realize this advancement. While education was to be universal, it was also to be sufficiently flexible to change with the changing needs and to help each student discover and develop his peculiar genius. As the nation would rapidly develop new opportunities, there would be a great need of leaders; education should be so conducted that there would be a strong stimulus toward leadership. Public education supported by the nation would be the surest and only means of effecting this. Universal support for universal education was inherent in democracy. If education were left to the precarious uncertainty of local encouragement instead of being promoted by the "wisdom and exertions of a whole nation," democracy would thereby be sacrificed. The United States had such a diverse population, being "inhabited by citizens blending together almost all the various manners and customs of every

[1] Knox, Samuel, *Essay on Education*, p. 72. 1799.

country in Europe," that unless a uniform, universal system of education were provided, no unity could be achieved. Freed from the bondage of religious dominance, we were in a position to set before the world an example of scientific control of all forces for human progress, which would reveal the great secret of happiness and achievement.

Samuel H. Smith's Plan for a National System of Liberal Education

In commenting upon the essays offered to the American Philosophical Society, the secretary of the organization said:

"Although none of the Systems of Education then under review appeared to them so well adapted to the present state of Society in this Country, as could be wished; yet considering the superior merit of two of the performances, the one entitled 'An Essay on Education'; the other, 'Remarks on Education: Illustrating the close connection between Virtue and Wisdom: to which is annexed a System of liberal Education'; the Society adjudged to each of the authors a premium of 50 dollars, and ordered the Essays to be published. On opening the sealed letters accompanying these performances, it appeared that the former was written by the Revd. *Samuel Knox* of *Bladensburg, Maryland;* and the latter by *Samuel H. Smith of Philadelphia*." [1]

The theme of this essay by Samuel H. Smith [2] was not born of one mind thinking in isolation, but of the minds of the leading statesmen and scholars comprehended in the American Philosophical Society. It was felt that the new mode of social life demanded a new form of social control,

---

[1] Smith, Samuel H., *Remarks on Education*, pp. 5-6. 1798. (Introduction in volume written by the secretary of the A. P. S.)

[2] Samuel Harrison Smith, 1772-1845, of Philadelphia, was a member of the American Philosophical Society. He attended the University of Pennsylvania. He was a student of the writings of Bacon, Milton, Locke, Rousseau, Sullivan, Rollin, Clark, and evidently a friend of Samuel Knox, for he quotes from his work before it was published. He made considerable use of Quintillian. In Philadelphia he edited a magazine called the *New World*. Later in 1800 he established *The National Intelligencer*, which he continued to edit until 1810.

that of intelligent opinion. The best means for this was a system of education, thorough and universal.

The principle stated, "of the most extensive *utility*," gives a clue to the general feeling of dissatisfaction with education as it was in the United States at that time, an education divorced from the immediate needs, both of the pioneer life and of the new type of social control that had so recently been established.[1] It is evident from these and other writings that *utility* was not to be interpreted in the narrow sense of the development of material resources but in the sense of the development of citizens who would have an appreciation of the values represented in the political as well as in the economic revolution.

It will become evident as we proceed in the exposition of this plan that at the time "virtue and wisdom" also carried the import of a new system of education, both political and economic, that would be suited to the unique conditions of the United States. The further principle, that this system of education was to be *liberal,* is also characteristic of the general attitude in the early state period. It would seem to be a paradox that education must be humanitarian, nationalistic, and individualistic. This paradox disappears, however, as soon as we grasp the fact that according to the most liberal thinkers of that period there should be developed in this country a nation largely free from the disintegrative prejudices of Europe with its narrow sectionalism, a nation with a humanitarian culture. The nationalism that was to be developed here was to be one that would represent a synthesis of life values irrespective of racial and religious differences. Such a universal culture did not exist in any other country, and hence the distinguishing characteristic of American culture would be freedom for the fullest possible human development.

[1] Smith, Samuel H., *Remarks on Education*, pp. 5-6. 1798.

Education should be the means for the development of citizens who would have the highest regard for life values from whatever source and who would cherish their own nation as the instrument through which the development of this ideal might be realized. It is not accidental that democracy has flourished where the scientific attitude has prevailed, granting, by its impartiality and disinterestedness, an opportunity for the freeing of human genius in whatever proved to be of social value.

Impartial and universal character of the new type of education. With a clear conception of the difficulties attending the creation of such a system of education, the author felt that there must be a fearless originality. He who would propose the breaking down of national distinctions as they existed in Europe, and the creating of an education that would be impartial and universal, must of necessity himself be free from those limitations and prejudices that tended to build up walls of distinction between the European nations and classes. This "capacity of original reflection," of objectively standing apart from and viewing the various cultures in order to improve upon them by bringing together the best that was in each, would call for him to "oppose with intrepidity the prejudices of the living" and also to "look upon the sentiments of the dead with distrust." [1] "He must have the courage to rend the veil that intercepts the light of truth." [1] It would require heroic endeavor to break from the traditions of the present, and to realize the ideal of the broadest possible improvement of the race.

Relative character of educational aims. Smith simplified the educational problem by relating it to two aims: to make men virtuous and to make men wise. We are told that "the terms virtuous and wise" are not "susceptible of absolute definition." [2] The idea of virtue is that man is a

---

[1] Smith, Samuel H., *Remarks on Education*, p. 9. 1798.
[2] *Ibid.*, p. 10. 1798.

being who acts, and virtue is thus synonymous with action. In order that action might be intelligent and helpful it must be guided by wisdom. It is evident that each of these vary in relation to environment and to each individual. Both of these are variables. Thus seeing what is best and doing what is best are relative. The New World offered a very different environment from that of Europe, and the democratic interpretation of life had no parallel in the history of mankind. Since the individuals who compose the nation would certainly vary, and since the nation would continually change environmentally, a system of education was needed, that would be constantly modified to meet the needs of the fluidity of life, and not one that would be invariable.[1]

Variables and flexibility in education. Where the social system was fixed there could be a fixed form of education, but where the principles of change and of variation must obtain, the almost impossible task of creating a system of education that would re-adapt itself, at least as readily as the "striking analogies" found in nature, must be undertaken.[2] The author was anxious that education should promote differentiation and not uniformity, since he saw in differentiation a possibility of contributing maximally to progress. It was clearly evident to the author and other writers that education had suffered but slight change since the middle ages, while the life of man had suffered changes innumerable.[2]

Great but limited power of education. Samuel Smith was familiar with the writings of Rousseau in which the power of education was apparently considered absolute. He was also acquainted with the opposite school that believed that education could function but slightly. Smith took the middle ground and said that "the power of education, however great, has doubtless its limits."[2] Both in France and in the

[1] Smith, Samuel H., *Remarks on Education*, p. 10.   1798.
[2] *Ibid.*, p. 13.   1798.

United States the dominating opinion was that man could be indefinitely perfected by educational means. Smith seems to have believed in the possibility of man's indefinite progress, providing customs and environment in general were not opposed to that progress. He was certain that a well planned educational régime would further the development of man for effective living. This was evidently the faith of the members of the American Philosophical Society.

Necessity of education because of the nature of man and society. It was obvious "that the crude wisdom which nature bestows is unequal to the production and government of virtue, such as man in his pursuit of happiness discovers it to be his interest to practice; and that to insure this desirable object, it is necessary that the original faculties of the mind should be vigorously exercised, extended and strengthened." [1] This contingency of virtue upon wisdom is stressed throughout the treatise, as is also the contingency of the success of education upon the kind of individual and the kind of environment. It was believed that man was made for growth, but Smith did not seem to see this as clearly in detail as Webster, yet he did see that since the European systems stood for tradition or, at most, the continuance of the *status quo,* it would not do to continue the practice of the past, which had been that of transporting systems from the Old World. None such could be adequate to meet the needs of a republic, especially a republic on American soil. Smith saw the significance of individual differences; the differences of environment in the narrower sense of New England versus Virginia; and of the still narrower and further differences in social status and occupation. Both the nature of man and the nature of society called for a variable form of education. The contrast between the fixed modes of life in Europe and the variable life in the New World must find

[1] Smith, Samuel H., *Remarks on Education,* pp. 15-16. 1798.

its counterpart in education. There could be no final forms.
Variables that would always continue to be such were the
determiners.[1]

Indefinite progress to be made through sciences and arts.
The evolution of society was seen to have been manifestly
related to the development of the sciences and the arts. It
will be remembered that at the opening the author saw the
necessity for an objective scientific attitude if there were
to result in the New World a growth unhampered by the
superstitions and prejudices of the Old World. Indefinite
progress could alone be effected through the scientific attitude. The scientific attitude was a matter of education, just
as were superstitions and prejudices, and "In proportion to
the cultivation of science and arts has the happiness of man
advanced in the nation which cultivated them." [2] It was
clear that "the origin of new and permanent regards, the
parents of a thousand new virtues" proceeded from the suggestions to man from these sources for the "improvement of
his situation." It was further observed that "this improvement seems susceptible of endless extension"; so the conclusion was reached "that reason in alliance with virtue ad-
mits of progression without termination, and that the purity
of the last is best secured by the strength of the first." [2]

This evolutionary character of virtue, its endless development in relation to time and place, might be accelerated
greatly through a form of education that had for its chief
aim the perfecting of man and society. "A reciprocity of
wants" thus being developed, there would be created a solidarity of human interests that would make for the extension of human happiness.

Humanitarianism—cosmopolitanism. The virtues that
would make for the greatest happiness of mankind, for the

[1] Smith, Samuel H., *Remarks on Education*, pp. 10, 13, 15-16, 20.
1798.
[2] *Ibid.*, pp. 17-18. 1798.

greatest intercommunication, for the furtherance of peace, would be those that would cause man to view "the whole world as a single family," in other words, "those which are unconnected with any particular time, person or place." [1] Such virtues would lift "the mind to an elevation infinitely superior to the sensation of individual regard, superior to the ardent feelings of patriotism." [1]

This humanistic strain, or world outlook, was quite general. It is worthy of note that this putting of national patriotism below humanitarianism did not cause the American Philosophical Society to refuse the prize to this essay. This broader view was also characteristic of Coram, Knox, Chipman, Webster, and others. There was to be created here a new type of national spirit, a national spirit that had for its motif the creation of a humanitarian attitude. This humanitarian spirit undoubtedly had its origin in the almost universal desire to overcome the many and terrible wars that were so general in the eighteenth century, and also to overcome the struggle between the classes that issued in the most cruel of all these wars, the French Revolution.

It will be remembered that the American Philosophical Society, which was most representative of the American spirit at that time, welcomed the royal refugees from France and thus demonstrated its catholic spirit.

Capacity for progress the unique characteristic of man. By nature man had been endowed with the capacity for indefinite improvement. The other animals were undoubtedly superior to man in their equipment for the preservation of the species but "to him alone the capacity of gradual and large improvement" had been given.[2] From this standpoint man was most "lavishly" and "bountifully" provided for. It was reiterated that this capacity could find its fullest realiza-

[1] Smith, Samuel H., *Remarks on Education* p. 19. 1798.
[2] *Ibid.*, p. 20. 1798.

tion through science. It was man's genius for invention that separated him from the animal kingdom and that made it possible for him to manipulate the most varied environments and bend them to his purposes. To give man, then, the greatest possible freedom to achieve was to be the aim of American education.[1]

Utilitarian conception of virtue. The conception of virtue took its rise from the fact that the progress of man depends upon the scientific control of his environment. "As all knowledge is susceptible of practical application, and is abused when it does not receive such application, it is improper to fix any limits to the improvement of the mind, which in proportion to its extension is qualified to effect the general good."[2] Action was the end of education, not idle culture. A world which offered unlimited opportunities for effecting changes beneficial to mankind, made it obligatory upon man to use his opportunities for humanitarian advancement. At the root of all advancement was education, for without this man would but recapitulate his past or degenerate.

Philosophy must be pragmatic. The author quoted from Bacon: "'As for the philosophers, they make imaginary laws for imaginary commonwealths, and their discoveries are in the stars, which give little light because they are so high.' (Vol. 2, p. 537.)"[3] In America were needed philosophers who would see the intimate relation between virtue and environment. Here was to be developed a people who would not be led astray by imaginative contemplations but who would deal with conditions as they were, and see in them the instruments for possible richer living.

America to make a synthesis of goods. Environment was not to be interpreted in a narrow sense. Chauvinism, which

---

[1] Smith, Samuel H., *Remarks on Education,* p. 20. 1798.
[2] *Ibid.,* p. 21. 1798.   [3] *Ibid.,* p. 23. 1798.

saw patriotism as a narrow geographical or racial virtue, effectually shut out from man's development the various resources of the world at large. Here patriotism "would become a study and a rational principle. . . . Love of country would impel us to transfuse into our own system of economy every improvement offered by other countries."[1] This was to be the unique function of American democracy, this synthesis of cultures.

It will be remembered that Smith started by saying that we should approach the work of the forefathers with a questioning, critical attitude. His evolutionary conception of virtue, its relativity to time and place, made it impossible to set up finalities as ends. The future held changes, changes more profound and far-reaching than any that had been achieved in the past. If America could have a citizenship sensitive to change in an evolving country with unlimited resources, it must come through an education that would develop such a sensitivity. Here was to be a nation that would maximally change and not one that would merely coserve; or, rather, conservation would be through the use of all values, ancient and modern, for the realization of the ideal of progress through experimentation, both in the physical and psychical sciences for the control of the forces of nature. In this way social institutions would evolve simultaneously with the evolution of the physical sciences. Intelligent obsolescing would be constant.[2]

Function of reason in progress. It was seen "that reason is the only power which directs the passions to their fit objects, and determines the force with which they ought to be applied. Rousseau says, 'It is by the activity of our passions, that our reason improves.' "[3]

Thus the pragmatic conception of the origin of knowl-

---

[1] Smith, Samuel H., *Remarks on Education*, pp. 25-26. 1798.
[2] *Ibid.*, pp. 46-49. 1798.   [3] *Ibid.*, p. 27. 1798.

edge and of its use was natural in a country where man learned by doing and for doing.

Influence of Rousseau. Rousseau influenced decidedly the thinkers of the post-revolutionary period. As a courageous and daring thinker, Rousseau was greatly admired by Smith. Smith felt that there was need of such genius and daring in order to break with the practice confirmed by tradition, and to strike out along the new lines pertinent to the development of American democracy. He believed there should be courageously set forth "what ought to be"—not just "what is." Any one who would project an adequate scheme of education would be considered by many to be a fanatic. It required some one with such a mind as that of Rousseau: "The mind of Rousseau was, without doubt, a great one; it emitted as copiously as genius or fancy can desire, the sparks of a noble intellect, which dared to disdain the shackles of prejudice, and break the chains of ignorance." [1]

The influence of Rousseau is seen further when the position was taken that "refined happiness" is "designed for the mass of any nation" and that merely because "their subsistence depends entirely upon labour, and the productiveness of labour depends on the time devoted to it," there is no adequate reason for depriving those who labour of this "refined happiness." "It only requires a zealous disposition to embrace *what ought to be,* instead of clinging to *what is,* to disarm this objection of all its force." [2]

More education, more leisure. Smith argued: "Will not the habit of reflection and progressive improvement continually devise new means of accomplishing a given object? Have not the powers of machinery already given a new creation to manufactures? And is not agriculture equally susceptible of improvement?" [3] This speeding-up of production by the use of machinery would increase the hours of leisure.

[1] Smith, Samuel H., *Remarks on Education,* p. 32. 1798.
[2] *Ibid.,* p. 33. 1798. [3] *Ibid.,* p. 34. 1798.

Growth of man was to be the end, not production, and hence the end of production was in fact to be an "increase of the hours of reflection . . . as a leading feature in a system of republican education." He further concluded that "He, who thinks frequently, imbibes a habit of independence, and of self-esteem, which are perhaps the great and only preservatives of virtue." So he said "Let us consider this feature as new, and as one which would be happily constructive." It was, further, "the prerogative of political virtue to ennoble man." With this new conception of man as a being capable of unlimited progress through the manipulation of his environment for the ennoblement of man, and the conception of the function of the state as the furtherance of human progress, there appeared immediately the intimate connection between education and its national control for nationalistic and humanistic ends.[1]

This meant also that a system of continuation education was to be instituted so that man after leaving school would not cease to advance, but would look to the school as an agency through which he might avail himself of all of the most recent developments for the furtherance of his pursuits.[1]

Society's duty and right to educate. The conclusion is obvious that society is both obligated to educate and has the right to do so. This second supposition must be established. "Previously to any prospect of success, one principle must prevail. Society must establish the right to educate, and acknowledge the duty of having educated, all children. A circumstance, so momentously important, must not be left to the negligence of individuals."[2] There is added to this a note in the Appendix saying: "It is proper to remind parents, that their children belong to the state, and, that in their education, they ought to conform to the rules which

[1] Smith, Samuel H., *Remarks on Education*, p. 35. 1798.
[2] *Ibid.*, p. 39. 1798.

it prescribes." [1] This is quoted from a speech by Cambacérès on a civil code for France.

Energizing universal education. The principles of universal education should be energetic. There could be no half-hearted acceptance of the right and duty of society to educate if democracy were to prevail. We would be but a congeries of discordant elements unless such a principle were adopted and unless such a principle "should be in the highest degree energetic." [2] In a democracy, "This is a principle which cannot be too extensively embraced." [2]

Educability of all—minimal essentials. The doctrine that education was something for a few who would profit by it, was not a doctrine consistent with democracy. "Let us, then, with mental inflexibility, believe that though all men will never be philosophers, yet that all men may be enlightened." [3] Smith added in a note a quotation from Bacon's Works, " 'Let men endeavor an endless progress, or proficience in truth.' Vol. 2, p. 417," [4] Smith concluded that "The ideas already expressed, and those which succeed, must be understood as applicable to a system of general education. They only prescribe what is necessary every man should know. They do not attempt to limit his acquisitions. Wealth and genius will always possess great advantages. It will be their prerogatives, if properly directed, to carry improvement to its highest eminences." [3]

There would be no inflexible system of education. There must be differentials in relation to the individual and to the environment. "Considerable latitude must be allowed for the different degrees of natural capacity, and the varying shades of temper and bias." [3]

Aims of education. Two criteria are developed for a proper education: first, a scientific attitude toward the pres-

[1] Smith, Samuel H., *Remarks on Education*, p. 88. Note F, Appendix. 1798.   [2] *Ibid.*, p. 40. 1798.
[3] *Ibid.*, p. 41. 1798.   [4] *Ibid.*, p. 89, Note G. 1798.

ent; and, second, a historical appreciation of the development of the race. Under all circumstances the individual should become cautious in his thinking and be made capable of distinguishing those ideas that "are either absolutely true, or in the highest degree probable." [1] In this way alone could maximal progress be made.

Pre-school education—despotic authority. In viewing the conditions as they existed it could not be denied that there were certain elements that were very unfavorable to these conceptions of education. It was recognized that "First impressions are almost omnipotent . . . but not on that account the less secure," and, for this reason, the parents and nurses tyrannize "with despotic authority." This was characteristic of the whole system where ignorant nurses, mothers, and fathers generally passed on their prejudices to the unsuspecting youth throughout the years of infancy, and it is here that "the chains of virtue or vice are generally forged." [1]

Education of a national character must do something to protect "the infant mind . . . from conviction without proof." [2] For this reason an education should be given that would establish the open mind through habitual experimentation.

Curriculum: The 3 R's. Since "the elements of education, viz., reading and writing, are so obviously necessary" Smith felt that "it is useless to do more than enumerate them." He also assumed the same for "the first principles of mathematics, as at present almost universally taught." [3] For this reason he did not dwell upon reading, writing, and arithmetic.

For the many writers who have seemed to think that no broader conception of universal education obtained dur-

---

[1] Smith, Samuel H., *Remarks on Education,* p. 42. 1798.
[2] *Ibid.,* p. 43. 1798.   [3] *Ibid.,* p. 44. 1798.

ing this period, it is instructive to see this acceptance of those principles as established in order that the broader idea might be the more emphasized.

Curriculum: Geography. The first subject considered is geography. This was not geography in the narrow sense in which it is known today, but it rather comprehended a study of practically all of the factors that have to do with the ongoing of civilization, and corresponded to what has recently been defined as "human geography." Each citizen should know the strength and weakness of the various nations, and also the peculiarities of customs and resources. He should also know the varied life and resources of the various parts of the United States. Since in a republic the citizen determined the national policies, this knowledge would "involve great advantages" both for the mercantile and the agricultural development.[1]

Curriculum: Natural philosophy. Another subject that must become a part of universal education was that of natural philosophy. The nations of Europe had developed to the extent that they had made their agricultural and mercantile interests scientific. Natural philosophy was not alone to be considered from the standpoint of the growth of national wealth but of the growth of the individual as well.[2] Smith declared: "If we behold the farmer enlightened by the knowledge of chemistry, how wide a field of reflection and pleasure, as well as profit, would acknowledge his empire?" The same was true in regard to the "ingenuity of the mechanic" who "would not long remain passive." [3] He forcefully concluded that science applied to every activity of life would liberate not only the natural resources but man as well. At some length he developed the idea of *science for all in the service of all.*[4] This

---

[1] Smith, Samuel H., *Remarks on Education*, p. 44. 1798.
[2] *Ibid.*, p. 45. 1798. [3] *Ibid.*, p. 46. 1798. [4] *Ibid.*, p. 47. 1798.

humanitarian conception of science permeated the thinking of that day and seems to have had its rise in the influence of Bacon and Rousseau who were frequently quoted in this treatise. Smith's idea of the resources of man and nature developed through science and the arts for the progress of mankind was the ideal of the national system of education.

Curriculum: Functional view of history. Man needed to be liberated from "Fanaticism and superstition" and also needed to be enlightened in regard to the devastating character of war as an instrument "of vice and folly." This liberation could alone take place through a "greatly enlarged" and "liberal acquaintance with history."[1] If the youth were made acquainted with the factors that had caused mankind to progress or to deteriorate, he would become an intelligent critic of the elements active in his present environment. Geographical knowledge would not give such an insight; neither would science. History would alone seem to be the study that would give to man a notion of values, and of methods for their achievement. For these reasons, in a democracy history must be a part of universal education.

Aim of education: Power to grow, improvement. "The second leading object of education, should be to inspire the mind with a strong disposition to improvement."[2] This emphasis, upon attitude rather than content, is significant with the notion of *science for all in the service of all* and of experimentation as the method of progressive enlightenment and development. Life would become a continuous adventure, "banishing from the mind all those sensations of indifference, ennui, and vacancy. . . . It would give to existence a thousand new charms."[3] Science chained to the

[1] Smith, Samuel H., *Remarks on Education*, p. 46. 1798.
[2] *Ibid.*, p. 47. 1798.   [3] *Ibid.*, p. 48. 1798.

development of man in his immediate environment would no longer be a subject for "a few recluse students, too apt to mingle the illusions of imagination with the results of indistinct observation." No longer would the "reproach that theory and practice oppose each other" be entertained, for, when it will be possible to make "a whole nation to be tributary to science, then it will dawn with a new lustre."[1] In this manner individual and national growth would develop simultaneously.

"A vigorous spirit of research." Never before had there been offered such an opportunity for "a vigorous spirit of research."[2] It was illimitable, and the greatest national service could be rendered in this way. We must not forget that the author was here discussing universal, minimal essentials. Here would be a nation devoted to the noble employment of humanitarian improvement. With respect to education in the schools, "This progressive improvement would be promoted . . . by inspiring youth with a taste for, and an attachment to, science, so firm, that it should be almost impossible to eradicate it in the subsequent periods of life."[3] It is well to recall again the author's conception of continuous education.[4]

Science in the service of the nation. But this object (life attachment to science) would be assisted, more than any other consideration, by—

"Rendering knowledge as highly practical as possible."[3] Smith contended that "All science ought to derive its rank from utility." Because of its vital connection with national progress. "It merits a more extensive discussion." "The only criterion of its value" was "the real good which it actually does, or is capable of doing." By establishing a direct contact between education and life, science would

---

[1] Smith, Samuel H., *Remarks on Education*, p. 47. 1798.
[2] *Ibid.*, p. 48. 1798.   [3] *Ibid.*, p. 49. 1798.   [4] *Ibid.*, p. 35. 1798.

not be the occupation of the recluse, but would be the instrument of the statesman for effecting humanitarian progress. If the youth of the nation could be in schools dominated with this passion of national service, in behalf of mankind, citizenship would come to have world significance. Humanity would not be subjected to the devastation of wars, nor enchained by superstition and prejudice, but would be laboring intelligently for the achievement of the most worthwhile ends in life.[1]

Curriculum: Physics and the happiness of man. It was as much a national duty to prosecute science as it was to prosecute the Revolution. The aims of education were not different from those stated in the preamble to the Declaration of Independence. In order that "Physics" might be seen in relation to the happiness of mankind as realized through the development of the individual and the nation, it must be so taught that it will be evident in physics that "the happiness of mankind is in the highest degree increased by discoveries and improvements connected with agriculture and manufacture." [2] Youth were to be given opportunity to carry out projects as a part of education. School and life were not to be separated, for "Naked speculation is either unintelligible or uninteresting to the young mind. . . . From this plain view of the subject, it appears that in youth the addition of practical to theoretical knowledge would add to its charms." Furthermore, "In this case, the child would realize the connection between its present pursuits, and its future prosperity, and this impression could not fail to kindle new ardour in its youthful breast." [3]

Public versus private education. The arguments of Quintilian and Milton in support of public education were reviewed, as was also the position of Locke in support of

[1] Smith, Samuel H., *Remarks on Education*, p. 49. 1798.
[2] *Ibid.*, p. 50. 1798.   [3] *Ibid.*, pp. 51-52. 1798.

private education. The conclusion was unqualifiedly in favor of public education, because of the narrowness of parental solicitude, the general weakness of parents, the lack of competition in private education, and the overwhelming biases of parents; whereas in public education there is the constant stimulation of competition, the unbiased, objective attitude, and the possibility of bringing to play upon education all the available resources of the nation.[1]

Public education should begin at birth. That education of a public sort during infancy would be most advantageous was the strong conviction of the author, who quoted Quintilian at some length, comparing the advantages of beginning education at birth rather than at seven. If the mind could be free from bias and could be given an opportunity for reacting objectively to its surroundings, the results would show how far we come from being intelligent in our living, because of the unreasoning prejudices developed during infancy.[2]

Smith would also have science begin with languages and not deferred, because he believed that thus alone could language be seen in its relation to truth and not as an instrument for passing on dogmas. By a system of "concurrent inculcation" language would aid scientific thinking, and scientific experimentation would make language an instrument for conveying the discoveries made from time to time.[3] He believed with Montesquieu that progressive enlightenment was to be the characteristic of man, and hence he said that "From these considerations, it appears, that the earlier the mind is placed under proper regimen, the greater is the probability of producing the desired effects." [4] He continued: "Making an allowance of five years, for these

---

[1] Smith, Samuel H., *Remarks on Education*, pp. 59-63. 1798.
[2] *Ibid.*, pp. 56-57. 1798. [3] *Ibid.*, p. 57. 1798. [4] *Ibid.*, p. 58. 1798.

unavoidable sacrifices (to parental weakness or ignorant caprice) . . . we arrive at the period of life most proper for commencing a system of general education." [1]

Independent reflection and conduct—objective attitude. The necessary basis for intelligent living is found in public education because it "inspires a spirit of independent reflection and conduct," since "the child now finds itself placed in a situation free from rigid parental authority." [2]   To free the mind from superstition and bias by any means other than public education is practically impossible because the tutors will consider their own interest rather than the interests of the child, and because "Error is never more dangerous than in the mouth of a parent. . . . Prejudices are as hereditary as titles." [3]   The function of American education should be to liberate the mind by establishing the scientific attitude. Here we had no hampering traditions such as those that dominated Europe, so this desirable end could be achieved provided the child could be freed from the prejudices of parents.

Parental authority averse to progress. After stating the argument that public education exposes children to immorality, Smith said: "That is true; but is it so extensively true as to countervail the numerous advantages which have been but partially stated? Is it equal to the injury sustained by the mechanical adoption of parental error or vice? More mischief, more immorality, have sprung from this source, than from the one complained of." [4]   As long as one generation was to be bound by the prejudices of the other, no great progress could be made. Parental authority is averse to progress.

Organization for carrying out the proposed scheme. "It is

[1] Smith, Samuel H., *Remarks on Education*, p. 59.   1798.
[2] *Ibid.*, p. 63.   1798.   [3] *Ibid.* p. 64.   1798.   [4] *Ibid.*, p. 65.   1798.

proposed that a board of literature and science be established on the following principles:

> "It shall consist of fourteen persons skilled in the several branches of, 1. Languages. 2. Mathematics. 3. Geography and History. 4. Natural Philosophy in general. 5. Moral Philosophy. 6. English Language, Belles Lettres, and Criticism. 7. Agriculture. 8. Manufactures. 9. Government and Laws. 10. Medicine. 11. Theology. 12. Elements of taste, including principles of Music, Architecture, Gardening, Drawing, &c. 13. Military Tactics. And in addition, 14. A person eminently skilled in Science, who shall be President of the board." [1]

That the chairman should be "A person eminently skilled in science" is indicative of the author's objective point of view.

In order that this organization for the control of American education should be as secure and free as possible it was proposed that "The persons shall hold their office during life"; they should "receive a liberal salary, which shall render them independent in their circumstances"; and that "No removal shall take place unless approved by the suffrages of three-fourths of the colleges, three-fourths of the professors of the University, and three-fourths of the fellows of the University." [2]

This board was to have complete supervision over the national system of education:

> "It shall be the duty of this board to form a system of national education to be observed in the University, the colleges, and the primary schools; to chuse the professors of the University; to fix the salaries of the several officers; and to superintend the general interests of the institution." [3]

In order that research might be stimulated there should be a fund established under the control of this board "out

---

[1] Smith, Samuel H., *Remarks on Education*, p. 71. 1798.
[2] *Ibid.*, pp. 71-72. 1798.　　　　[3] *Ibid.*, p. 72. 1798.

of which premiums be paid to such persons as shall, by their writings, excel in the treatment of subjects proposed by the board for discussion, or such as shall make any valuable discovery." Such treatises should be read by members of the board and if deemed worthy should "be printed at public expense, and the author rewarded." [1]

Supervisory powers of the Board. This central board was "to determine what authors shall be read or studied in the several institutions and at any time to substitute one author for another." [1] In order that the best works might be available as widely as possible, the Board was to be given the authority to establish libraries wherever they should see fit, and to introduce all original publications into them. [2]

For effectively carrying out the plan proposed, the importance of the establishment of such an agency for control was evident. "It is not concealed, that on the establishment of this board, the utility, the energy, and the dignity of the proposed system are deemed greatly to depend." [3] That such a board would be faithful to its high responsibilities could not be doubted, since they would see "their immediate relation to the education of youth" and their general service to society through "the impulse given to science by their efforts." [4] Hitherto learning had been "under the management of men, either incompetent to its superintendence, or not interested in a sufficient degree." [3]

A new exposition required of the unique character of American institutions. The force of the uniqueness of American institutions lay at the basis of the establishment of such an American system of education, for "The radical ideas we have recently established, and which are in a great measure peculiar to us, claim a new and entirely different

---

[1] Smith, Samuel H., *Remarks on Education,* p. 72. 1798.
[2] *Ibid.,* pp. 72-73. 1798.   [3] *Ibid.,* p. 73. 1798.
[4] *Ibid.,* p. 74. 1798.

exposition from that which they have yet received."[1] Through this hierarchy of educational institutions the results of each fresh interpretation would be a force in moulding the character of the nation. There is no uncertain conception both of the relation of education to national culture and of the peculiar character of that culture.

Practicability of such a system. There could be no question then, about the desirability of such a system, but would it be practicable? In order that there might be no doubt upon this point a considerable analysis was given of how, through a system of public taxation duly proportioned, such a system could be supported; that it would not entail too great an expense; and that such taxation would be just. Furthermore, if we had the talent to work out a system of justice that would be universal, and a national form of government to execute this justice, there was no reason to believe that we were any less capable of initiating a national system of education such as that elaborated.[2]

Flexibility: Interest and capacity to determine education. While the outlines of the scheme presented would seem to stress uniformity, that was not the intention of the author. Any system of education to be most meaningful for the nation should be of "sufficient comprehensiveness" to include "every species of genius." No restriction should be placed upon capacities and interests. "The mind should be left free to chuse its favorite object, and when chosen should find the means of prosecuting it with ardour."[3] Toward this end the system of education advocated by Smith, was to be made universal through the economic support of youth as well as through the public support of schools. No system of education would be truly democratic that did not provide

[1] Smith, Samuel H., *Remarks on Education*, p. 76. 1798.
[2] *Ibid.*, pp. 76-77. 1708. Cf. pp. 82, 84-86.
[3] *Ibid.*, p. 78. 1798.

the economic means for each individual to prosecute education.

Effects of such a system on the individual, on the United States, on the world. The effects of the establishment of such a system of education would obviously be the making of the individual "a freeman in its truest sense"; [1] "the giving of perpetuity to those political principles so closely connected with our present happiness"; [1] and the making of "numerous improvements in our political economy." Since "Politics are acknowledged to be still in their infancy," it would be seen that "No circumstance could so rapidly promote the growth of this science as an universal illumination of the mind. The minds of millions centered in one point, could not fail to produce the sublimest discoveries." [2] Since "Nation is influenced as powerfully by nation, as one individual is influenced by another," it was to be expected that there would be progress along these lines throughout the world. [3] The United States was to become the example of a new kind of national culture, a culture that had at its root liberalism, freedom, scientific progress, and science used for the progress, both of individuals and of institutions. It would be nothing less than a base disregard of a sublime privilege to fail in such a venture as this. [4]

Democracy demanded universal education. "The diffusion of knowledge, coextensive with that of virtue," was an essential part of a "republican system of education." [5] First, a republic must be made "most tenacious of its rights" for this is the virtue of "an enlightened nation." [5] Second, a democracy differs from "many societies differently organized" in that "it is not the interest of such a society to perpetuate error." [5] When the success of the nation depended upon

[1] Smith, Samuel H., *Remarks on Education*, p. 82. 1798.
[2] *Ibid.*, p. 84. 1798. [3] *Ibid.*, p. 86. 1798.
[4] *Ibid.*, pp. 84-86. 1798. [5] *Ibid.*, pp. 36-37. 1798.

the advancement of its individual citizens, there was inevitably involved the greatest possible growth of these citizens. Third, a republic is characterized by open-avenues-ahead. Here "the sources of happiness are open to all without injuring any." [1] For this reason it devolved upon a republic to aid its citizens in every way in their advancement, economically, and intellectually. Fourth, since happiness is made "to depend on the improvement of the mind, and the collision of mind with mind" each individual must have that preparation which will give him the "capacity to think and speak correctly." [1] And last, "Under a republic, duly constructed, man feels as strong a bias to improvement, as under a despotism he feels an impulse to ignorance and depression." [1] This incentive ought to make every citizen support education liberally, since his own improvement depended upon the progress of others, for without the progress of others opportunities would be limited.

Reason for omission of female education and ornamental education. The author apologized for having omitted the discussion of female education and ornamental education. The first was omitted because of his anxiety to present a system that would be acceptable to all citizens and there seemed to be at that time too much division of opinion on female education to warrant its inclusion in the national system, if that system were to be adopted. The latter was deemed a matter of "expediency rather than necessity" and more immediately applicable to the wealthier class. He would, however, have ornamental education ultimately made universal. [2]

Summary of principles. After having elucidated in this way what he meant by virtue and wisdom, and after having shown that in this country a new type of social control had

---

[1] Smith, Samuel H., *Remarks on Education*, pp. 36-37. 1798.
[2] *Ibid.*, p. 77. 1798.

been established that demanded a new kind of education, an education free from bias and superstition and founded upon scientific procedure, the following summary of principles was given:

"*In the first place,* virtue and wisdom . . . possess an inseparable connection, and the degree and efficiency of the one . . . depend on the measure and vigor of the other." [1] Smith's idea of virtue was related to time and place, and his idea of wisdom was the correlate of this ability to see virtue as related to time and place, so "From this proposition the inference is deduced that a nation cannot possibly be too enlightened, and that the most energetic zeal is necessary to make it sufficiently so for the great interests of virtue and happiness." [1]

"*Secondly.* That it is the duty of a nation to superintend and even to coerce the education of children, and that high consideration of expediency not only justify, but dictate the establishment of a system, which shall place under control independent of, and superior to, parental authority, the education of children." [1] Neither the caprice of parents nor the accident of economic situation should be allowed to interfere with a national, universal and equal educational opportunity.

"*Thirdly.* The preference has been given at a certain age to public education over domestic education." [1] The private schools were not conducive to equalization of opportunities. Their tendency was to develop class distinctions, to build up antagonisms, and hence to subordinate one part of mankind in order that it might be exploited the more successfully.

"*Fourthly.* The period of education recommended has been fixed at an age so early, as to anticipate the reign of prejudice, and to render the first impressions made on the mind subservient to virtue and truth." [1] Parental despotism

[1] Smith, Samuel H., *Remarks on Education*, pp. 66-72. 1798.

over the mind of youth had hindered progress perhaps even more than the union of church and state. This parental despotism established before the youth had acquired the power of independent thinking prevented independence later in life. For this reason it was proposed that public education should begin early enough to obviate the limitations placed upon children by their parents.

This summary of principles was followed by twenty-two recommendations:

"I. That the period of education be from 5 to 18.

"II. That every male child, without exception, be educated.

"III. That the instructor in every district attend to the faithful execution of this injunction. That it be made punishable by law in a parent to neglect offering his child to the preceptor for instruction.

"IV. That every parent, who wishes to deviate in the education of his children from the established system, be made responsible for devoting to the education of his children as much time as the established system prescribes.

"V. That a fund be raised from the citizens in the ratio of their property.

"VI. That the system be composed of primary schools; of colleges; and of a *University*.

"VII. That the primary schools be divided into two classes; the first consisting of boys from 5 to 10 years old; the second consisting of boys from 10 to 18.—And that these classes be subdivided, if necessary, into smaller ones.

"VIII. That the instruction given to the first class be the rudiments of the English language, Writing, Arithmetic, the commission to memory and delivery of select pieces, inculcating moral duties, describing natural phenomena, or displaying correct fancy.

"IX. Flexible promotion.

"X. Adherence to established truth.

"XI. That the instruction given to the second class be an extended and more correct knowledge of Arithmetic; of the English language, comprising the plain rules of critiscism and composition; the concise study of General History, and a more detailed acquaintance with the history of our own country; of Geography; of the laws of nature, practically illustrated. That this practical illustration consist in an actual devotion of a portion of time to agriculture and mechanics, under the superintendence of the preceptor. That it be the duty of this class to commit to memory, and frequently to repeat, the constitution and the fundamental laws of the United States."

"XII. That each primary school consist of 50 boys."

XIII. One boy to be annually chosen on the basis of "Industry and talents" out of the second division of the primary to be sent to college.

"XIV. That students at college so promoted be supported at the public expense. . . .

"XV. That the studies of the college consist in a still more extended acquaintance with the above stated branches of knowledge, together with the cultivation of polite literature.

"XVI. That each college admit 200 students.

"XVII. That an opportunity be furnished to those who have the ability, without interfering with the established studies, of acquiring a knowledge of modern languages, music, drawing, dancing, and fencing. . . .

"XVIII. That a National University be established, in which the highest branches of science and literature shall be taught. That it consist of students promoted from the colleges. That one student out of ten be annually chosen for this promotion. . . .

"XIX. That the student so promoted be supported at the public expense, and be lodged within the walls of the University; remaining so long as he please on a salary, in consideration of his devoting his time to the cultivation of science or literature, in which last case, he shall become a fellow of the University.

"XX. The number of professors in the College, and the University is not fixed; but it is proposed that the last contain a professor of every branch of useful knowledge.

"XXI. It is proposed that the professors be in the first instance designated by law; that afterwards, in all cases of vacancy, the professors of the college chuse the preceptors of the primary schools, and that the professors of the University chuse the professors of the colleges.

"XXII. For the promotion of literature and science, it is proposed that a board [1] of literature and science be established. . . ." [2]

Summary. The approval by the American Philosophical Society of Smith's essay on a national system of education, is an evidence of the liberal conceptions of that organization. Smith took the point of view that one who should propose an adequate system, must divest himself of fear and prejudice, —for such a system must be free from the limitations of local, racial, and religious prejudices,—and he must be dominated by an objective, universal aim. The scientific attitude should be the chief aim of American education. The openminded, impartial outlook that would put to the test of utility the most sacred creeds and customs and consider nothing as beyond question and scientific investigations, was the *sine qua non* of democracy. Such a system must be in every way flexible. If there were to be the greatest progress, growth must be the end of education. The chief emphasis must be upon invention, experimentation, personal initiative, discovery, resourcefulness, and flexibility of institutional life in order that "the power of growth" might become greater. The business of education would be to discover the individual's capacities, to discover the natural laws governing his development, to train the individual in

[1] *Cf.* p. 159.
[2] Smith, Samuel H., *Remarks on Education*, pp. 66-72. 1798.

the methods of scientific procedure, and to cause him to see that individual and social progress could best be achieved through a creative society with indefinite progress as its, aim. To assure this openminded scientific attitude the state should take charge of the child before parents could instill dogmas and superstitions inimical to progress. The nation was obligated to enforce the principle of universal education and to provide the means necessary for all to prosecute it. Economic provision was a necessity. Each citizen should be given the greatest possible opportunity to achieve. Man's genius for invention was what separated him from the other animals. Democracy must harness this genius for humanitarian progress. In the development of this power of invention lay the future of mankind. In order that man might continue to grow in effective living after he left school, some means of continuation education should be provided. In order to energize universal education a Board of Education should be established that would have supervisory and certifying powers. This board should represent the best scholarship and genius of the nation. A vigorous spirit of research into whatever would make for the progressive improvement of the nation, should be supported and stimulated as a part of the national system of education. This humanitarian scientific type of education should become the unique character of the nation. We were obligated to set such an example before the world.

CHAPTER FIVE

French influence in the United States. The plans of Lafitte and Du Pont de Nemours are representative of the French influence in American thinking, previous to 1800. Due to the difficulties arising with France at that time, this influence was somewhat checked. The extent of this French influence has been indicated in connection with the activities of the American Philosophical Society, which represented one phase of the French influence. Lafitte was in sympathy with the Agrarian movement in France, as is shown in his agrarian outlook upon the problem of education in the United States.

Lafitte du Courteil's National Plan of Education

Lafitte du Courteil,[1] professor in the Academy of Bordentown, Pennsylvania, offered a plan of national education in 1797 which he announced as a "PROPOSAL To demonstrate

---

[1] Amable-Louis-Rose de Lafitte du Courteil was professor of the French language, mathematics, geography, history, etc., and master of drawing at the Academy of Bordentown, Pennsylvania. He was a close observer of American life and institutions and travelled widely. Lafitte was a student of the colonial policies and government of the various European countries, and was also a student of government in the ancient republics. Because of his having been appointed to draw up petitions to the French government in 1776 and in 1787 for a defence of the military schools, he became greatly interested in the private and public schools of France and their methods of instruction. Upon his advent in America his chief attention was given to the conditions of education that prevailed here.

the necessity of a NATIONAL INSTITUTION in the *United States of America* for the *Education of children of both sexes.*" To this argument for a national system of education he added, "A PROJECT OF ORGANIZATION." [1]

Agrarianism. The demand of America seemed to be for a kind of education that would help the people generally to perceive the opportunities of agricultural development. Furthermore, Lafitte believed that it was in agriculture that any nation laid its most wholesome foundations. Through the institution of a proper system of education he believed that the nation might create such inviting social and economic conditions in the country that "the country would be abundantly populated with true American patriots." [2] He said: "The country is more particularly the object of my solicitude; because it is through it that a state has a positive consistency. But in the country, the children are entirely left to themselves, and they eat the most unwholesome food." [2] He argued also that the development of manufactures would make the American dependent on Europe and this dependency on Europe would make them more European than American, whereas, if agriculture were to predominate, "All nations would come to the United States for the necessary supplies of a thousand objects; this republic, thus made populous and fertile, under the shade of the olive and the shepherds' crook, would in all ages be admired by the universe." [3]

Neglect of education. Practically "All the youth of both sexes is absolutely neglected. From one extremity of America to the other, the children are seen running about the streets alone, and dispersing themselves in the country, without their parents ever knowing, or informing themselves where they have been." [4]

---

[1] Lafitte du Courteil, *National Plan of Education*, p. 1. 1797.
[2] *Ibid.*, p. 10. 1797.   [3] *Ibid.*, p. 13. 1797.   [4] *Ibid.*, p. 19. 1797.

One thing that was responsible for this condition was the private schools, for in the private schools the masters sought to please the parents and the children, and both of them were indifferent. The remedy lay in changing the nature of education offered and also in establishing effective control for equalizing opportunities. He concluded: "The summary of what I have just said is, that there is not a true national character in the United States of America, not any of those public establishments which announce a nation, and that the education of the youth of each sex is almost nothing, and the houses of instruction very defective."[1] This neglect of education must continue unless general provision were made.

Vivid contrast between cities and country. Lafitte had travelled up and down the Atlantic Coast from Boston to Charleston, and had observed in these travels what he called "afflicting contrasts." In the cities there was a certain degree of opulence and luxury, and a fair provision was made for education. But, "If after this first examination of the cities, this observer travels through the country, then his heart will be truly wounded."[2] Because of the scattered condition of the population in the rural districts children were allowed to grow up without any educational opportunities. The parents seemed to take but little interest in their offspring except as they were of immediate value in doing the work of developing the farms. The abundance of land, which should have been an inspiration for the development of the intelligence of youth, had apparently proved to be the opposite. Lafitte would have had the government offer considerable inducements to overpopulated Europe in order that these far stretches of unoccupied land might become populated, and in that way the greater density of

[1] Smith, Samuel H., *Remarks on Education*, p. 23. 1797.
[2] *Ibid.*, p. 5. 1797.

population would create a greater interest in educational institutions.

Lack of national institutions—education. Both in the country and in the city, there was one thing that stood out: There were no "public establishments such as announce an organized nation." The most surprising lack of these public establishments was the fact that there was "no national institution for the education of subjects." [1] If educational opportunities were to be provided for city and country, and if the inhabitants were to have in some small degree a common culture such as would give them a truly national spirit, a system of national education must be instituted.[1]

Conditions responsible for lack of institutions. Lafitte thought that it would not be wise to depict in detail the true conditions, for it would be generally thought that he lacked prudence and delicacy since, "the colours and features would be too strong, not to cause any person to be revolted, and that too much truth would spoil all." [2] The country abounded with agricultural opportunities that were neglected, while in the city were to be found side by side, misery and luxury; but there could be no true democracy where such inequality existed, inequality between the classes in the cities and the broader inequality between the cities and the country. Undoubtedly, the scattered condition of the population was responsible to a large extent for the lack of educational provision, and also in the country the struggle for subsistence was of such a character in many instances as to preclude the necessity of education and to discourage the refinements of cultured living.

Tendency toward division through isolation. In his travels Lafitte had observed "the essential difference of habit of almost every family." As a consequence, "From this

[1] Lafitte du Courteil, *National Plan of Education*, p. 6. 1797.
[2] *Ibid.*, p. 7. 1797.

results evidently a perpetual and constant estrangement for the reason, that we have already exposed, from a national character." [1] If, then, we cherished the development of a unity that would assure the perpetuity of the nation and that would tend toward an American culture as opposed to the European culture, this could best be accomplished through national supervision and control of education.

State control of education. Nothing less than absolute control of this matter on the part of the state would meet the demand. "To say to fathers and mothers that their children are subjects of the state, and were born to become members of the republic; is what they know, and nobody pretends to deny: But to tell them that the consequence of this principle, is, that the direction and immediate inspection of the education of children belongs to the jurisdiction of the government, will not be perhaps so generally avowed." [2] Excessive individualism due to certain economic and social conditions peculiar to America seemed to be responsible for this lack of appreciation of the meaning of education for all youth. Parents must see that their children are, first, children of the state and, second, that the state has a right to direct their education. [2]

Necessity of a national education. A study of the ancient republics showed that they had flourished or disintegrated according to the degree of attention which they had given to education. These ancient republics had in many ways a superior unity to that existing in the United States, a unity of race and common culture and customs and habits, while in America the greatest differences existed. For this reason, "On account of the difference of the elements which form the population of the United States of America, an institution of national education is there evidently more necessary

[1] Lafitte du Courteil, *National Plan of Education*, p. 18. 1797.
[2] *Ibid.*, p. 23. 1797.

to form a proper character, than it was in the republics of antiquity. This institution is absolutely necessary to make and arouse principles of patriotism to be inoculated in the heart of infancy; to strengthen the bonds of an union which needs to be incessantly solicited, in an immense republic, composed of divers peculiar states." [2] They could not depend upon the advantages the ancient republics had in common traditions and in the smallness of nations. The United States of America demanded the establishment of a national system of education to a far greater extent than did the ancient republics.[2]

National institution necessary for effective administration of instruction. To make education that controlling principle which it must be to insure the success of the republic, a national institution must be provided, for: "It is impossible, for any establishment, except a *national institution,* to be able to unite the different branches of instruction, and the objects which it renders necessary." [3] There could not be common aims, common procedures, and common provisions without this national organization.

One thing was evident, that the instructors were not here respected in any high degree; and until the instructors were given a place in the national life somewhat in accord with the service that they rendered the youth of the nation, the youth would not be guided by them into constructive citizenship. Instructors were to be given the dignity of national servants in order to accomplish this end. With national supervision there would come also the national certification of instructors, which would guarantee a higher quality of service and would be a challenge to those having real ability. Thus from whatever standpoint a national

---

[1] Lafitte du Courteil, *National Plan of Education,* p. 24. 1797.
[2] *Ibid.,* pp. 24-25. 1797.   [3] *Ibid.,* p. 25. 1797.

institution was considered, it would be necessary for an effective administration of education.[1]

Advantages of a national institution. Evident advantages would be gained through nationalizing education. First among these would be "The foundation of a national character and union." [2] A second advantage would be that of "Creating that institution in a manner the least expensive." [1] In the third place, by equally distributing the burden of education all would be able to participate in its benefits and in the end all would be more able to support it.[2] And in the fourth place, private schools were not conducive to nationality and unity.[3] If "you will form a national character possess yourselves of the earliest infancy," through the establishment of a compulsory system of national education.[4]

National education at an early age. The principle of nationalism demanded that education be begun "at the earliest age" because "it is essential in the formation of a national character." The earlier association of youth would tend in this way to erase "the differences belonging to the origin of each family." Genius would be seen not to belong to one class or race, but to all levels. In such an institution, "merit alone would count" because of the "thousand means of comparison." Family pride would give way to national pride. Local interests would be over-shadowed by the great national interests.[5]

Curriculum. Education might be divided into four periods: from six to twelve years, largely devoted to the fundamentals; [6] from twelve to sixteen years, in which would be formed chiefly the ideas of life and social processes; [6] from sixteen to eighteen years, in which would be created a

---

[1] Lafitte du Courteil, *National Plan of Education*, pp. 25-28.   1797.
[2] *Ibid.*, p. 29.   1797.   [3] *Ibid.*, p. 30.   1797.
[4] *Ibid.*, p. 32.   1797.   [5] *Ibid.*, p. 31.   1797.
[6] *Ibid.*, p. 34.   1797.

stronger sense of social obligations and in which their training would be in making all training useful to society;[1] and
the last period, from eighteen to twenty-five years, should
be devoted to specialization for the different professions.[1]

Location and organization. The plan, then, in general,
might be conceived to be as follows: First, control should
be "under immediate direction of Congress"; second, a
central higher institution was to be near the center of the
United States; third, adequate provision for instructors and
tutors was to be made in the careful selection of directors
and faculty and other officers; fourth, education of a liberal
and national character should include both sexes: and, fifth,
the whole was to be maintained at public expense.[2]

Universal provision for national education. By making
such a universal provision for education all would be made
to realize that "Every inhabitant of the country shall have a
right to have his children educated."[3] It would also become
a part of public faith that it was not only a right, a privilege,
but also a national duty to see that all were educated. Such
a scheme of instruction would make it possible for all to
equally share in the responsibilities of government and to
equally share in the results of the discharge of such
responsibilities.[3]

Universal support. The burden of such a system of
education need not be insupportable. The author suggested
that a general tax might fairly equalize the burden according
to each one's ability to bear it, and that such equalization
would be just. There could be a tax on certain commodities
that were not necessities of life, such as tea, coffee, etc., and
there might be taxes on certain liveries and carriages of
the city. If necessary, further support might be gained from
the establishment of lotteries.[4]

---

[1] Lafitte du Courteil, *National Plan of Education,* p. 35. 1797.
[2] *Ibid.,* pp. 37-40. 1797. [3] *Ibid.,* p. 49. 1797. [4] *Ibid.,* pp. 53-55. 1797.

Summary. The main contention of Lafitte was for a system of education that would provide equal opportunities for education in the country and in the cities, and would raise continually the standards of living in the country. He believed that the ultimate success of a nation depended upon the development of the rural life and resources, and he saw the inequalities of opportunities in the country as the source of ultimate failure of American democracy. The development of manufactures would tend toward dependence upon Europe and would bring into the United States monarchical influences. The United States had no great "establishments such as announce an organized nation"; especially did it lack a national system of education. The mothers and fathers must be made to acknowledge that it was not alone the privilege of the state to educate its youth but it was the obligation of the state to do so. A national institution was necessary for effective administration of instruction. Such an institution should have absolute control of certification of all instructors. This would give to the instructors that dignity which was necessary to give them due control of youth. The children should be placed in the public schools at a very early age in order to establish the national spirit and to obviate parental neglect and mal-education. In such schools merit alone would count, and peculiar family origins would be forgotten. Family pride would give way to national pride. A national system of education could more adequately and easily be supported than could local systems and private schools.

Du Pont de Nemours' Plan for "National Education in the United States of America."

Du Pont de Nemours' contact with Quesnay. Du Pont de Nemours [1] was an exponent of the eighteenth century

[1] Pierre Samuel Du Pont de Nemours, 1739-1817, intimate friend of Franklin, Jefferson, and other Americans, was political economist and statesman during the critical period in France. He studied medicine but

physiocratic philosophy. He was a member of the Société d'Agriculture de Soissons. François Quesnay, the chief exponent of the Physiocratic philosophy, sent for Du Pont after reading his essay on *Richesse de l'Etat* and in Du Pont's Memoirs we are told, "for eleven years he was my master, my instructor, my father." [1] That one whose thinking was so moulded in the fashion of the Physiocrats should be asked to write a plan of national education in the United States of America was undoubtedly due to the fact that Jefferson as well as Franklin and other Americans were profoundly influenced by that philosophy. It was the philosophy that saw in education the almost omnipotent force for the fashioning of man.

Du Pont's contact with Turgot and Franklin. Du Pont worked intimately with Turgot for a number of years and

gave up this calling because of his connections with Quesnay, Turgot, and others who were leaders in the reconstruction movement in France. In 1772 he was called to become secretary of the council of public instruction in Poland, which office he held until he was recalled by Turgot to assist him. He was active in negotiating the independence of the United States in 1782. This interested him most vitally in the outcome of the democratic movement in the United States. In 1790 he was made president of the constitutional assembly of France. While he was sympathetic to the movement for freedom, his adherence to monarchial ideals of government caused him to be imprisoned in 1794 and later forced his exile to America in 1799. Jefferson had discussed with him the problem of making national provision for education in the United States. In answer to Jefferson's request he wrote the plan here used, and it was published in 1800 under the title of "Sur l'éducation nationale dans les Étatus Unis d'Amerique." He was made secretary of the French government in 1814 and finally became councillor of state. Upon Napoleon's return he again fled to America. He was one of the first to give expression to the idea of progress in his "De l'origin et progrès d'une science nouvelle" which was published in London and Paris in 1767. In 1768 was published in Paris "Physiocratie, ou constitution naturelle du gouvernment le plus avantageux au genre humain." He also wrote many works that dealt with technical economic problems. The friendship of Du Pont with Jefferson continued from their first meeting until Du Pont's death in America.

[1] Du Pont de Nemours, *National Education in the United States of America*, p. vii. 1800. (Throughout this treatise the references are to the translation made in 1923, for convenience. The original was used by the author before the translation appeared.)

edited a paper in support of Turgot's doctrines. In 1766 he was called to Poland by Stanislas Poniatowski, the King of Poland, to become secretary of the council of public instruction. When Turgot became financial minister in France he sent for Du Pont to come back to work with him, and at the close of Turgot's régime we are told: "Du Pont retired to his estate near Nemours and occupied himself with the education of his two sons, the development of his estate, the translation of Ariosto, and his Memoirs of Turgot." [1]

In 1782 when Franklin was laboring for the recognition of the United States, Du Pont assisted him and was made Councillor of State because of his services in the treaty involved and also in the French-English treaty of commerce. Perhaps the best reward that he gained from these services was the intimate friendship with Franklin and Jefferson, two leading Americans who were representatives of the New American spirit. Thus Du Pont de Nemours had a somewhat direct knowledge of the problems facing the United States, and was not writing simply as a casual visitor in the United States in 1800. He knew also the problems in France and the difficulty in meeting them.

Du Pont de Nemours in America. In 1799 Du Pont came to America and settled in New York. He frequently visited Jefferson in Philadelphia, and Jefferson undoubtedly visited him in New York City. It was during this time that they worked out together the scheme of education proposed by Du Pont. It was written in French because Du Pont could not write in English but many of the Americans at that time could read French. [2]

Du Pont's treatise written at the request of Jefferson. To those who persist in thinking of Jefferson as opposed to the

---

[1] Du Pont de Nemours, *National Education in the United States of America*, p. viii-ix. 1800.   [2] *Ibid.*, pp. xii, xiii. 1800.

broader national conception of education, and to those who feel that perhaps one of the great differences between him and Washington was that of a national system of education headed in a national university, it may be instructive to find that in 1800 Du Pont wrote this treatise on National Education in the United States of America at Jefferson's request.[1] We are fortunate in having this treatise made available through its translation by Bessie Gardiner Du Pont, a member of the Du Pont family.

In the preface to the translation it is said:

"This is something more than the educational ideas of a learned Frenchman. It probably contains the theories of both Jefferson and Du Pont de Nemours modified to form one carefully detailed plan. It was written before Jefferson's election to the presidency, when as vice-president he was living in Philadelphia and Du Pont de Nemours was in New York and they had frequent opportunities of meeting. They had been warm friends for more than fifteen years; they were both eager students of Greek and Latin and mathematics,—Du Pont was the better educated in scientific subjects, Jefferson in modern languages; both were thoughtful and honest patriots; each had seen the institutions of his country shaken to their foundations by the most important revolutions in history and each had played an important part in those revolutions. It was inevitable that two such men should try to formulate a plan to educate their country-men for their new opportunities."[2]

It is further said that Du Pont "had the approval of that great statesman and of his worthy successor."[3]

The similarities between Jefferson's plan of education for the state of Virginia and Du Pont's national system.[4] While it is not the intention here to delineate the plan proposed by Thomas Jefferson for the state of Virginia, it may be

---

[1] Du Pont de Nemours, *National Education in the United States of Amerca*, p. iii. 1800.

[2] *Ibid.*, pp. v-vi. 1800. [3] *Ibid.*, p. iii. 1800.

[4] No further discussion of Jefferson's ideas are given here than is necessary to indicate his probable belief in a national system of education. His plans for Virginia have been treated by others.

well to notice some of the similarities between that plan and the one by Du Pont. There need be no inconsistencies between the national conception of Du Pont in which there is a high degree of centralized control and the plan offered by Jefferson for his own state. Some of the similarities are so obvious that there can be no doubt of mutual influence in thinking.

The exigencies of the times caused Jefferson to support local control. The idea that Jefferson was opposed to centralized control is probably a mistaken conception. It is known that he believed in a high degree of centralization. For instance, in 1785 in a letter to Colonel Monroe he advocated the regulation of trade by Congress, and in the same letter opposed a "plan of opening our land offices, by dividing them among the States, and selling them at vendue," because he believed "It separates still more the interests of the States, which ought to be made joint in every possible instance, in order to cultivate the idea of our being one nation, and to multiply the instances in which the people shall look up to Congress as their head." [1] Jefferson represented the democratic element of the back country, and he always worked on the principle of expedience. It was probably for this reason that the system of education which he recommended was based largely upon local control. It was expedient to offer such a system as would appeal to his clientèle. No doubt the exigencies of the times were the chief reason for this phase of Jefferson's proposal. It is likely that he suggested to Du Pont the offering of his national scheme of education with a hope that it might gain acceptance even with those who were opposed to centralization.

Jefferson a believer in American education. In a letter to

---

[1] Washington, H. A., *The Writings of Thomas Jefferson*, Vol. I, p. 247. 1853.

J. Bannister, Jr., in 1785 Jefferson raised the question: "Why send an American youth to Europe for education? What are the objects of an useful American education?" [1] He did not conceive that there would be any advantage derived from sending young men to Geneva, for he said: "The late revolution has rendered it a tyrannical aristocracy, more likely to give ill than good ideas to an American." [1] He believed that every part of liberal education could be as well acquired in America as in Europe, excepting, perhaps, "the habit of speaking the modern languages." [1] He believed that the youth of the nation would be demoralized by going to foreign countries for their education. For instance, "If he goes to England, he learns drinking, horse-racing, and boxing. These are the peculiarities of English education." [1] His experience in Europe had apparently caused him to turn against European education. He said that before he went to Europe he suspected that certain evils might have existed and that residence there had convinced him "that an American, coming to Europe for education, loses in his knowledge, in his morals, in his health, in his habits, and in his happiness." [2] Furthermore, the trusted leaders in America "are those who have been educated among them (Americans), and whose manners, morals, and habits, are perfectly homogeneous with those of the country." [3]

Republican principles of government peculiar to America. In writing to T. M. Randolph, Jr., in 1787, Jefferson congratulated him upon the fact that he had fixed upon politics as his principal pursuit. Jefferson believed that America would most immediately be benefitted through this

[1] Washington, H. A., *The Writings of Thomas Jefferson*, Vol. I, p. 467. 1853.
[2] *Ibid.*, Vol. I, pp. 468-469. 1853.
[3] *Ibid.* Vol. I. pp. 468-469. 1853. Ford, Paul Leicester, *The Writings of Thomas Jefferson*, Vol. I, pp. xxi, xxii. 1892.

avenue. He said: "She has much for you to do. For, though we may say with confidence, that the worst of the American constitutions is better than the best which ever existed before, in any other country, and that they are wonderfully perfect for a first essay, yet every human essay must have defects." [1] The labor of perfecting American institutions required an education of a unique type, the kind of education that could alone be given in the United States. [2] In 1788 he wrote Mr. Izard that he considered the United States fortunate in that "every description of interest is in favor of national and moderate government." [3] The spirit that prevailed in America was favorable to such changes as would be found necessary, since "we are yet able to send our wise and good men together to talk over our form of government, discuss its weaknesses and establish its remedies with the same *sang-froid* as they would a subject of agriculture." [3] We had given to the world an example "of changing our form of government under the authority of reason only, without bloodshed," [3] and this bid fair to become the prominent principle in American life. [4] Jefferson believed that education should be of such a character as to make this principle of change permanent. By change Jefferson referred to form and not to any possible change of principle. In this he stood in contrast with Webster on the Bill of Rights. [5]

Education forward-looking; Jefferson's plan. It is not necessary here to enter into the details of the system sug-

[1] Washington, H. A., *The Writings of Thomas Jefferson*, Vol. 1, p. 175. 1853.

[2] Ford, Paul Leicester, *The Writings of Thomas Jefferson*, Vol. VII, p. 455. 1896. Vol. X, p. 4. 1899.

[3] Washington, H. A., *The Writings of Thomas Jefferson*, Vol. II, p. 429. 1853.

[4] *Ibid.*, Vol. III, p. 390. 1853.

[5] *Cf.* p. 209.

gested by Jefferson, but it is worth while to note [1] his sentiments: "The Gothic idea that we are to look backwards instead of forwards for the improvement of the human mind, and to recur to the annals of our ancestors for what is most perfect in government, in religion and in learning, is worthy of those bigots in religion and government, by whom it has been recommended, and whose purposes it would answer. But it is not an idea which this country will endure." [2] Jefferson said he had two great features in mind in his educational proposals: 1. That of general education, to enable every man to judge for himself what will secure or endanger his freedom. 2. To divide every county into hundreds, of such size that all the children of each will be within reach of a central school in it." [3]

Education a national duty. In 1806 Jefferson went so far as to advocate that there be added to the constitutional federal powers such matters as "public education, roads, rivers, canals." [4] If these were made matters of federal control, "By these operations new channels of communications will be opened between the States; the lines of separation will disappear, their interests will be identified, and their union cemented by new and indissoluble ties. Education is here placed among the articles of public care." [5] It would appear from such sentiments as this that Jefferson in reality was in favor of federal control of education and that the plan offered for his own state took its character immediately from the outlook of the democracy of the back-country.

Du Pont's plan for a national system of education might be considered to be not only consistent with Jefferson's ideas,

---

[1] Washington, H. A., *The Writings of Thomas Jefferson*, Vol. III, p. 317; VI, 564, 656, 566. 1853.

[2] *Ibid.*, Vol. IV, p. 317. 1853.

[3] *Ibid.*, Vol. V, p. 525. 1854.

[4] Ford, Paul Leicester, *The Writings of Thomas Jefferson*, Vol. III, p. 494. 1897.

[5] *Ibid.*, Vol. III, p. 494. 1897.

but also an expression of Jefferson's greatest desires. By the plan coming from another, no undue prejudice would be raised because of party prejudice, and no political ridicule would be involved because of charges against him for apparent inconsistency. Du Pont's plan may be accepted as substantially Jefferson's view.

Du Pont's view of the educational status in the United States in 1800 as compared with that of Europe. It was natural that a European, accustomed to the educational conditions prevailing there, should see in the United States conditions that seemed advanced. Du Pont said that there was "a large number of primary schools" and that "THE UNITED STATES are more advanced in their educational facilities than most countries." Hence he said:

"Most young Americans, therefore, can read, write, and cipher. Not more than four in a thousand are unable to write legibly— even neatly; while in Spain, Portugal, Italy, only a sixth of the population can read; in Germany, even in France, not more than a third; in Poland, about two men in a hundred; and in Russia, not one in two hundred." [1]

The United States was rather to be compared with

"England, Holland, the Protestant Cantons of Switzerland . . . because in those countries the Bible is read; it is considered a duty to read it to the children." [1]

An illuminating side-light is thrown in the following:

"In America, a great number of people read the Bible, and all the people read the newspaper. The fathers read aloud to their children while breakfast is being prepared—a task which occupies the mothers for three-quarters of an hour every morning. And as the newspapers of the United States are filled with all sorts

Du Pont de Nemours, *National Education in the United States of America*, p. 3. 1800.

of narratives—comments on matters political, physical, philosophic; information on agriculture, the arts, travel, navigation; and also extracts from all the best books in America and Europe—they disseminate an enormous amount of information, some of which is helpful to the young people, especially when they arrive at an age when the father resigns his place as reader in favor of the child who can best succeed him." [1]

This is undoubtedly a somewhat roseate picture of conditions as they existed at that time, as will be seen by reading the first two chapters of Fitzpatrick on educational conditions as they existed in the state of New York in his monograph "The Educational Views and Influence of DeWitt Clinton."

Conditions in America favorable to broad education if not to high culture. The author viewed with enthusiasm the conditions existing in this country for he said, in contrast with Europe:

"They are now at that fortunate time when every man must increase his talents by some knowledge of all crafts; when the race grows enlightened, strong and vigorous; when families can live in comfort, can enjoy freely and leave for their descendants the dew from the skies and the richness of the earth, which depend on the whims of no one." [2]

This mode of living in which man was not confined to some small division of labor as was the case in Europe, where resourcefulness was joined to the privilege to labor and to possess, and where each person exercised himself in several arts, was conducive to growth and culture.

Development of the nation. There could be no object more worthy of national education than the development of the nation, for "That which the nation should most carefully develop is the nation itself." By a thorough system

[1] Du Pont de Nemours, *National Education in the United States of America*, p. 4. 1800.
[2] *Ibid.*, pp. 121-122. 1800.

of education the nation "should save its citizens both from the temptation of treating others unjustly and from the weakness of submitting to oppression." The main feature of such an education must be moral and for this reason, "The school books that of necessity begin all education; those from which children learn to write and read, should therefore contain all the principles of morals, the ethics of law, the fundamental ideas of duty, the maxims of wisdom, the proverbs of common-sense. No such book now exists."[1] There must be a system of national education with nationalism as its object.

Education as growth and power of growth—child responsibility in control. Du Pont did not conceive education to consist in the mastering of facts, but rather in the development of the power of growth:

> "The real aim of education is less to give the children positive facts than to keep them constantly developing, working themselves and by themselves to observe and to understand. For that wonderful habit once made part of their lives will never be lost and will grow with the growth of their minds."[2]

While it is true that this ideal of education as growth and as power of growth was not a universal one in the United States, conditions were such as to develop thought and initiative and inventiveness, and to stimulate that power of growth which was to be cherished above all else, and Du Pont said: "It has been those children who have always thought and advanced who have become great men actuated by a constant desire for more thought and further advancement; who from thirty to sixty years, sometimes till death, make strides that astonish the world, and what is better, that illuminate it."[2]

[1] Du Pont de Nemours, *National Education in the United States of America*, p. 154. 1800.
[2] *Ibid.*, p. 24. 1800.

As an example of the type of school that should be founded in America he cited the school of Chevalier Pawlett. Because of its suggestive principles of democracy, for learning "by and for doing," and for the recognition of the necessity of developing a sense of responsibility through having responsibility placed upon the pupils, a brief sketch will be given of this institution.

Pawlett, we are told, "spent sixty thousand francs yearly, before the French Revolution, in supporting a school in Paris for two hundred children who were received when they were eight or nine years old and taught until they were fifteen. There were no instructors except those who taught the older pupils; who in turn taught their younger comrades." [1] These pupils were given twelve *sous* a day and each was to buy his own food and clothing with this sum, to pay for heat, light, paper, pens, pencils and other necessities, and "the whole to be administered by themselves." Pawlett said the children "proved themselves worthy. Their discipline was admirable, their thoroughness perfect. They chose their own officers and obeyed them promptly. Punishments were ordered in council with unprotested justice." [2] We are told that the benefactor each evening was given statements, both moral and financial. Du Pont declared: "That was a wonderful example of what childhood can do, by and for itself." [2]

Learning by and for doing. The principle, then, of learning by doing and for doing should be at the basis of American education. In other words, as in the Pawlett school, "they learned to talk, by use; and they will also have learned the important truth that all use is founded on reason, or at least has a reason." [3] American education would profit by

---

[1] Du Pont de Nemours, *National Education in the United States of America*, pp. 25-26. 1800.
[2] *Ibid.*, p. 26. 1800.   [3] *Ibid.*, p. 31. 1800.

this method. America afforded a wide range of opportunity for the use of this principle in education. It not only furnished the opportunity but also demanded such a type of education because of the general diffusion of responsibility to every citizen. He conceived clearly the relation of method in education to the making of virile, responsible citizens.

Pupil experimentation. In order that this education might function immediately, pupils should be stimulated to undertake and conduct projects involving experimentation, projects that should be their own, and, if possible, of such a character that they would continue their experiments outside of school during their period of training. There is constant recurrence of this problem of bringing the school more directly into contact with real life. Du Pont believed that the school should be as nearly as possible a place where the child could *live,* and be directed in the carrying forward of natural life projects.[1]

Self-government for self-development. In a democracy where external controls were reduced to a minimum, inner controls must be established. Practice should be given in self-government that would lead to the establishment of happiness. The youth should learn "all the pleasure of using their rights of citizenship, to select those whom they sincerely believe to be the best and most competent."[2] Furthermore, after the most competent had been selected, they would learn that "The principle of obedience will be finer and nobler when they have themselves been the commanding officer. These children will eventually serve the State better, because, having learned to exercise some authority themselves, they will realize the importance of respecting it always."[3]

[1] Du Pont de Nemours, *National Education in the United States of America,* p. 72. 1800.
[2] *Ibid.,* p. 46. 1800.   [3] *Ibid.,* pp. 46-47. 1800.

In the small circles of the schools it would be easy to observe the results of action, since each "likes to show that he is of value." No place would offer a better opportunity for him to see "that his vote counts for something." Hence, since "Every reasonable being . . . feels a certain dignity to which he holds fast," there would be that satisfaction through self determination that would lead to the highest degree of respect for the thing created. In such an institution there could be no unequal justice on the part of masters in fostering privileges. This basic character training would best take place through the placing of individuals in positions of responsibility. For this reason it was held that "To consult children on all matters on which they may have an opinion seems to me to be so good a way to form their judgment, to accustom them to decide for themselves and to reason, to give them character, that I would not hesitate to allow them to vote on all matters." [1]

Learning by doing; self-government. Hence, a different type of school organization would be necessary, one in which the responsibilities of conduct and of activity rested with the pupils themselves, for "Let them be the nation and the nation can never be equalled except by imitation." In this way "Their general intelligence will be developed; their judgment, their imagination, their character, their reasoning powers, their honesty will be found." [2]

Learning to judge character. The primary school was to be a place that would stimulate in every way a comprehension of the forces that determine human conduct. Not least among these would be that of gaining the approval of their fellows through living according to proper standards. This could not be learned through books so well as through activities conducted by the pupils, for in these activities "they

---

[1] Du Pont de Nemours, *National Education in the United States of America*, p. 47. 1800.   [2] *Ibid.*, p. 156. 1800.

will learn to judge each other fairly, to show their appreciation to work and to excel, to try to deserve approval." [1]

Integration of studies; methods to be like life. At that time, grammar, ethics, algebra, geometry, arithmetic, and physics were all abstract bits of life. If children can learn them in a natural way, "They will exercise their own logic and their minds will become accurate. They will understand objects before they concern themselves with signs and words—which will be given them not as arbitrary forms, but as welcome assistance." [1] Learning, then, would be by experimentation, whether in physical science or in social science.

Correlation and integration—continued growth throughout life. If education were to function in real life, it must be through a correlation or integration such as exists in real life. When learning takes place on this basis, "the *philosophy of knowledge* will remain with them; they will use it with profit all their lives and will be accepted everywhere as educated men, able to learn more every day, and to recognize and appreciate those who are even better informed than themselves." [2] By "philosophy of knowledge" is here meant understanding its relation to the problem of effective living, and effective living here is conceived of as that which leads to a continuous growth throughout life. This continuous growth could be achieved maximally only as the pupils were led to see that the social heritage and the present environment were elements to be used in working out more effective control. [3]

Selection and education of geniuses. That education should be differentiated to some extent would be recognized by all. It would not be possible for all to be leaders. There must be, then, some way of providing for the selection and

---

[1] Du Pont de Nemours, *National Education in the United States of America*, p. 156. 1800.
[2] *Ibid.*, pp. 157-158. 1800.   [3] *Ibid.*, pp. 24-26. 1800.

education of geniuses, because "genius is rare; it must not be stifled. So soon as a child shows a spark of it, he must be cherished, and care taken that he is never refused opportunities that may help him to become a light in the world." [1] Any adequate economy of government would recognize that "A single day of an educated man of genius is of more value to the world than the labor of a hundred thousand average men for a year." Since, "Sciences are the keys to the treasures of nature," these geniuses should be carefully "trained to use them rightly." [1]

For those whose families were able to provide higher educational advantages some provision must be made that would cause them to stimulate the youth to get the utmost education "suitable to his age and ambitions." "And if his own family cannot, the larger family—the community—must adopt the child, rather than lose the great man into whom he may grow." [1]

Number of geniuses chosen. If the secondary schooling were to continue for a period of seven years, there might be twenty students a year chosen, to be supported by the State; "seven in each college, if twenty are established; fourteen, if the State of Virginia is limited to ten colleges." "I would prefer the smaller number because, general and fundamental instruction being assured in the primary schools with their carefully chosen books, I believe that for literary and scientific instruction *quality* is better than *quantity*." [1] Hence it would probably be better if a smaller number of colleges were established in order that higher salaries might be paid to the professors; also, in this way superior men would be enlisted. Furthermore, this would stimulate men of ability "to give their lives to professorships." [2]

Secondary schools and colleges. The principle of national

---

[1] Du Pont de Nemours, *National Education in the United States of America*, pp. 55-56. 1800.

[2] *Ibid.*, p. 59. 1800.

supervision should not alone be applied to the primary schools but also to the secondary schools and colleges. Perhaps there might be greater freedom on the part of the professors in the secondary schools and colleges to choose the books which were to be used for "The national feeling that will be established, the definite foundation that will be given to education will suffice to prevent any professor in the higher schools from choosing any books of instruction or suggesting such forms of essays as would conflict with the methods of the primary schools and would displease fathers, mothers, legislators, and public opinion." [1] The foundation, then, of national culture rested mainly with the primary schools.

Curriculum for the colleges. The courses in the colleges should consist chiefly of "four languages with their literature; and what is far more useful, fourteen true sciences of which the great part are not yet taught in the colleges of Europe." [2] These four languages would probably be "Greek, Latin, French and German." [3] Courses should be given in mathematics of such a nature as could be applied immediately to mechanics, hydraulics, architecture, navigation, etc. This country with its development yet before it, would certainly need the best instruction possible in chemistry, physics, natural history, and the principles of zoology and botany. Advanced courses should be given in *"the law of nature"*, political economy, history, geography, "and to crown all, *national law.*" There was needed in this respect a reformation of education in America such as would make it a truly rational education related to national prosperity. [4]

Pragmatic basis of method. In line with the pragmatic conceptions of education each of the studies would be taught in its relation to immediate application for the solution of

[1] Du Pont de Nemours, *National Education in the United States of America*, p. 53. 1800.
[2] *Ibid.*, p. 157. 1800. [3] *Ibid.* p. 59. 1800. [4] *Ibid.*, pp. 63-65. 1800.

problems that had to do with social welfare. Geometry would be taught in relation to astronomy, "for the construction of ships and for navigation," and for national defense. Botany, chemistry, and anatomy would be taught in connection with medicine and surgery. Mineralogy would be immediately applied to chemistry and "subterranean geometry" for the development of the mineral resources of the country, "And the study of law will be subordinate to the science of statesmanship." [1]

Suggested distribution of college courses. A tentative distribution of the work was indicated which is illustrative of the new emphasis upon science. There should be the following "Classes or Courses": [2]

"Greek—language and literature,	678 lessons.
"Latin—language and literature,	727 lessons.
"Moral philosophy and French,	832 lessons.
"Mental science, logic and German,	781 lessons.
"Geometry, algebra and physico-mathematics,	729 lessons.
"Chemistry and other natural sciences,	677 lessons.
"Natural and national law, political economy and history,	573 lessons."

Scholarly and practical education. There should be no clash between the scholarly professions and practical living. It is true that some must of necessity be trained in "more detailed instruction than is necessary for those who want only an ordinary literary and scientific education," but "The higher schools will be practical as well as scholarly." [3] This pragmatic outlook upon education was a correlate of pioneer experience where the problems descended upon all for solution rather than upon a few.

Estimated cost of system as it might be carried out in the one state of Virginia. If education were instituted on this

[1] Du Pont de Nemours, *National Education in the United States of America*, pp. 158-159. 1800.
[2] *Ibid.*, p. 78. 1800.   [3] *Ibid.*, p. 158. 1800.

basis, "it would be the best national education that has ever existed in any country", and from this estimate given for Virginia, "one may judge, in proportion to the population, the wealth, the capacity of the sixteen other states, the cost of public education in the whole, of the United States." The following is the itemized, estimated cost:[1]

"To the Principal .... 500 dollars.
"To each professor 300 dollars, and for six 1,800
"To each assistant professor 200 dollars, and for
    two 400
"To the cook 200
"To three other servants 150 dollars each 450
"For annual prizes and the upkeep of the buildings 150
    "Total yearly for each college .... 3,500 dollars.
"And for the ten colleges .... 35,000 dollars.
"To which add the cost of one hundred and forty
    pupils of the State, or fourteen for each insti-
    tution, allowing 150 dollars each 21,000
"If one adds the higher special schools which will
    cost as much as three colleges 10,500
"And the support of fifty State pupils at these spe-
    cial institutions 10,000
"The national education of Virginia will cost..... 76,500 dollars."

It was deemed best that instead of the states supporting special universities that there "be only one such establishment in the United States, that it would be at the capital— at Washington City, and supported by the Union. Each State could send there at its own expense a certain number of pupils."[2] This would reduce the estimated cost above "in that State to *sixty-six thousand dollars.*"[3] Hence the establishment of a national system of education according to the plan suggested would not over-tax any of the inhabitants and would provide free education from the primary school through a national university.[4]

[1] Du Pont de Nemours, *National Education in the United States of America*, pp. 94-95. 1800.
[2] *Ibid.*, p. 95. 1800.   [3] *Ibid.*, p. 96. 1800.   [4] *Ibid.*, pp. 95-96. 1800.

A further estimate is given of the expense per pupil of each state: [1]

	"*Pupils Supported by the State*	
	Food	100 dollars.
	Laundry	6
	Heat and lights	6
Amount to be paid by the State for each of these pupils 150 dollars.	Paper and other small expenses	5
	To the professor of ancient languages, who instructs two classes	4
	For each of the other professors three dollars	15
	The assistant professors	4
	Each servant one dollar	4
	Total	150 dollars."

The only item not included in this is that of clothing, because it was thought "in the United States there is no family so poor that it cannot clothe its child if the State supplies his education and support." [1]

The conception here of the necessity of state provision for the support of the individual in order to equalize opportunity and to further the highest interests of the state, was quite general.

What is meant by University. Du Pont said: "I would not therefore give the name *University* to the special schools, though it may have a useful side; namely, that of adopting accepted standards, and of convincing Europeans as well as Americans that youth can be as well taught in America as in Europe." [2]   The term was to be applied rather to the whole system of schools: "It will include our *primary schools,* our *colleges,* and our *special schools.*"   All of these institutions were to be but "branches of our public education.   And the special schools will be only the summit or the comple-

[1] Du Pont de Nemours, *National Education in the United States of America,* p. 99.   1800.
[2] *Ibid.,* p. 125.   1800.

tion." The name "University," would be applied to all grades in the national system.[1]

Provision was to be made by law for a "General Council" and for "Committees of Public Instruction." There should be *special schools* for the most advanced studies." Also, *"colleges,* of which the object is chiefly to develop literary and scientific men." As a foundation for the whole system, "the primary schools . . . will give the most important knowledge to all citizens." All of these should "together constitute the University of North America." [1]

Four schools should comprehend the higher institution, which was to be located at Washington City, "One of medicine; one of mines; one of social science and legislation; one of geometry and the sciences that it explains." Besides these schools, and accessory to them, "there will also be the public library, the museum, the botanical garden, the quarters of the General Council of Education, and the philosophic society." Du Pont believed that "this palace of science" would be "one of the monuments with which the eighteen States would wish to embellish their capital." [2]

The approximate cost of such an institution would be about $11,100. Four principals should receive $4,000; the other eleven professors $6,600; a porter to clean the rooms $200; and other epenses $300.[3]

General organization of Council of Education. There must of necessity be a general organization of each public establishment. In education this would be State Committees and a National Council. "This Council and these Committees will be the agent of the Government for the administration of everything concerned with education; and in matters that concern legislative bodies or Congress, the Council

---

[1] Du Pont de Nemours, *National Education in the United States of America,* p. 125. 1800.
[2] *Ibid.,* p. 126. 1800.　　　　[3] *Ibid.,* p. 142. 1800.

and Committees will be the proper petitioners for laws and appropriations that may contribute to the progress of their work." [1]

Duties of Council of Public Instruction. There should be a high degree of centralized control in "THE PARTICULAR COMMITTEES AND GENERAL COUNCIL OF PUBLIC EDUCATION." Within each State there should be selected by the Legislature "a committee of six or seven members to administer public education within its own State." The members of this committee should be men highly qualified for the position and "They should be chosen for seven years, after that period one should retire each year, but should always be eligible for re-appointment." [2]

The nature of their functions is best appreciated by giving the following:

"In each State the Committee of Education appointed by the Legislature should supervise all the national instruction; appoint the Principals of colleges; give its approval to professors and assistant professors; dismiss them, as well as the Principals themselves; keep informed of all that is being accomplished; preside, by one of its members or by an authorized Commissioner, with the municipality and local public officers, at the distribution of prizes; present to the Legislature every year an account of the work of colleges and schools; publish the names of pupils to whom prizes are awarded; suggest, in the form of a petition, such laws or appropriations as may be necessary for education. The Committee should also inspect the free schools, which may not open without its consent, after submitting their plans, their books and papers; and it may close them if their principles become dangerous or their methods improper. Finally, the Committee should select one member to join in forming the General Council of Education of the United States; he may be a member of the Committee or not; may even be a member of Congress, or not." [3]

[1] Du Pont de Nemours, *National Education in the United States of America*, pp. 160-161. 1800.
[2] *Ibid.*, p. 151. 1800.   [3] *Ibid.*, pp. 151-152. 1800.

Here it will be seen that nothing less than national inspection of free schools was contemplated. These could not be opened without the consent of the "General Council of Education," and this council had absolute power to close any school. The teachers were to be certified by this central organization. The care of the whole system, which would mean a supervision of all national instruction, was contemplated.[1]

Since the above Committee was to "select one member . . . in forming the General Council of Education of the United States", this General Council was to contain as many members as there were states in the Union, and it would have the ultimate direction of education throughout the United States. Each State Committee would render an annual report to this central organization from which would be made up "a report to Congress on the situation and progress of education in the whole of the great American republic." Along with these reports they "should suggest to Congress, always in the form of a petition, whatever it may believe helpful for the advancement of knowledge." Hence, "The whole educational system should be directly or indirectly in touch with the legislative body and the administrative power. The Government should be everywhere to protect everyone." [2]

The General Council of Education should select its own presiding officer from among its members, and he was to be "elected for three years by the votes of a majority of his colleagues, confirmed by the Senate and always re-eligible." [2]

Here then was conceived a plan of education which thoroughly knit together the educational interests of the Union, and this plan was written at the suggestion of Thomas Jefferson and had his approval.

[1] Du Pont de Nemours, *National Education of the United States of America,* pp. 151-153. 1800. [2] *Ibid.,* p. 153. 1800.

Summary. Du Pont saw in the United States conditions favorable to broad education. These conditions were such as to demand a national control and support of universal education from the lowest to the highest institutions. A peculiar code of ethics or principles obtained in the democratic form of control, which demanded a peculiar type of education. The principle of growth was inherent in democracy, and the real aim of education must be to stimulate this growth, to keep the youth of the nation "constantly developing." The habit of continual growth should be so firmly established that it would "never be lost." In order that each might become sensitive to responsibility and its noble discharge, the school should be a place where the youth would live naturally, not artificially, and where in this natural association and endeavor each would be actually living in a democracy. General and natural diffusion of responsibility must be an essential principle of American education. Achievement, self-government, experimentation, were fundamental in the national system. If learning were to take place on this natural basis, then "the *Philosophy of knowledge* will remain with them; they will use it with profit all their lives." Because of the demand for intelligent guidance in national development there should be a careful selection and nurture of geniuses. Since the principle of national supervision must be extended to the colleges and the higher institutions as well as the lower grades, the whole system could be directly related to the immediate economic and social problems. The most scholarly education would be immediately practical. To administer such a system effectively, there should be a "General Council" and "Committees of Public Instruction." The latter would be organized in each state. Control would in this way be both democratic and highly centralized. Such centralization would be necessary for effective administration.

CHAPTER SIX

WEBSTER'S NATIONAL SYSTEM OF DEMOCRATIC EDUCATION

1. *Life and Writings of Webster*

Characteristics of the period from 1770 to 1800. Since Noah Webster [1] was the chief proponent of and worker for educational reconstruction during this period, his life and

[1] Noah Webster, 1758-1843, came of New England stock, being a descendant of John Webster, Governor of Connecticut, 1656-1657, and on his mother's side from Governor William Bradford of Plymouth. Webster graduated from Yale in 1778, and was admitted to the bar in Hartford in 1781. He taught a classical school at Goshen, New York, 1782-1783. Here he discovered the need of better textbooks of English, and started the *Grammatical Institute*. The *Sketches of American Policy* were written in 1785. He established the *American Magazine* in 1788, and wrote his *Dissertations* in 1789. He published the *Essays* in 1790. The *Minerva* and *Herald* were started in 1793. He assisted in the founding of Amherst in 1821, and was made President of the Board of Trustees. He went abroad in 1824-25 to Paris and Cambridge. In his Big Dictionary of 1828 there were given about 40,000 definitions that had not appeared earlier in any dictionary. He was honored by the Abolition Society in 1790; the Massachusetts Historical Society in 1792; the Whig Society of North Carolina in 1795; the American Academy of Arts and Sciences, Massachusetts, in 1799; the Academy of Medicine, Philadelphia, in 1800; the New York Historical Society in 1809; received the degree of LL.D. from Yale College in 1823; the American Philosophical Society of Philadelphia in 1827; the Royal Academy of Science, Paris, in 1829; received the degree of LL.D. from Middlebury College in 1830; the Columbian Institute, Washington, in 1831; the Society of Adelphi in Union College in 1830; the Philoclean Society of Rutgers College in 1831; the Phi Gamma Alpha Society of Hamilton College in 1834; Dickinson College, Carlisle, Pennsylvania, in 1837; the Royal Society of Northern Antiquaries, Copenhagen, in 1831; the Connecticut Historical Society in 1839; the Georgia Historical Society in 1839; the Michigan Historical Society in 1840; the Historical Society of New Haven in 1841; the National Institute of Washington in 1842; and the American Oriental Society, Boston, in 1842.

political conceptions are given in more detail. His political conceptions are also typical of the thinking out of which arose the plans here discussed. Webster lived during a time of change. It was a period in which institutions that were venerable were attacked with absolute unreserve by many of the more radical. Researches were made in every field of science and the scientific method as conceived in the eighteenth century was applied to every field. It was a time when through the many inventions there came a revolution in industry and transportation. The great democracies of the United States and of France were born out of a new political philosophy. All the institutions of church and state were being brought to the test of scientific thinking. Webster was a student of these changes and tried to discover their relation to the political revolution that had taken place in the United States.

Political-educational and philological-educational aspects of Webster's life. The life of Noah Webster may be divided into two periods corresponding in general to his predominant interest: First, in the political-educational aspect before 1800; and second, in the philological-educational aspect from 1800 until his death. Before 1800 he was an advocate of openminded investigation and experimentation. During this period he was a pragmatist in his conception of morals, and held a critical attitude toward religion.[1] About 1800 his religious activities began. This was about the time also, of the beginning of his conservatism in politics. He became a contender for religious and political dogmas rather than experimentation. Throughout his life he was a writer, journalist, editor, lecturer, lawyer, teacher, political pamphleteer, and philologist. As editor he published the *American Magazine* which was of short duration. He later published the *Minerva* and the *Herald* which were changed re-

[1] Unpublished *Diary*, April 20, 1785.

spectively to the *Commercial Advertiser* and the *New York Spectator*.[1] In these he was an advocate of the principles of the Federalists. All who have found it necessary to study and consult Noah Webster have been impressed by his genius and his indefatigable labors. Because of the popularity of Webster's spelling book and of his dictionary, his place in the evolution of the political life in the United States has been obscured. Beginning with his *Sketches of American Policy* in 1785 he became one of the truly great pamphleteers following the Revolution. As a writer it is said that if his journalistic essays in the *Minerva* and the *Herald* alone were published, they would make over twenty large volumes. His journalistic essays covered a wide range of topics, but that which most commanded his interest was the unique character of American life and political thought. This was fundamental in all of his educational writings and in his conception of the duty of the nation in its relation to the education of American youth. During the time that he published the *American Magazine* he worked out analytical and critical summaries of the leading issues of the *Federalist*. This was what probably led the Federalist party later to choose him as the most likely agent for the furtherance of their purposes.[2]

Webster's ambitions. Some of Webster's leading ambitions were the following: First, to form a distinctive American character; second, to create a consistent national tongue; third, to work out an adequate political philosophy that would be humane in character, and universal; fourth, to create a flexible institutional control as a means for the realization of these humanitarian ideals of life; and fifth, fundamental to it all, was the establishment of a system of education. His aim was to mould the American character along humanitarian

---

[1] Hudson, Frederick, *Journalism in the United States from 1690-1872.*
[2] *The American Magazine*, p. 506. 1788.

lines. Nearly all of his work was related to one or the other of these basic aims.

Education of Noah Webster. The statement made by Scudder that Webster "was not so much opposed to foreign culture as he was absolutely ignorant of it"[1] may be put down as absolutely untrue. As a matter of fact Webster was a student of the development of institutions in this country as well as in France and England. In his *History of the French Revolution* he manifests a general knowledge of the history of France and of the philosophies of some of the leading French writers. In his *Letters to Dr. Priestley* we find that he was acquainted with the writings of Turgot, Brissot, Perthion, and the Duc de Rockfocault.[2] In his criticism of these he said that "Such men by the way do not pass for politicians in the United States— They know nothing about true politics, or the act of governing—and to their blunders must be ascribed the miseries of the French people, during the revolution."[3] He was also familiar with the writings of the Abbe Raynal and Adam Smith.[3] He had quite mastered the political writings of the leading men in the United States. He was also familiar with the leading writers on education from Plato, Tacitus, Cicero, Quintilian, down to his own day. He seems to have digested such writers as Ascham, Montesquieu, and Rousseau. Webster had read Rousseau's *Émile* and *Le Contrat Social.*[4] The writings of Dr. Price he valued highly and he said that Price had anticipated him in many of the things that he had intended to publish himself.[5] With Thomas Paine he was

---

[1] Scudder, Horace, *Life of Noah Webster.* pp. 50-51. 1882.
[2] Webster, Noah, *Letters to Dr. Priestley,* p. 10. 1800.
[3] *Ibid.,* p. 10. 1800.
[4] *American Magazine,* p. 86. Jan. 1788. *Essays,* pp. 19, 20, 21, 22, 23, 25, 27, 30. 1788.
[5] Webster, Noah, *Sketches of American Policy,* pp. 2, 27. 1785; Unpublished *Diary,* Ford Collection, January 22, 1785.

directly acquainted. He said, "The continent was electrified by his writings—the minds of the people were prepared for the great event" through the publication of *Common Sense* in 1775. The vividness of Noah Webster's account of Paine's influence shows how much he must have been stirred at the time. He noted in his Diary on February 27, 1786, that he was introduced to Thomas Paine, and also introduced to Mr. Rittenhouse.[1]

During practically the whole of his career Webster travelled up and down the Atlantic coast and went as far south as Charleston.[2] During his travels it was his custom to meet all of the leading political and educational men. It is noted for instance that they conversed "upon the great question, What are the means of improving & establishing the Union of the States?"[3] He met Franklin and discussed the political and educational issues of the day, and with Franklin's permission lectured in the University of Pennsylvania.[4] He had been in Washington's home more than once and had played cards with him.[5] It was also his habit to submit whatever he had written to such men as Washington and Adams for their criticism. In this way he knew the governors of the states, presidents of the colleges, the leading political writers and gained in a most direct manner what might be called the superior part of his education for leadership in American thought. Webster wrote Priestley that he had made one "journey of eight hundred miles through the Eastern states, in various directions."[6] When he published his *Essays* in 1790 he had practically all of the leading men of that day as subscribers for the volume.

---

[1] Unpublished *Diary*, February 27, 1786, Ford Collection.
[2] *Ibid.*, May 30, 1785, July 18, 1785, Ford Collection. Skeel, Emily E. F., *Notes on the Life of Noah Webster*, p. 501.
[3] Unpublished *Diary*, Jan. 20, 1785, Ford Collection.
[4] *Ibid.*, April 17, 1786, Ford Collection.
[5] *Ibid.*, May 20, 1785, November 5, 1785, Ford Collection.
[6] Webster, Noah, *Letters to Dr. Priestley*, p. 4. 1800.

The vital part of Webster's education as noted by Scudder was that of the nature of his training in self-government: "English freedom, which had forced its way to these shores, had grown and increased under the fostering care of self-government and native industry. He had been born and brought up in a New England country village, the type of the freest and most determinate form of local government; he had been educated at a democratic college; he had shouldered his musket in a war for the defense not of his State alone, but of his country." [1] Scudder does give Webster credit for having "had a singular faculty of being the first in time in many departments of literary industry, and constantly to have anticipated other people." [2] He further says that "Webster, with his self-reliance, his indifference to the past, his consciousness of destiny, his courage and resolution and quick fitting into his country's work, stands easily as the first aggressive American in our literature." [3]

Contradictions in Webster's philosophy. At the same time that Webster was a Jacobin in his real attitude toward institutions, he was by force of circumstances a defender of Hamiltonian federalism. Until about 1800 he was an advocate of a free expression of differences of opinion, and yet he condemned those who held views that seemed to threaten the constitution. He called them perverters of the truth and said they were underhanded in their methods. He contended for peace but was most Puritanical in his condemnation of those who opposed his views. Undoubtedly most of these clashes were unconscious divergencies,—clashes between his interests and his ideals; his friendships and his inexorable habit or tendency to put everything to the test of impartial science; his private and his public life. In general

[1] Scudder, Horace, *Life of Noah Webster*, pp. 118, 19-20. 1882.
[2] *Ibid.*, p. 68. 1882.
[3] *Ibid.*, p. 289. 1882.

Webster was broad, international; but by circumstances he was national in his suggested solutions of national problems. These dualisms seemed to have occasioned no particular difficulty. The fortunes of the French Revolution coupled with certain religious contacts and the fervor of religious revivals, made almost a complete change in Webster's outlook. He became as eloquent a conservative as he had been a defender of openmindedness and scientific procedure against the impostures of superstition and religion. We are not concerned here with his thinking following this change. During the period covered in this treatise his mode of thinking was that of the experimenter in every field. No institutions were considered too sacred for investigation.

Webster's disillusionment. In 1800 Webster wrote Dr. Priestley, "The theories of Helvetius, Rousseau, Condorcet, Turgot, Godwin and others, are founded on artificial reasoning, not on the nature of man; not on fact and experience. . . . Between these theories and the old corrupt establishments, there is a *mean,* which probably is the true point of freedom and national happiness." [1] This change of view from his earlier position when he believed in the doctrines of Rousseau, began to take form in his reactions to the French Revolution about 1793. He wrote further to Priestley in answer to Priestley's proposal for a liberal form of recall: "I am sure, sir, you have not been eye witness to so many freaks of the populace as I have, or you would not think such a provision very well calculated to secure wisdom and justice." [2] He was sure that if Priestley were to attend the popular assemblies in this country and get "a view of their passions, folly, precipitation, and sometimes violations of law and justice" that it would cure him of many errors. Webster had lost his earlier faith in "the wisdom and purity

[1] Webster, Noah, *Letters to Dr. Priestley,* p. 21. 1800.
[2] *Ibid.,* p. 14. 1800.

of popular councils." [1]   He recalled that it was the contact
with Mr. Genet in 1793 that had first altered his view of the
French Revolution, even though he said that "the bulk of
the people in America, in the strength of their prepossessions
for a Republican government, and in their honest credulity,
continued to think well of the views of the French Re-
formers, until two or three years later." [2]   He continued:
"For myself, sir, I can assure you, that in 1793, I was a
warm admirer of the French reformation; and in some pieces
which I wrote for the public papers, will be seen my zeal
to apologize for the excesses." [2]

In Noah Webster's copy of the *Sketches* we find in the
margin some very illuminating notes.   One says, "The three
first Sketches contain many chimerical notions—adopted in
the enthusiasm of the revolution; but which can never be reduced to practice.   N. Webster.   1800." [3]   Many marginal
comments inserted in a copy of his work, *Examination of
the Principles of Federal Government,* show the same change.
Some further marginal notes are interesting: "These ideas
are too democratic & not just.   Experience does not warrant
them." [4]   "Many of these notions taken from Rousseau's
SOCIAL CONTRACT, are found to be chimerical." [5]   In the
Sketches he declared: "It will be said that I have described a system of government, excellent in theory, but impracticable." [6]   He came in ten years to say it himself.   In
an unpublished letter from Asher Robbais to Webster in
1785 it was said: "I had almost forgotten to mention the
Gov.'s sentiments of your political piece.   He says that it
displays genius & learning, but that your notions are too
democratic for him."   In the blank page opposite this,

[1] Webster, Noah, *Letters to Dr. Priestley,* p. 14.   1800.
[2] *Ibid.,* pp. 5-6.   1800.
[3] Note on page 2 of Webster's copy of the *Sketches.*
[4] *Ibid.,* Note on page 6.
[5] *Ibid.,* Note on page 7.   [6] *Ibid.,* p. 11.

Webster wrote, "Note Feb'y 1800—The sentiments of that pamphlet are too democratic for the author. This was Sketches of American Policy.—We grow wiser with age. N. Webster." [1] It may be noted that almost simultaneously with the bloody episodes of the French Revolution it became of material interest for Webster to further the principles of the Federalists. This matter of convenience may have influenced him somewhat.

2. *Webster's Theory of Government*

Webster conceived his mission in life to be that of a corrector of errors. He seemed by constitution to be a reformer. He thought of himself as the prompter in plays, and said, "The PROMPTER is *the man who, in plays,* sits behind the scenes, looks over the rehearser, and with a moderate voice, corrects him when wrong, or assists his recollection, when he forgets the next sentence." [2] While many saw in him the confirmed egoist, in truth, he spent his life very largely in what he judged to be service to mankind. He was active in reforming both politics and education. Within these fields he was one of the chief publicists of the time. Webster was also the most considerable educationist after the close of the Revolution. From his point of view government and education were inseparable. For this reason it will be well to analyze his theories of government.

Fixed versus flexible institutions. Can one generation legislate for another? In 1789 Thomas Jefferson wrote from Paris in a letter to James Madison saying that "The question of whether one generation of men has a right to bind another, seems never to have been started, either on this or our

---

[1] Unpublished manuscript. 1785. 1800.
[2] Webster, Noah, *The Prompter,* preface, p. iii. 1791.

side of the water." [1] This seemed rather strange to Jefferson since, "It is a question of such consequence as not only to merit discussion, but to be placed also among the fundamental principles of any government." [1]

The central idea in Webster's early thinking was that of constantly evolving institutions. At the center of this, again, was the idea of nationalism, a nationalism not of a fixed character but plastic in its essential nature. He was living in the midst of most rapid changes in state, religion and industry. To accept unchallenged these institutions was considered a crime; in fact, to preserve institutions unchanged was impossible. Since old forms must be made into new, the question was no longer that of preservation of form but rather of value. The dominant idea in *The Sketches* and also in Webster's controversy with Jefferson about a Bill of Rights, was flexibility according to the principles of utility or the exigencies of circumstances.

Bill of Rights. The question of the Bill of Rights represented a chief difference between the conception of Webster and that of Jefferson. In answer to the dissenting members of the Philadelphia convention, where the question had been hotly discussed as to whether or not there should be attached to the constitution a long Bill of Rights, Webster said: "As a supplement to that article of your bill of rights, I would suggest the following restriction: 'That Congress shall never restrain any inhabitant of America from eating and drinking, at *seasonable times,* or prevent his lying on his *left side,* in a long winter's night, or even on his back, when he is fatigued by lying on his right." [2] This would seem to be the doctrine of *laissez-faire,* but elsewhere Webster showed how thoroughly he believed in social controls.

[1] Unpublished Letters in Noah Webster Collection, September 6, 1789, Ford Collection.
[2] Webster, Noah, *Essays,* p. 149. 1787.

Economic basis of freedom. Human freedom could not exist without a sound economic basis. Enslavement could be quite as complete through the failure of the individual to have an adequate economic support as it had ever been under the most despotic forms of government. This economic basis of freedom was held by Webster to be far superior to many of the more popular issues: "The liberty of the press, trial by jury, the Habeas Corpus writ, even Magna Charta itself . . . are all inferior considerations, when compared with a general distribution of real property among every class of men." [1] If Webster were living now he would undoubtedly include all property, since personal and business property now equally create aristocracy. He went so far as to say, "An equality of property, with a necessity of alienation, constantly operating to destroy combinations of powerful families, is the very *soul of a republic.*" [2] While he was an adherent of the principles of the eighteenth century liberal philosophy, he did not go so far as to believe that a complete absence of control that would allow men's natures to act freely would in any way solve the problem. He said, "*Virtue,* patriotism, or love of country, never was and never will be, till men's natures are changed, a fixed permanent principle and support of government." [2] His use of the phrase, "equal distribution of landed property", was decidedly socialistic, and he said, "The system of the great Montesquieu will ever be erroneous, till the words *property or lands in fee simple* are substituted for *virtue,* throughout his *Spirit of Laws.*" [2] It will be recalled that this was prior ot the French Revolution, which took its radical socialistic course because of the great inequalities in Europe. His extreme position is seen in the following: "A general and tolerably equal distribution of landed property is the whole

[1] Webster, Noah, *Examination into the Leading Principles of the Federal Constitution*, pp. 47-48. 1787.
[2] *Ibid.*, p. 47. 1787.

basis of national freedom."[1] Freedom in this sense meant economic independence in the achievement of the ends that were deemed worthy by the individual. In this he took the position of those who believed in the origin of society in social contract. He did not, then, stand for the *laissez-faire* conception of society: "In a free government, every man binds himself to obey the *public voice,* or the opinions of a majority; and the *whole society* engages to protect each individual. In such a government a man is *free* and safe."[2] He would not go so far as to contend for the liberty that is characteristic of the savage, but believed in civil society and such a civil society as that in which "political liberty consists in *acting conformably to the sense of a majority of the society.*"[2] He disagreed with those who believed "that liberty consists in *a power to act without any control.*"[3] The controls should be such, however, that each would have his opportunity to determine his economic interests and to share in all of the advantages of the society of which he was a member.

He said, "In attending to the principles of government, the leading idea that strikes the mind is that political power depends mostly on property." For this reason, "government will take its complexion from the divisions of property in the state."[4] In order that the individual would be protected in his property rights, he must have it in fee simple; in other words, he must have practically an undisputed possession of lands.[5] This should be characteristic of a republican form of government, for "In despotic states, the subjects must not possess property in fee," since "an exclusive

---

[1] Webster, Noah, *Examination into the Leading Principles of the Federal Constitution,* p. 47. 1787.
[2] *Ibid.,* pp. 40-41. 1787.
[3] *Ibid.,* p. 40. 1787.
[4] Webster, Noah, *Essays,* p. 326. 1790.
[5] Webster, Noah, *Examination into the Leading Principles of the Federal Constitution,* p. 48. 1787.

possession of lands inspires ideas of independence, fatal to despotism." [1] Webster believed that economic forces were largely the determining factors in making for a democracy that would be self-respecting. "The basis of a democratic and a republican form of government is a fundamental law, favoring an equal or rather a general distribution of property." [2] So long as man remained economically superior or inferior there would be a large portion who would fail to achieve independence in any real sense. Citizenship should carry with it the responsibilities of government and the protection of those things that were fundamental to individual welfare. The individual should be subordinated neither to a state nor to a class.

Religion and liberty. At the time that Webster wrote the *Sketches* he was a liberal thinker and held consistently the critical attitude toward all institutions, religious and civil. He held that religion was the offspring of ignorance and for this reason was the great support of monarchy. His definition of religion was indicative of his general viewpoint: "Religion, by which I mean superstition, or human systems of absurdity, is an engine used in almost all governments, and has a powerful effect where people are kept in ignorance." [3] If the American Revolution meant anything, it meant a break with this exploitation of humanity through ignorance. Webster said, "The American constitutions are founded on principles different from those of all nations, and we must find new bonds of union to perpetuate the confederation." [3] We shall find later how fundamental this conception was to Webster's idea of the function of the school. The source of power would no longer be the ignorance of the people but rather in their intelligence—a people trained to intelligent and critical citizenship. In this new democracy "All power

[1] Webster, Noah, *Essays*, p. 326. 1790.
[2] *Ibid.*, p. 327. 1790.
[3] Webster, Noah, *Sketches of American Policy*, p. 30. 1785.

is vested in the people."[1] Power was not vested in the
people artificially; "this is their inalienable right." The question that arose out of such a principle was "how this power
shall be exerted to effect the ends of government."[1]

Basic principles of Webster's philosophy. Webster
claimed originality for his conception of government as it was
developed in *The Sketches*. In the fly-leaf of his copy of the
Sketches is a note written in 1800 and signed by Noah
Webster in which he said, "The following sketches were
written in the month of February, 1785, before any proposal
had ever been made to new model the government of the
States."[2] He also noted that "In May I carried one copy of
them to Virginia & presented it to Ge. Washington. Mr.
Madison saw and read it at the General's soon after."[2] He
noted further that "in November of the same year, he, in
conversation with me, expressed a warm approbation of the
sentiments it contains."[2] Webster elsewhere jotted another
marginal note about 1800 in the same copy saying that the
principles that found expression in *The Sketches* were not
based upon a sound view of mankind but were due to an
unreasoning acceptance of the liberal philosophy of Europe.[2]

The Sketches were offered because there had been certain
forcible attempts to establish a monarchy. Webster wrote
Hamilton: "It was agreed, in case of civil convulsion, to
rally the officers and soldiers of the late army, and with the
help of supplies to be furnished by some rich merchants,
to give a government to this country by force."[3] This was
a "project . . . concerted among certain military characters
in the year 1785, when Joel Barlow, who then was ripe for
the establishment of a monarchy, was sent as an agent from

---

[1] Webster, Noah, *Sketches of American Policy*, p. 30. 1785.
[2] Webster's copy of the *Sketches*, pp. 2, 6, 7, 11. 1785 and 1800.
Letters to Dr. Priestley, p. 21. 1800. Unpublished mss. *Letter from
Asher Robbais to Noah Webster.* 1785. 1800.
[3] Webster, Noah, *A Letter to General Hamilton*, p. 5. 1800.

Connecticut to Boston, to make some arrangement with the military gentlemen in that state." [1]

The basic principles of the *Sketches* were: The doctrine of "natural law"; the relativity of law to the natural exigencies of life; and, hence, the need for modifiable, flexible institutions.[2] Webster was decidedly opposed to "hereditary honors" and "superiority of birth." Aristocracy was not considered in harmony with the law of nature. Superiority of birth was in every way artificial.[3] Another principle was that of freedom of action. In a democracy controls should be from within and not from without.[4] The source of power in government was in unity of sentiment.[5] The unquestioning acceptance of religious and monarchical forced controls was in no way consonant with the principles of democracy. Only as long as military force and superstition continued were exterior controls sufficient. He said: "These two instruments of despotism, superstition and a military force" had commanded "peace and subordination" even during the American Revolution, but the time had come for a revolt against the continuance of such principles. In some ways Noah Webster was a philosophical anarchist in his outlook, but he believed in a scientific, constructive iconoclasm.[6]

Webster held that the constitution should be a changeable instrument and that it was to be defended only as a tentative solution of the problem of social control in the United States.[7] These principles led to his emphasis upon a type of education that would make possible a constant readjust-

[1] Webster, Noah, *A Letter to General Hamilton*, p. 5. 1800.
[2] Webster, Noah, *Essays*, pp. 47, 51, 59, 63, 68, 69, 70, 71. 1790; *Sketches of American Policy*, pp. 15, 18, 31. 1785; *Examination into the Leading Principles of the Federal Constitution*, p. 48. 1787.
[3] Webster, Noah, *Sketches of American Policy*, pp. 18, 24, 25, 26. 1785.
[4] Webster, Noah, *Essays*, pp. 151, 152, 153. 1787.
[5] *Ibid.*, pp. 72, 76, 78. 1787.
[6] Webster, Noah, *Sketches of American Policy*, pp. 12, 13. 1785.
[7] *Ibid.*, pp. 31, 32. 1785.

ment of institutional control according to the exigencies of locality and time.[1]

3. *Relation of Theory of Government to Education*

Identity of interests of legislators and of the people. One of the sources of biased legislation had been the separation of the interests of the legislators from those of the people. In any form of aristocratic government it was to the interest of the aristocracy to legislate in such a fashion as to build up their own interests at the sacrifice of the interests of the people. For instance, education had been guarded as the privilege of the aristocracy because in this manner they could continue their dominance. The aristocracy had also very largely freed themselves from the responsibilities of taxation. The support of the government had rested upon the common people. There should be no privileged classes in America; all should share equally the burdens as well as the privileges. In order that this might be true, there must be an identity of interest between the legislative body and the people. The legislators would then "involve themselves, their families and estates in all the mischiefs that result from such laws" as were enacted.[2] *"A union of interests between the governors and governed"* was essential to prevent the growth of inequalities which would be fatal to democracy.[3]

This doctrine involved a correlate. This correlate was that the legislature should be the supreme power and "invested with all the authority of the State."[4] So long as the matter of elections by the people were carefully guarded, no one could doubt "That a legislature should have unlimited

---

[1] Webster, Noah, *Essays,* p. 80. 1787.
[2] Webster, Noah, *Sketches of American Policy,* p. 40. 1785.
[3] Webster, Noah, *The American Magazine,* p. 76. January, 1788.
[4] *Ibid.,* p. 75. January, 1788.

power to do right." [1] The unlimited safety of the interests of the people did not rest in limiting the powers of the legislature. It rested rather upon a union of interests. "This union of interests depends partly on the laws of property; but mostly on the *freedom of election*." [1] No legislative body should have the right to continue itself in power beyond the time set at the time of its election. Furthermore, the people had what amounted to the modern principle of "recall" in that it was their privilege to discontinue the legislature by popular vote when the legislature ceased to function for the interests of the people. This union of interests in reality meant that the nation itself became in a very direct way the legislative body because the people became the ultimate determiners of the policies of the legislature. The educational implications of this particular feature of the American government were evident to Noah Webster.

An intelligent electorate with freedom of debate. It was held, "A perfect freedom of debate is essential to a free government." [2] No citizen was to be debarred the privilege of criticizing to the utmost every institution that had to do with human welfare. With a people trained to see the implications of democracy, there could be no doubt about the progress of liberty without the loss of stability. With such an intelligent electorate the act of the majority would be "the most perfect and only practicable method of legislation." [2] Thus far, Webster declared, "We have no perpetual distinctions of property, which raise one class of men above another." Again, "We suffer no hereditary offices or titles." Furthermore, "We are not under the direction of a bigoted clergy." [3] We were free in this manner from the limitations placed upon the people by large land-holding classes

[1] Webster, Noah, *The American Magazine*, p. 76. January, 1788.
[2] Webster, Noah, *Sketches of American Policy*, p. 34. 1785.
[3] *Ibid.*, p. 39. 1785.

and the superstitions fostered by religious bigotry, and could thus act in harmony with the highest possible degree of intelligence. Those who were in office were not separate from the people: "Their interest is the same with the people." [1] "Such principles form the basis of our American governments." [2] However, even these articles could not be effective unless "the people *are wise enough to maintain the principles* of the confederation." [3] In the margin of Webster's copy of the *Sketches of American Policy* we find in 1800 the word "true." Also, it was at this time that he underlined the above. The principle of distribution of power in the whole electorate involved three things: first, the people must be educated; second, "A law without a penalty is mere *advice"*; and third, "a magistrate, without the power of punishing, is a cipher." [4] Power there must be, but it must be a power resting within the people rather than one divorced from them.

Webster's idea of democracy. The use of the term democracy was very specific with Webster. It meant to him that the people were the law-making body. This conception held true for a representative democracy as well as for the direct democratic control in small communities, because by frequent elections the people in reality made the laws directly. This conception of the direct connection between the people and social control influenced Webster's thinking very greatly and determined his notions of education and of flexible government. He gave the following definition: "By *democracy* is intended a government, where the legislative powers are exercised directly by all the citizens, as formerly in Athens and Rome." [5]

Evolutionary character of institutions and morals. The difficulty in American thinking had been that the difference

[1] Webster, Noah, *Sketches of American Policy*, p. 40. 1785.
[2] *Ibid.*, p. 39. 1785.   [3] *Ibid.*, p. 41. 1785.   [4] *Ibid.*, p. 44. 1785.
[5] Webster, Noah, *Letters to Dr. Priestley*, p. 9. 1800. Cf. pp. 214, 215.

had not been recognized between the struggle in England "against the encroachments of Kings and Barons, or against any power independent of the people" and the attempt in the United States to create an efficient instrument through which the people could act.[1] Webster declared that the contention for a Bill of Rights under such circumstances as obtained in England under the rule of barons or monarchs was perfectly intelligible, "but a Bill of Rights against the encroachments of an elective Legislature, that is, against our own encroachments on *ourselves,* is a curiosity in government." [1] He said that he would undertake to prove "that a standing *Bill of Rights* is absurd because in a democracy no constitution can be unalterable." [2] "The present generation have indeed a right to declare what *they* deem a *privilege;* but they have no right to say what the next generation shall deem a *privilege.*" [2] In such a form of government a legislature "has the same right to repeal a law this year, as it had to make it the last." In the ultimate analysis it was clear that "If therefore our posterity are bound by our constitutions, and can neither amend nor annul them, they are to all intents and purposes our slaves." [2] No one could deny that the following generation could not determine the laws that had been passed by the former. Then by what right could this generation legislate for the next? If American life stood for freedom it could only do so on the basis that all of its institutions were proper subjects of change. "Most institutions in society, by reason of an increasing change of circumstances, either become altogether improper, or require amendment." [3] We shall see later how Webster advocated an education for resourcefulness in the bringing about of desirable changes.

The experience of certain states had proved the impossi-

---

[1] Webster, Noah, *Essays* p. 45. 1788.
[2] *Ibid.,* p. 47. 1788.   [3] *Ibid.,* pp. 47-48. 1788.

bility of fixing once for all how they should be controlled. For instance, Webster said that "Pennsylvania and Georgia, have suffered under bad Constitutions, till they are glad to go through the process of calling a new Convention." [1]   It was fortunate that in these cases the inertia of the people had not been so great as to delay the matter until a revolution was necessary.   They had come to recognize that "government originates in *necessity* and *utility*." [2]   There was one principle that was necessary and that was that the right of election "cannot be alienated without changing the form of government." [3]   It was but a *"species of bigotry"* that made possible the continuance of peculiar forms of government or a peculiar faith, unchanged.   This species of bigotry was not a thing to be despised, however, it was rather to be directed: "This passion, when corrected by candor, benevolence, and love of mankind, softens down into a steady principle, which forms the soul of a nation, *true patriotism*." [4] Determination of what this principle should be or what form it should take was the problem that interested many following the Revolution.   Webster saw it perhaps most clearly and said, "I consider our *union*, and consequently our *strength* and *prosperity*, as depending more on mutual *interest* and mutual *concession*, than on the force of the national constitution." [5]   This made it the business of the state to provide such a system of education as would direct the energies of the nation along the lines of common interests and to create a spirit of mutual concession that would make possible united effort.   Webster had seen what an energetic and fervid effort was required to unite the heterogeneous elements at the opening of the Revolution to get the Colonists to act together.   He had also seen the rapid and almost in-

[1] Webster, Noah, *Essays*, p. 52.   1788.
[2] *Ibid.*, p. 56.   1788.   [3] *Ibid.*, p. 59.   1788.
[4] Webster, Noah, *Miscellaneous Papers*, p. 26.   1794.
[5] *Ibid.*, p. 47.   1794.

stantaneous disintegration as soon as the common danger was removed. He sought now to supply a cement to the discordant parts. Some believed that he was an anarchist in his tendencies, but he said, "He (referring to himself) has not however imbibed the modern philosophy that rejects all ancient institutions, civil, social, and religious, as the impositions of fraud; the tyranny of cunning and ignorance, and of power over weakness." [1] He saw the weakness of the French Revolution in its acceptance of the doctrine that man was perfect until debased by institutions, and declared that he was not convinced that men were "capable of such perfection on earth, as to regulate all their actions by moral rectitude, without the restraints of religion and law." [1] While he did not go to this extreme he did recognize that those who were reactionary were through their policies, if continued long enough, preparing for another revolution. He observed, "It is astonishing to observe how slowly men get rid of old prejudices and opinions. The feudal ideas of allegiance, which make fidelity in the subject an obligation or grateful return for the protection of the prince, still prevail." [2] He observed further that if this doctrine which was finding expression through those who were advocating the establishment of a monarchy in order to bring about more effective control, were to prevail, it would in the end destroy the very purpose for which the Revolution had been fought. "When the spirit of the government is lost, the form must change." [3]

Custom opposed to change. The dominance of custom grew out of the inertia of mankind rather than out of the efficiency of custom to meet certain demands of social control: "CUSTOM, with an iron rod, rules four fifths of

---

[1] Webster, Noah, *Miscellaneous Papers*, p. 21, 1794.
[2] Webster, Noah, *Essays*, p. 381. 1788.
[3] *Ibid.*, p. 331. 1788.

mankind." [1]   The general tendency was to say, *"Let us go
on in the good old way—it will do for the present."* [2]   Custom was like gravitation; it was always easier to go down
hill. The American Revolution was an attempt to break
with the tyranny of custom. The Revolution had grown
out of a critical attitude, and if that critical attitude had
been justifiable and advantageous in connection with the
Revolution, why should it not be continued? [3]   Adherence
to custom was contrary to the very principles of American
life. "Custom is the plague of wise men, and the idol of
fools." [4]   It was time to recognize that "Integrity without
knowledge is weak, and generally useless." [5]   In the *Grammatical Institute* many of the selections have to do with instilling patriotism, but it was a patriotism that found its
chief interest in the development of American life rather
than in the continuance of the *status quo.*

Tyranny of opinion and custom. If the Declaration of
Independence were to have fundamental meaning it would
be through the development of an independence in dress,
habits, thinking, literature, arts, language—in fact, a sufficient break with the traditions of Europe to mean a modification of them to meet the exigencies of American life. [6]
He said: "We are groaning beneath the tyranny of opinion;
a tyranny more severe than the laws of monarchies, a dominion voluntary indeed, but for that reason, more effectual." [7]
It was in this voluntary nature of subservience to foreign
customs and a foreign outlook that Webster saw the need
for a new type of education. He argued that "The revolution in America is not yet complete." [8]   A political revolu-

[1] Webster, Noah, *The Prompter*, p. 30. 1791.
[2] *Ibid.*, p. 32. 1791.
[3] Webster, Noah, *Essays*, p. 92. 1788.
[4] Webster, Noah, *A Grammatical Institute*, Part III, p. 14. 1785.
[5] *Ibid.*, Part III, p. 37. 1785.
[6] Webster, Noah, *Essays*, pp. 81-118. 1787.
[7] *Ibid.*, pp. 91-92. 1787.   [8] *Ibid.*, p. 92. 1787.

tion without the attendant changes in modes of life meant simply the establishment of the old order in America. This slavishness which was manifested in the keeping of foreign institutions and manners was one of the chief objects of Noah Webster's attack. He tried to give to American youth the necessary challenge to free themselves from bondage to modes of thinking and acting that were foreign to them. He asked, "Have the ladies in America no ingenuity, no taste? Do they not understand what dresses are best adapted to the climate, what dresses are most convenient and elegant?" [1] In planning for this "revolution of manners" there was no need for the sacrifice of any value, but without such a revolution all of the unique values of American life would be sacrificed.[2] The times were chaotic largely because there was not a national spirit. Without a national spirit there would be continually developing antagonisms and irregularities that would make impossible any high degree of cooperative effort. We needed to establish an independent monitary system as well as independent customs of life. Failure to recognize this principle had caused a general demoralization: "Such are the consequences of a variable medium: neglect to industry; application to irregular commerce; relaxation of principles in social intercourse; distrust of individuals; loss of confidence in the public; and of respect for laws; innumerable acts of injustice between man and man, and between State and the subject; popular uneasiness, murmurs and insurrections." [3] There could be but one remedy for such irregularities—the creation of a national consciousness. This could not be attained by imitation of foreign institutions. Imitation of foreign institutions had a tendency to bring into America the very things that should have been obliterated in the Revolutionary struggle. It was

---

[1] Webster, Noah, *Essays* p. 92. 1787.
[2] *Ibid.*, p. 93. 1787.   [3] *Ibid.*, p. 112. 1787.

curious to see the degree to which this slavishness to European customs had gone. When a young man "has worn an elegant suit of clothes for six weeks; he might wear it a few weeks longer, but it has not so many buttons as the last suit of my lord——: He throws it aside, and gets one that has." [1]

Basis of stability. Unchangeable forms of government could never be stable, for they must become obsolete as soon as conditions changed. Constant revision of institutional forms was the only possible way of avoiding revolution. Scudder in his *Life of Noah Webster* says concerning the *Sketches of American Policy,* "It is curious in the opening pages, to see how, in his theories of government, he is led away by the popular and alluring philosophy of Rousseau and Rousseau's interpreter, Jefferson. . . . In the earlier pages of his 'Sketches' he lays down his Theory of Government, which is, in brief, that of the *contrat social,* but presented in a homely form, which brings it nearer to the life of men." [2] He notes further that Webster's conception of the most perfect practicable system of government is that in which "the right of *making* laws is vested in the greatest number of individuals, and the power of executing them in the smallest number." [2]

Webster did not seem to be aware of any inconsistencies in his doctrine of the state of nature and the natural basis of laws with the social contract theory. The two were held to be consistent because man is, according to Webster, an egoistic creature dominated by self-interest. For this reason he enters into the social contract in order to act "in conjunction with other interests for its (self-interest's) own sake." [3]

Inevitability of change; education to determine the character of change. Certain assumptions were implied in the

[1] Webster, Noah, *Essays,* p. 91. 1787.
[2] Scudder, Horace, *Life of Noah Webster,* pp. 119-120. 1882.
[3] Webster, Noah, *Sketches of American Policy,* p. 4. 1785.

contention for the Bill of Rights and unalterable constitutions. One was that "the Convention which frames the government, is *infallible"* and the other was "that future Legislatures will be *less honest, less wise,* and less attentive to the interest of the State, than a present Convention." [1] Webster argued that "The first supposition is *always* false, and the last is generally so" and he said that the implication "of *perfect wisdom* and *probity* in the framers" was "both arrogant and impudent." [1] He recognized the possibility of making succeeding generations wiser by means of a system of education. He not only saw the possibility of greater wisdom being developed but believed it was the duty of the state to make men wiser and more free so that they would change the present forms of government into better.[1] Change was inevitable: "Unless the advocates for unalterable constitutions of governments, can prevent all changes in the wants, the inclinations, the habits, and the circumstances of people. They will find it difficult, even with all their declarations of unalterable rights, to prevent changes in government." [2] The fact was that "Government originates in necessity, and takes its form and structure from the genius and habits of the people." [3] The only way to proceed then would be to recognize that government "will assume a new form, in spite of all the formal sanctions of the supreme authority of a State." [3]

Unalterable constitutions and education for progress. It was but natural that those whose immediate interests were embodied in forms peculiar to the old order should seek to obviate any high degree of change. Security of property interests seemed to demand unalterable provision for their continuance, and the contention for an unalterable constitution took its rise chiefly from these economic interests.

[1] Webster, Noah, *Essays,* p. 63. 1788.
[2] *Ibid.,* p. 64. 1788.   [3] *Ibid.,* p. 66. 1788.

Strange as it may seem, Jefferson became a proponent for fixed institutions in certain respects. In the constitutional debate in Virginia in 1776 the extreme conservatives had gone so far as to propose, "in the House of Delegates to create a Dictator, invested with every power, legislativ, executiv and judicial, civil and military."[1] Again, "In June, 1781, under a great calamity the proposition was repeated, and was near being passed."[1] Webster took issue with the proposed fixed institutions but did not take issue with the idea of creating a dictator if that were found to be expedient, because he had faith that the creators of the dictator would also depose him when the crisis was passed.[2] In other words, Webster stood for the greatest freedom in the creation of any form of government that might be deemed necessary or expedient under the circumstances. When the disintegrative forces were in the ascendancy it might be necessary to create an absolute power to prevent disintegration.

Educational implications of constitutional revision. The recognition of the principle of change was fundamental in Webster's educational thinking. He believed that "A government which is perpetual, or incapable of being accommodated to every change of national habits, must in time become a *bad* government."[3] However, it was not to be argued that changes in government would bring about good government unless popular provision were made for educating the legislators. The legislators in a democracy were the people and since circumstances and habits were continually changing it would be illogical for any assembly to make ualterable laws. How could one assembly have greater authority than another? Thus, "One Assembly cannot pass an act, binding upon a subsequent Assembly of equal authority."[3] Jefferson was not a consistent supporter

[1] Webster, Noah, *Essays*, p. 70.   1788.
[2] *Ibid.*, p. 71.   1788.   [3] *Ibid.*, p. 61.   1788.

of his own position: "Mr. Jefferson himself, in the very next sentence, (after his statement concerning authority of assemblies in Notes on Virg. p. 197) assigns a reason, which is an unanswerable argument in favor of my position, and a complete refutation of his own." [1]

Mode of education and form of government. The title of one essay in the *American Magazine* was "The IM- PORTANCE of accommodating the MODE of EDUCATION to the FORM OF GOVERN'MENT." [2] This essay showed the maturity of thought due to Webster's various contacts with the political and educational leaders of the day, and also his direct knowledge of conditions throughout the United States. He attacked the subject from two points of view: "First, as it respects arts and sciences. Secondly, as it is connected with morals and Government." [3] He sought to find out "what errors may be found, and what improvements suggested, in our present practice." [3]

Among the defects noted, the chief one was that of the failure of education to function in a republican form of government. The system that prevailed had been largely transported from Europe and had functioned very well while the colonists were members of a monarchy, but they had thus far failed to institute a system of education in harmony with democracy. [4] We were not here to inspire servile fear in youth, but rather to lead them into an understanding of the principles of democratic control. It was extremely hazardous to have a mode of education that was out of harmony with the mode of government. "The impressions received in early life, usually form the characters of individuals; a union of which forms the general char-

[1] Webster, Noah, *Essays,* pp. 61-62. 1788.
[2] Webster, Noah, *The American Magazine,* p. 311. 1788.
[3] Webster, Noah, *On Education of the Youth in America,* p. 3. 1788. *Essays,* 1790.
[4] *Ibid.,* p. 24. 1788.

acter of the nation." [1] If, then, the youth were to grow into citizens capable of furthering democracy, it must be by means of an education suited to democracy.

Hence Webster said: "When I speak of diffusion of knowledge, I do not mean merely a knowledge of spelling books and the New Testament. An acquaintance with ethics, and with the general principles of law, commerce, money and government, is necessary for the yeomanry of a republican state." [2] He said further that the youth should be taught "The history and transactions of their own country; the principles of liberty and government." [3]

In writing to Dr. Priestley he recognized that democracy was indigenous in America, for "It is a form of government which has grown out of our state of society which is interwoven into all the habits of life and opinions of our citizens." [4] This pre-revolutionary basis of democracy should be made a part of the social inheritance of American youth.[5] Webster did not believe that a form of government could exist independent of a correlative form of education. He believed that a republican form of government was best for the United States as long as there was education of a proper character. He said, "It appears to me that a free government arises naturally out of a state of society, like that which exists in America; but that the state of society, in most parts of Europe, will not admit of that form, or will render it impracticable." [6] This was written after Webster had been disillusioned by the results of the French Revolution. It is to be noted that Webster's disillusionment in this respect in no way checked his confidence in education as the most effective instrument for

[1] Webster, Noah, *On Education of the Youth in America*, p. 1. 1788.
[2] *Ibid.*, p. 25. 1788.   [3] *Ibid.*, p. 26. 1788.
[4] Webster, Noah, *Letters to Dr. Priestley*, p. 10. 1800.
[5] Webster, Noah, *Essays, On Education of Youth in America*. 1788. *Essays*. 1790.
[6] Webster, Noah, *Letters to Dr. Priestley*, p. 8. 1800.

social control. It simply changed his conception of the kind of education needed.

Female education. In a democracy female education must be given special attention since "Their influence in controlling the matters of a nation" was in many ways more considerable than that of the males.[1] Mothers were in a vital way the determiners of the outlook of youth upon life and of their conceptions of democracy. For this reason, "Their own education should therefore enable them to implant in the tender mind, such sentiments of virtue, propriety and dignity, as are suited to the freedom of our government."[1] Female education must be much broader than that generally comprehended in girls' schools. It should comprehend geography, magazines, newspapers, history, science, all that constituted a liberal education.[2] It could happily be said that "The women of America (to their honor it is mentioned) are not generally above the care of educating their own children."[3] Their share in determining the broader aspects of education demanded that "in a system of education, that should embrace every part of the community, the female sex claim no inconsiderable share of our attention."[3]

False ideas at boarding schools. The type of education that prevailed in the boarding schools was largely that of Europe, being ornamental instead of useful. A false evaluation resulted and women were educated to be inefficient as far as American life was concerned. Webster said, "This ambition to educate females above their fortunes pervades every part of America."[4] As a matter of fact, it was perhaps better not to send a young woman away to school than to send her under prevailing conditions, for in the schools she learned to despise essential occupations and to

[1] Webster, Noah, *On Education of the Youth in America*, p. 27. 1788.
Essays. 1790.   [2] *Ibid.*, p. 29.   1788.   [3] *Ibid.*, p. 27.   1788.
[4] Webster, Noah, *The American Magazine*, p. 369.   1790.

revel in mere adornments and pleasures. "This fatal mistake is illustrated in every large town in America." [1] Women must be educated for serious occupations and not for frivolities.

Also, private schools for young men, supported by the wealth of the country, were demoralizing in their tendencies. They did not give the student a serious outlook upon life nor instill the principles of service. After recounting in detail the elements of a system of education that made dancing the highest accomplishment for the young man, and dressing the highest accomplishment for the young lady, he said, "By following this plan, which is now indeed very much practiced, your son will be a *man,* at twelve, a boy all the rest of his life." [2] Not much was to be expected of the private schools in the United States.

Pragmatic basis of educational method. A friend wrote Noah Webster concerning a youth whom he wished to be directed toward a successful life. This youth had been "till within a few years, under the watchful eyes of very attentiv parents; from whom he had received much better advice and much more of it, than the generality of parents" were wont to give. [3] This youth had been taught by them "to regard truth with a steady attachment; in short his education till their deaths, was such as might with propriety have been called rigidly virtuous." [3] The guardian of this youth was rather puzzled to find that after a rigid parental authority was gone, he seemed to be without the ability to control himself. He felt that the youth's education had been most adequate and rigid, and he sought a way out of his difficulty through writing to Noah Webster. Webster replied, "He has had good precepts indeed but of

[1] Webster, Noah, *The American Magazine*, p. 370. 1790.
[2] *Ibid.*, p. 163. 1788.
[3] Webster, Noah, *Essays*, p. 247. 1790.

how little weight are precepts to young people! Advice to the young sometimes does good; but perhaps never, except good habits, have been previously formed by correct discipline, in manners, or by a mechanical attention to honest employments."[1] Webster saw the need of reform in American education along the lines of providing serious endeavor for the youth of the nation. He went on to say, "I venture to affirm that grave advice never yet conquered a passion, and rarely has restrained one so as to render a sprightly youth, in any degree serious."[1] The great criticism of the school practice of his day was that it was unrelated to life; it was a mere memorization of facts and words and a repeating of them to a master. He argued that "I have ever thought that advice to the young unaccompanied by routine of honest employments, is like an attempt to make a shrub grow in a certain direction by blowing it with a bellows. . . . The only effectual method perhaps is to keep young persons from childhood busy in some employment of use and reputation . . . perhaps by *nothing else.*"[1] Webster held that "We are the creatures of habit."[1] This divorcement of school life from worthy occupations was perhaps the most serious defect in the schooling that existed at that time. It had a tendency to cause a gentleman "to disdain business," and for any young man who had suffered the consequences of such a system, "his friends have only to whistle advice in his ears, and wait till old age, experience, and the death of his passions, shall change the man."[1] America afforded the best opportunity that could be imagined for the cultivation of worthy habits through serious employment. This would not mean a sacrifice of a broad education. It would mean, rather, that education would become a vital part of life.

Webster held that "The spirit of a government springs

[1] Webster, Noah, *Essays*, p. 247. 1790.

immediately from the temper of a people" and if that people were trained in youth in serious employment and to the discharge of real responsibilities, the habits most essential to the development of the nation would be thus formed.[1] This principle was held to be especially essential in the education of females in America.

The business of education. Webster believed that while man inherited his passions, it was "the business of education to restrain and direct the passions to the purposes of social happiness." [2] For instance, such a great movement as the French Revolution, "the noblest ever undertaken by man," was made abortive because education had not freed the human mind sufficiently to achieve its purposes: "The feudal and papal systems were tyrannical in the extreme; they fettered and debased the mind; they enslaved a great portion of Europe." [2] Because of the lack of general education there had been established in France, instead of a free republic, "a *military aristocracy,* the most bloody ever recorded in history." [3] To obviate such evils it would be necessary to establish a system of education that would diffuse its power throughout the masses.

Provision for early instruction in democracy. In *The Little Reader's Assistant* the attempt was made to bring out rather forcibly the differences in meanings of various kinds of governments, and it emphasized the advantages and implications of democracy. The stories were such as to cultivate interest and pride in American history and things. The last part was "A Federal Catechism, Containing a short explanation of the Constitution of the United States of America." [4] Here was an attempt to instill into the minds of American youth the principles of democratic life.

[1] Webster, Noah, *Essays*, p. 69. 1790.
[2] Webster, Noah, *Miscellaneous Papers*, p. 21. 1794.
[3] *Ibid.*, p. 22. 1794.
[4] Webster, Noah, *The Little Reader's Assistant.* 1790.

4. *Nationality and Education*

Schools the nurseries of inequality and the enemies of liberty. Webster observed that there had taken place in this country a very "injurious change of Opinion . . . on the Subject of Education." That which was "known to hav excited the earliest and most anxious solicitude" of the fore-fathers, had been neglected by their posterity. The fore-fathers had "regarded Colleges as the best schools of Wisdom and Virtue" while "we consider them as nurseries of Inequality, the Enemies of Liberty." The reason for this change in attitude was that the colleges and higher institutions of learning had largely been patronized by the affluent, while the education of the poor had been neglected. This had caused a feeling that education was necessarily an instrument of dominance on the part of aristocracy. The only way to overcome this prejudice was to provide equality of economic opportunity as well as educational equality.[1]

Anarchy and distraction. As a result of the failure of higher education to be democratic, there came the anarchical conditions following the Revolution. In the preface to the essays published in 1790 Webster apologized for the freedom of language which appeared in his earlier essays. He said, "This freedom of language will be excused by the frends of the revolution and of good government, who will recollect the sensations they hav experienced, amidst the anarky and distraction which succeeded the ·cloze of the war."[2] Out of this anarchy grew Webster's conception of a national system of education whose chief function was to be the Americanization of the whole people in such a way as to cause them to use and not to abuse the new privileges which they had gained. The school was to assume the burden

[1] Webster, Noah, Unpublished Manuscript, Ford Collection.
[2] Webster, Noah, *Essays,* preface. 1790.

of unifying the nation. It was also to create a sense of the new responsibilities due to the new relation to the world at large as an independent nation established on the basis of a new interpretation of social control.[1]

Education the means of uniting organically the forces of the nation. What was needed in this new type of social control was the elimination of the "dissocial passions" and prejudices. A proper system of "Education will gradually eradicate them and a growing intercourse will harmonize the views of all the citizens."[2] The faith of Noah Webster that America was to make this vital contribution to the world was evident throughout his writings. He wrote to Dr. Priestley, "be assured, Dr. Priestley, that the parent is yet to derive some scientific improvements from the child. Some false theories, some errors in science, which the British nation has imbibed from illustrious men, and nourished from an implicit reliance on their authority, are to be prostrated by the penetrating genius of America."[3] This was a task far more arduous than that of winning the Revolution through physical contest.

National unity and purposeful endeavor. During the Revolution the nation had been engaged in a vast, serious and arduous endeavor to gain freedom. This had given rise to "the enthusiasm which was called *public spirit, heroic virtue, and love of country.*"[4] Immediately upon the close of the Revolution it seemed that all of this noble spirit had been "absorbed in the general steady principle, private interest."[4] This was perhaps due to the fact that when the long and arduous struggle for freedom was over, there was a failure on the part of the nation to engage in national endeavors having sufficient challenge to continue the spirit

[1] Webster, Noah, *Essays,* preface. 1790.
[2] Webster, Noah, *Sketches of American Policy,* p. 45. 1785.
[3] Webster, Noah, *Letters to Dr. Priestley,* p. 90. 1800.
[4] Webster, Noah, *Essays,* p. 82. 1787.

that had reigned. "A fundamental mistake of the Americans has been, that they considered the revolution as completed, when it was but just begun." [1] Webster believed that the Revolution gave an opportunity to work out good in the future through education and experience rather than that the Revolution had purchased a final good as a simple result. Freed from foreign despotism and given the opportunity to work out fresh values in a new environment, the colonists might have been enlisted in the more arduous task of creating these fresh values for civilization and for humanity. [2] According to Webster, there seemed to be a failure to recognize those necessities for continuing the task that had been begun. He saw in it challenges far superior to any that had been involved directly in the Revolution. The delusion that the prize was obtained had caused America to be surprised at the disappointing results. [3] Had the statesmen who so ably conducted the Revolution set themselves with equal energy to the task of education, they would have seen in the youthful nation a force that might be successful in its struggle against what Webster considered a decaying civilization. To consider the achievement of freedom as a closed task was but to destroy it, while if the nation realized the possibilities of achieving freedom, civil war would give way to unified effort, and quarreling and cavilling would give way to a general tranquillity that would harness the energies of the nation in furthering the purposes of the Revolution. [3] Webster deprecated the American tendency to imitate Europe. Europe was considered by him to be senile, decaying; America needed to recognize that she must make her declaration of independence such as to liberate her energies for the creation of new modes of thinking and living. [4]

Nationalism.   Scudder refers slightingly to Webster's

---

[1] Webster, Noah, *Essays*, p. 84.   1787.
[2] *Ibid.*, p. 83.   1787.   [3] *Ibid.*, p. 81.   1787.   [4] *Ibid.*, p. 91.   1787.

Americanism and nationalism without giving any just reasons for his disparagement. He seems to think that the nationalism of Webster was of a very rude sort and that one must look elsewhere for a finer analysis of nationality.[1] That nationalism was not a mere "posture" with Webster is evident throughout the whole of his writings.

Webster clearly defined some of the new objectives peculiar to American life. He indicated an enrichment of the curriculum and a change in content for the realization of these new objectives. He indicated also a change in method more in harmony with democratic institutions, and showed to some extent at least how the elementary schools, secondary schools, and higher schools might be reshaped so that the interests of the nation might be integrated in one ideal. To continue the form of education that had largely prevailed while the states had been colonies under a monarchical form of government that bred an aristocracy and class divisions was to miss the very spirit of the declaration of independence: "This appears to me a most glaring solecism in government. The constitutions are *republican,* and the laws of education are *monarchical.* The *former* extend the civil rights to every honest and industrious man; the *latter* deprive a large portion of the citizens of a most valuable .privilege." [2]

Nature of Webster's nationalistic conception. Webster was consistently American. His training had been such as to give him a decided American bias. He contended for independence in American thinking and even in the formation of a peculiar type of language and manners. In 1785 he declared, "America is an independent empire, and ought to assume a national character. Nothing can be more ridiculous, than servile imitation of the manners, the language,

[1] Scudder, Horace, *Life of Noah Webster,* p. 228. 1882.
[2] Webster, Noah, *Essays,* p. 24. 1790.

and the vices of foreigners." [1] It seems that one of the chief motives in the writing of the *Sketches* was that of urging upon the American people the necessity of creating institutions peculiarly adapted to conditions that had been created largely through the divergence of the experience of the Colonists from that of Europe. In the formation of a national government it was natural that there would be a tendency to keep the forms of government that had dominated European life. This would be a serious mistake, for such institutions would only continue the unfortunate circumstances that had driven the colonists away from Europe and had caused them to face the harshness of life in a new country. Webster placed national interest above all else. He said that "As a member of a family, every individual has some domestic interests, as a member of a corporation, he has other interests; as an inhabitant of a state, he has more extensive interests; as a citizen and subject of the American empire, he has a national interest superior to all others." [2] Nationalism involved from this viewpoint a new set of loyalties, loyalties peculiar to the democratic form of government.

A new type of character was to be formed through education. A change in the aim of education necessarily involved a change in content. This change in the aim of education was derived from the change in the nature of government and the changed general outlook upon life peculiar to democracy. The system of education should be such as to include an appreciation of the evolution of American institutions, a knowledge of the nature of government in a republican state, and habituation in democratic ways of thinking. [3] Finally, education was to be in harmony with the

[1] Webster, Noah, *Sketches of American Policy,* p. 47. 1785.
[2] *Ibid.,* p. 48. 1785.
[3] Webster, Noah, *Essays,* p. 23. 1787.

simplicity of American life and was to be mainly for utility rather than ornament.[1]

American national character not yet formed. Webster believed in an indigenous type of education. He urged: "It is an object of vast magnitude that systems of education should be adopted and pursued, which may not only diffuse a knowledge of the sciences, but may implant, in the minds of American youth, the principles of virtue and liberty."[2] Education was to be such as to "inspire them with just and liberal ideas of government, and with an inviolable attachment to their own country."[2] He recognized that "Our constitutions of civil government are not yet firmly established; our national character is not yet formed," and believed it to be the highest mission of the state to form such a character through the establishment of a national system of education.[2]

When he wrote the *Sketches of American Policy*, in 1785 he believed that "general education of youth is an article in which the American states are superior to all nations." This he attributed to the fact that "This institution is the necessary consequence of the genius of our Governments."[3]

Formation of national character. During the early state period there seems to have been a failure to develop a national character. Among the numerous associations formed at this time for the promotion of national interests, we find, for instance, that Noah Webster was interested in the "ASSOCIATION of AMERICAN PATRIOTS for the purpose of forming a NATIONAL CHARACTER."[4] Webster was always active where national interests were concerned. The weak

---

[1] Webster, Noah, *On Education of the Youth in America*, p. 27.   1788; *Essays*, p. 247.   1790; *The American Magazine*, pp. 369, 370.   1790.
[2] Webster, Noah, *On the Education of the Youth in America*, p. 3. 1788.
[3] Webster, Noah, *Sketches of American Policy*, p. 28.   1785.
[4] *Connecticut Herald*, May 17, 1808.

resistance to the abuses of American interests on the seas was due to this lack of nationality. The Association of American Patriots became one of the propaganda institutions for whatever reforms were deemed urgent at the time.

Nationalistic conception of education. Webster was one of the first to emphasize the nationalistic conception of education. In 1788 he wrote, "During the course of ten or twelve years, I hav been laboring to correct the popular errors, and to assist my young brethren in the road to truth and virtue; my publications for theze purposes hav been numerous."[1] In the same essay he declared, "I am attached to America by birth, education and habit; but abuv all, by a philosophical view of her situation, and by the superior advantages she enjoys, for augmenting the sum of social happiness."[2] In looking back over these ten years he said: "Much time haz been spent, (in urging social reforms) which I do not regret, and much censure incurred, which my heart tells me I do not deserve."[3] This philosophical point of view may be considered the key to the unremitting endeavors of Noah Webster for the establishment of institutions and agencies for world progress, especially may it be considered the key to his increasing devotion to education. Webster was quick to perceive the implications of democracy and the relation of education to these implications. The fact of Noah Webster's nationalistic conception of education is clearly established in the opening paragraphs of his essay, "On the EDUCATION of YOUTH in AMERICA" in which he showed how the Greeks, the Scythians, the Persians, the Chinese, and other empires of Asia used education to further national ends.[4]

Change in content for national culture. American con-

---

[1] Webster, Noah, *On Education of the Youth in America.* 1788.
[2] *Ibid.,* p. 5. 1788. [3] *Ibid.,* pp. 6, 8, 9. 1790. [4] *Ibid.,* pp. 1-3. 1788.

tent should have precedence since "a knowledge of our own country is most interesting to our citizens." [1]   For this reason in the first two volumes of the *Elements of Useful Knowledge* the chronological order was disregarded, and all that had to do with "the American continent, and especially of that part which is comprehended within the limit of the United States . . . takes place of all other parts of this system, and forms the substance of the two first volumes." [1]   When we think of the great labor involved in the preparation of this content we observe with what enthusiasm Webster worked for the Americanization of the school system.

As early as 1787 Webster said, "A selection of essays, respecting the settlement and geography of America; the history of the late revolution and of the most remarkable characters and events that distinguish it, and a compendium of the principles of the federal and provincial government, should be the principal school book in the United States." [2] If the youth of America were to fix their attention upon "the interests of their own country," this would assist them "in forming attachments to it, as well as in enlarging the understanding."   This was in harmony with the principle announced by "the great Montesquieu, that the laws of education ought to be relative to the principles of government." [2]   In America "every child . . . should be acquainted with his own country.   He should read the books that furnish him with ideas that will be useful to him in life and practice.   As soon as he opens his lips, he should rehearse the history of his own country; he should lisp the praise of liberty, and of those illustrious heroes and statesmen, who have wrought a revolution in her favor." [2]

In the introduction to the *American Magazine* in 1787

[1] Webster, Noah, *Elements of Useful Knowledge,* preface.   1802.
[2] Webster, Noah, *On Education of the Youth in America,* p. 23.   1788.

Webster announced as his purpose the gathering together of such materials as would develop in this country an interest in its literary products, in its geography and history. He said, "The Editor is determined to collect as many original essays as possible; and particularly such as relate to this country, and contain useful and curious discoveries in the history or geography of America, or ingenious remarks upon the science of government, and the peculiar institutions and customs of the people in the different States." [1] His own essays on government which were later published in the volume of 1790 came out in the *American Magazine* under the signature of Giles Hickory.

Broad character of nationalism in the United States. While it was necessary to stimulate a high degree of attachment to the interests of the United States, these interests were not to be considered as separated from the humanitarian values to be ultimately wrought out through a world-wide progress. Because of this need for openmindedness to truth from all sources, the need for humanitarian spirit, the broadening influence of science should become a chief part of American education.[2] Since, 'Science liberalizes men and removes inveterate prejudices," it is the best instrument for destroying "Every prejudice, every dissocial passion." From whatever viewpoint, national or world-welfare, "Education or a general diffusion of knowledge among all classes of men, is an article that deserves peculiar attention." [2]

It will be remembered that Webster offered in his *Sketches of American Policy* suggestions for more effective government because of the weakness of the confederation. It was perhaps the first rather elaborate argument in behalf of a stronger constitution, a closer union in order that the gov-

---

[1] Webster, Noah, *The American Magazine.* 1788.
[2] Webster, Noah, *Sketches of American Policy*, p. 44. 1785.

ernment might be more effective. In this argument he said, *"Provincial* interest is inseparable from *national* interest" and they would stand or fall together. He urged that "These things demand our early and careful attention: a general diffusion of knowledge; the encouragement of industry, frugality, and virtue; and a sovereign power at the head of the States."[1] Thus early he saw as the prime necessities of effective democracy: education and centralization; intelligent election and sufficiently powerful execution; liberty and nationality. Neither liberty nor nationality could be achieved without an especially devised system of national education.

In the *Massachusetts Centinel* in 1786 there was an announcement of a series of lectures to be given by Mr. Webster, on "the *English Language* and on *Education.*" In these lectures were discussed the "Different Dialects of the Eastern, the Middle and Southern States" and also "Some differences between the English and Americans." He argued that there were "Reasons why the English should not be our standard, either in Language or Manners." The last lecture was on: "General Remarks on Education. Effects in our mode of Education. Influence of Education on Morals, and of Morals on Government. Female Education. Connection between the Mode of Education and the Form of Government. Effects of European Education in America. Tour of America a useful Branch of Education. Conclusion."[2] In his diary we find the following: "Feb. 11. 13. 1786. Read my 4 and 5 Lectures to a crouded audience. Read my last Lecture to a crouded audience whose applause is flattering."[3] This lecture was developed later into his essay on Education published in 1788 in the *American Magazine,* and later included in the *Essays.*

[1] Webster, Noah, *Sketches of American Policy,* p. 44. 1785.
[2] *Massachusetts Sentinel,* July 12, 1786.
[3] Unpublished *Diary,* Feb. 11, 13, 1786, Ford Collection.

Establishment of American opinions and principles. In a letter to Pickering in 1786 Webster avowed his intention: "I shall make one *General* effort to deliver literature and my countrymen from the errors that fashion and ignorance are palming upon Englishmen." [1] The American language was to be delivered from "the dupes of a strolling party of players, who, educated in the school of corruption, have no profession, but to make people laugh, and who, dependent on opinion, for subsistence, must conform to caprice at the expense of every principle of propriety." [1] The opportunity was to be given America to make a choice between a language constructed upon scientific principles and one which was the result of base accident. "The question will then be, whether the Americans will give their opinions and principles as well as their purses to foreigners." [1]

Unity and harmony promoted through a national language. In the preface to the *American Spelling Book* Webster said that its purpose was "To diffuse an uniformity and purity of language in America, to destroy the provincial prejudices that originate in the trifling differences of dialect and produce reciprocal ridicule." [2] He went on to say that the harmony of the United States depended upon the creation of such a medium. It became, then, the duty of the nation to establish schools upon some uniform basis for the annihilation of these differences. He argued that "Nothing but the establishment of schools and some uniformity in the use of books, can annihilate differences in speaking and preserve the purity of the American tongue." [3] The promotion of national spirit and unity was apparently his chief objective in the publishing of the *Institutes*. In his *Dissertations* he said, "A sameness of pronunciation is of considerable consequence in a political view" for it was

[1] Webster, Noah, Unpublished Manuscript.
[2] Webster, Noah, *The American Spelling Book*, preface. 1784.
[3] Webster, Noah, *Dissertations*, p. 19. 1789.

obvious that "provincial accents . . . have an unhappy effect upon the social affections."[1] Social harmony depended upon the erasure of peculiarities that arose out of sectionalism. For this reason, he argued that "political harmony is therefore concerned in a uniformity of language."[2] Furthermore, national solidarity was required in order that we might command the respect of other nations: "Our honor requires us to have a system of our own, in language as well as government."[2] We were sufficiently isolated from Europe to develop this medium of expression with comparatively slight hindrance.[3] "As language is the medium of all social intercourse . . . it is of great importance that its general principles should be well understood by those who superintend the education of youth."[4] There was a real demand in America for this new departure in language: "In this country new objects, new ideas, and association of ideas, compel us, either to invent new terms, or to use the English words in a new sense."[5] A national language was a necessity, not simply a convenience.

There were special reasons why such a separate language should be developed. It would have a tendency to enlarge the publications of books in our own country and "Besides this, a *national language* is a band of *national union*. Every engine should be employed to render the people of this country *national;* to call their attachments home to their own country; and to inspire them with the pride of national character." He contended that "America is in a situation most favorable for great reformations. . . . The minds of men in this country have been awakened." For many reasons, *"Now* is the time, and *this* is the country, in which we may expect success in attempting changes favorable to

[1] Webster, Noah, *Institutions*, p. 19. 1789.
[2] *Ibid.*, p. 20. 1789.   [3] *Ibid.*, p. 22. 1789.
[4] Webster, Noah, Unpublished Manuscript. *A Letter to Governors, Instructors, and Trustees of the Universities*, p. 3. 1798.
[5] Webster, Noah, *A Letter to the Hon. Pickering*, p. 8. 1878.

language, science, and government." [1] Since the time was so opportune he urged, "Let us, then, seize the present moment and establish a *national language* as well as a national government." [1] Again: "I am confident that such an event is an object of vast political consequence." [1] It would have a tendency to unite the various sections of the country and to erase class distinctions: "A correct orthography would render the pronunciation of the language as uniform as the spelling in books. . . . All persons, of every rank, would speak with the same degree of precision and uniformity." [1] By the introduction of this language "The simplicity of the orthography would facilitate the learning of the language. It is now a work of years for children to learn to spell." [1] This national tongue should be phonetic and should eliminate all silent letters. By making the language phonetic there would be a saving of one page in every eighteen. This would be a great convenience and economy. [1]

Design of the Grammatical Institute. The design of the *Grammatical Institute of the English Language* was to provide a "Method of EDUCATION designed for the use of *English* Schools in AMERICA." [2] It was Webster's purpose to "frame a Grammar of our own language upon true principles." The grammar most generally used was that of Mr. Dilworth, which was, "to use the words of an eminent scholar and critic, 'A mere Latin Grammar, very indifferently translated.' " [3] It was Webster's object, "In the choice of pieces" to be "attentiv to the political interests of America." He considered it a great fault of the schools that "the writings that marked the Revolution, which are perhaps not inferior to the orations of Cicero and Demosthenes, and which are calculated to impress interesting truths upon young minds, lie neglected and forgotten." [3] Recogniz-

[1] Webster, Noah, Appendix to *Dissertations*. 1789.
[2] Webster, Noah, *Grammatical Institute*, p. 1. 1784.
[3] *Ibid.*, p. 2. 1784.

ing the value of these addresses and documents "written at the commencement of the late Revolution" he desired to make them available to the youth of America because they contained "such noble sentiments of liberty and patriotism." The schools could have no nobler function than "to transfuse them into the breasts of the rising generation."[1] The comprehensive character of the *Institute* may be seen from this statement: "The design of this Grammatical Institute is to furnish schools in this country with an easy, accurate, and comprehensive system of education in the English language."[2] Webster said that "the most ardent wish of the author is to promote the interest of literature and harmony of the United States."[3]

In the preface of Part III of the *Grammatical Institute* Webster said, "This part completes the system I had proposed to publish for the use of schools. To refine and establish our language, to facilitate the acquisition of grammatical knowledge, and diffuse, the principles of virtue and patriotism, is the task I have labored to perform."[4] An examination of the three parts of the *Grammatical Institute* impresses one with the significance of Webster's attempt to change the motive or spirit of American education as well as its content. Throughout is manifested the fact that he had seen the limitation of an education that had for its sole purpose the winning of a social status or the meeting of an economic necessity. The purpose of education was to establish the fundamental equalities that would exist in humanity if they were allowed to express themselves, and to create an appreciation of the principles of democracy as announced in the Revolution. This required an independence from European thinking, a type of thinking free from racial and other long established prejudices. The

[1] Webster, Noah, *Grammatical Institute,* preface. 1784.
[2] *Ibid.,* Part I, p. 6. 6th ed. 1787.
[3] *Ibid.,* Part I, p. 8. 6th ed. 1787.   [4] *Ibid.,* Part III, p. 5. 1785.

ultimate aim of such an education was humanitarian unity rather than national unity, but the latter must be achieved first, yet so achieved that the humanitarian values would not be lost through the creation of narrow national prejudices. The outlook upon life should be as broad as the laws of nature. This was the announcement made by Webster in the *Elements of Useful Knowledge,* which was copyrighted in 1802 and was representative of Webster's earlier thinking.[1] It would be by following the order of nature through a recognition of her established laws that man would rise above the distortions of peculiar faiths and superstitions. It is significant that a selection from Thompson, the great nature poet, gives the key to his volume.[1]

[1] Webster, Noah, *Elements of Useful Knowledge,* Vol. I, preface. 1802.

Recommendations of *The Grammatical Institute:*

"Having examined the first part of the new Grammatical Institute of the English Language, published by *Mr. Noah Webster,* we are of opinion that it is preferable, in plan and execution, to Dilworth's or any other Spelling Book, which has been introduced into our schools.

"Subscribed by the following Gentlemen.

> The Hon. Oliver Wolcott, Esq.
> Rev. Ezra Stiles, D.D., President of Yale College.
> Rev. Elizur Goodrich, D.D.
> Rev. Patrick Allison, D.D., Maryland.
> Col. George Wyllys, Secretary of State.
> Hon. Stephen MixMitchel, Esq.
> Col. Thomas Seymour, Mayor of Hartford.
> Gen. Samuel H. Parsons.
> Hon. John Treadwell, Esq.
> Rev. Samuel Hopkins.
> Col. Samuel Wyllys.
> Ralph Pomeroy.
> John Trumbull.
> Rev. Timothy Dwight.
> Rev. Eliphalet Steele.
> Rev. Nathan Strong.
> Rev. Nathan Perkins.
> Rev. Joseph Buckminister.
> Mr. Andrew Law.
> Daniel Lyman, Esq.
> Chauncey Goodrich, Esq.
> Joel Barlow, Esq."

Preface to the *Grammatical Institute.* Very strong recommendations were given by Joseph Willard, Topping Reeve, and Benjamin West, all influential men of that period.

Over-specialization cramps the mind. We were fortunately situated in the United States in the opportunity for the immediate service of a general education. We had not suffered here, and would not for some time, the vicious results of over-specialization. Webster said: "One further remark, however, which I cannot omit, is that the people of America are necessitated, by their local situation, to be more sensible and discerning, than nations which are limited in territory and confined to the arts of manufacture." [1] Special conditions existed in Europe which were not in harmony with the broader humanitarian type of education. Webster saw the evil effects that grew out of the economic situation in Europe: "In a populous country, where arts are carried to a great perfection, the mechanics are obliged to labor constantly upon a single article. Every art has its several branches, one of which employs a man all his life." [1] This specialization had been carried so far that "A man who makes heads of pins or springs of watches, spends his days in that manufacture and never looks beyond it." [1] It was obvious that such specialization was "the means of perfecting the arts," but it could not be denied that this "cramps the human mind, by confining all its faculties to a point." [1]

Minimal essentials: constants and variables. Even though he contended against over-specialization, Webster did not hold that what was considered at that time a cultural education should be continued. He declared, "Indeed it appears to me that what is now called a *liberal education* disqualifies a man for business." [2] The encyclopædic type of education that prevailed was an impossibility since "The greatest genius on earth, not *even* a Bacon, can be a perfect master of every branch." [3] To attempt a mastery of all fields of

[1] Webster, Noah, *Sketches of American Policy*, p. 29. 1785.
[2] Webster, Noah, *The American Magazine*, p. 161. 1788.
[3] *Ibid.*, p. 160. 1788.

knowledge meant that there would be no sufficient mastery of any one branch for immediate use. Besides the learning which was necessary for a common intercourse, "lads should be directed to pursue those branches which are connected more immediately with the business for which they are destined." [1] This need not mean the neglect of general culture for "There are some arts and sciences which are necessary for every man." [1] Schools should in some way provide for the giving of those skills peculiar to different lines of endeavor and combine these with all the education that would be necessary for fruitful living. For instance, "It would be very useful for the farming part of the community, to furnish country schools with some easy system of practical husbandry," while he advocated "French, Italian, or such other living language for young men in the mercantile line" and also "commercial courses including the study of law (commercial), trade relations, insurance, etc." [1] In order to become most useful citizens the youth must be prepared for the broader responsibilities of citizenship in a democracy, but along with general education there must be special training of such a character as to make the youth efficient in lines of business.

In discussing the Revolution in France, Webster said that it was the chief function of the historian and the statesman "to discover, if possible, the *causes* of great changes in the affairs of men; the *springs* of those important movements, which vary the aspect of government, the features of nations, and the very character of man." [2] In analyzing out the causes of the French Revolution and especially the causes of its failure to materialize and the causes of its excesses, he found as one of the chief factors that while France "had illuminated a portion of its inhabitants" it

[1] Webster, Noah, *The American Magazine,* p. 160. 1788.
[2] Webster, Noah, *Miscellaneous Papers,* p. 1. 1794.

"had not dissipated the gloom that was spread over the mass of the nation." [1]   The remedy for this lay in a universal provision for a broad type of education that would unchain the minds of all.   In France, "The philosophical researches of Voltaire, Rousseau, and the Abbe Raynal, had long before unchained the minds of that part of the French nation who read; a respectable class of men.   These men understood the errors of their government and the nature of liberty," but the weakness of the French republic lay in the fact that the multitude had been neglected.[1]   In France the philosophers had rejoiced at the necessity of breaking down "the whole machine of despotism, involving all the privileged orders in the proposed renovation." [2]   While it was true that "the *ecclesiastical* state was so interwoven with the *political*" that it called for "deranging the whole fabric;" France was unprepared for carrying through such a régime. "Superstition and enthusiasm" must be replaced by scientific knowledge in order that permanent reforms might result.[2]

Education should take place within the United States.   It would be a great mistake to send the youth of America to Europe for their education.   "This was right before the revolution; at least as far as national attachments were concerned; but the propriety of it ceased with our political relation to Great Britain." [3]   Serious consequences would arise if this practice were to continue: "In the first place, our honor as an independent nation is concerned in the establishment of literary institutions, adequate to all our own purposes; without sending our youth abroad, or depending on other nations for books and instructors." [4]   Webster could not conceive why America "after the heroic achieve-

[1] Webster, Noah, *Miscellaneous Papers,* p. 9.   1794.
[2] *Ibid.,* p. 10.   1794.
[3] Webster, Noah, *On Education of the Youth in America,* p. 39.   1788.
[4] *Ibid.,* p. 31.   1788.

ments of the late war" should "send to Europe for men and books to teach their children A B C." [1] Second, a more serious result would be that foreign attachments would be formed. He argued: "Every person of common observation will grant, that most men prefer the manners and the government of that country where they are educated. Let ten American youths be sent, each to a different European kingdom, and live there from the age of twelve to twenty, and each will give the preference to the country where he has resided." [1] There could be no doubt that "Ninety-nine persons of a hundred who pass that period in England or France, will prefer the people, their manners, their laws, and their government to those of their native country," and "Such attachments are injurious, both to the happiness of men and to the political interests of their own country." [1] Webster did not believe that foreign travel should be eliminated from education, but he held that "A boy who lives in England from twelve to twenty, will be an *Englishman* in his manners and feelings; but let him remain at home until he is twenty, and form his attachments, he may then spend several years abroad, and still be an *American.*" [2] This would very generally be true because of *"the influence of habit."* [2] Third, a further evil result would be that if the youth of America were educated in foreign universities and schools they would become accustomed to receiving institutions as final.[3] If we did not have institutions that were as good as those of foreign nations, it was the business of our nation to establish such schools, and "to furnish them with professors of the first abilities and most assiduous application, and with a complete apparatus for *establishing theories by experiments.*" [3] This experimental attitude would be sacrificed unless such schools were established. "Nature

---

[1] Webster, Noah, *On Education of the Youth in America*, p. 31. 1788.
[2] *Ibid.*, p. 32. 1788.   [3] *Ibid.*, p. 34. 1788.

has been profuse to Americans, in genius, and in advantages of climate and soil. If this country, therefore, should long be indebted to Europe for opportunities of acquiring any branch of science in perfection, it must be by means of a criminal neglect of its inhabitants." [1] Fourth, the chief reason for having youth educated in the United States was "The difference in the nature of the American and European governments." Our ways of reasoning and thinking were very different from those of Europe and, since "Men form modes of reasoning, or habits of thinking on political subjects, in the country where they are bred," we would have here as a result of sending youth abroad an *"infinite variety of national opinions and habits"* which would be very difficult to change.[1] "It is therefore of infinite importance that those who direct the councils of a nation, should be educated in that nation" and that "their first ideas, attachments and habits should be acquired in the country which they are to govern and defend." [2] Webster declared that "When a knowledge of their own country is obtained, and an attachment to its laws and interests deeply fixed in their hearts, then young gentlemen may travel with infinite advantage and perfect safety. . . . My meaning is that *men* should travel, and not *boys*." [2]

Travel in America. Instead of sending youth immediately to travel in foreign countries after they had completed the usual course, it would be well that they should become acquainted with their own country: "It is time for Americans to change their usual route and travel through a country which they never think of or think beneath their notice; I mean the United States." [2] While the States had been a part of the British empire it was natural that "our interests, our feelings were those of Englishmen; our depen-

---

[1] Webster, Noah, *On Education of the Youth in America,* p. 34.   1788.
[2] *Ibid.,* p. 35.   1788.

dence led us to respect and imitate their manners, and to look up to them for our opinions."[1] At that time, "We little thought of any national interest in America" and "we had no common interest, we little thought of improving our acquaintance with each other, or of removing prejudices, and reconciling the discordant feelings of the inhabitants of different provinces."[1] But now these circumstances had been changed: "Independence and union render it necessary that the citizens of different states should know each others characters and circumstances; that all jealousies should be removed; that mutual respect and confidence should succeed, and a harmony of views and interests should be cultivated by a friendly intercourse."[1] For this reason, "A tour through the United States ought now to be considered a necessary part of a liberal education. Let them spend twelve or eighteen months in examining the local situation of the different States; the rivers, soil, the population, the improvements and commercial advantages of the whole." During these travels there should be "an attention to the spirit and manners of the inhabitants, their laws, local customs and institutions." Any one who had travelled widely knew that "The people of America, with all their information are yet extremely ignorant of the geography policies and manners of their neighboring States."[2] Even those of the higher classes "have not so correct information respecting the United States, as they have respecting England or France. Such ignorance is not only disgraceful, but it is materially prejudicial to our political friendship and federal operations."[2] Webster closed his appeal for education within the United States by saying, "Americans, unshackle your minds, and act like independent beings."[2]

Educational conditions in the United States. No one was more familiar with the general status of education in the

[1] Webster, Noah, *On Education of the Youth in America,* p. 35. 1788.
[2] *Ibid.,* p. 36. 1788.

United States before 1800 than Noah Webster. He had
come into direct contact with all the different types of
schools, public and private. He had travelled extensively
in nearly every state in the union. The picture that he
gave of educational conditions was not generally compli-
mentary to the supporters of education. In describing
the conditions that existed in Maryland, he declared "The
body of the people are ignorant. I once saw a copy of
instructions given to a representative by his constituents,
with more than a hundred names subscribed; three-fifths
of which were marked with a cross because the men could
not write." [1] The evidence here was unchallengeable and
the conditions that existed in Maryland were only too
general throughout the United States. Concerning the
schools in the state of New York, he said, "Many parts
are either unfurnished with schools, or the schools which
they have are kept by low ignorant men, and are frequently
worse than none. This remark may be extended to a large
proportion of the United States." [2] His statement concerning conditions existing in Maryland and in New York
may be considered fairly representative of the status of
education following the Revolution. In 1788 he said "There
are not more than two States in the thirteen, where one
half the freemen read the public papers." [3] In writing to
Dr. Priestley he gave a more favorable picture of educational
conditions in New England: "The truth seems to be that
in the Eastern States, knowledge is more diffused among
the laboring people than in any country on the globe." [4]
In these states, "they read not only the bible, and newspapers, but almost all read the best English authors, as the
Spectator, Rambler, and the works of Watts, Doderidge, and

[1] Webster, Noah, *Essays*, p. 260.   1788.
[2] Webster, Noah, *The American Magazine*, p. 227.   1788.
[3] Webster, Noah, *Essays*, p. 74.   1788.
[4] Webster, Noah, *Letters to Dr. Priestley*, p. 23.   1800.

others." But even here he declared that "in the higher branches of literature . . . learning is superficial to a shameful degree." [1] Largely "The learning of the people extends to a knowledge of their own tongue, of writing and arithmetic sufficient to keep their own simple accounts." [1]

Practicability of a national system of education. A national system of education for the furtherance of national culture was in no way an impossibility:

> "Such a general system is neither impracticable nor difficult; and excepting the formation of a federal government that shall be efficient and permanent, it demands the first attention of American patriots. Until such a system shall be adopted and pursued. . . . Until Legislators discover that the only way to make good citizens and subjects, is to nourish them, it cannot be known to what degree of perfection society and government may be carried. America affords the fairest opportunities for making the experiment, and opens the most encouraging prospect of success." [2]

Summary. Noah Webster's early training and experience gave him a uniquely American outlook. He very early began to work for the realization of a distinctive American character, a national tongue, flexible institutions that would make for, rather than against, national freedom of development, and a system of education that would train citizens in the scientific, objective, humanitarian attitude. His main stress was upon flexible institutions that would be democratic so that there could be a maximal development of the experiment being made in democracy. He believed that the utmost of freedom should be encouraged in social experimentation. Influenced by Helvetius, Rousseau, and Thomas Paine during the period following the Revolution, he sought to make permanent the philosophy of change and reconstruction that had dominated during the war against Great Britain. The essence of democracy lay in the change

---

[1] Webster, Noah, *Letters to Dr. Priestley*, p. 23. 1800.
[2] Webster, Noah, *On Education of the Youth in America*, p. 26. 1788.

from external control to control from within, from the
control motivated by fear to that motivated by a sense of
values, from acceptance on authority to a scientific, experimental attitude. Each generation was to be engaged in
furthering human progress through scientific procedure and
not in following the obsolete laws and customs of past
generations. The tyranny of opinion and custom was to
be broken. The United States were peculiarly free from
the venerable institutions of European nations, and here
could be perfected the various institutions that were essential to human progress. Change was inevitable. In the
United States the nation could work out a broad, scientific,
humanitarian basis of social control. Changes would not
then be the result of caprice or accident, but of scientifically
controlled procedure. A mode of education must be created
that would respect every human value and that would raise
up a body of creatively constructive citizens. A national
system of education would be the only adequate means for
forming such a national character.

CHAPTER SEVEN

SUMMARY

Philosophical basis of education: Indefinite perfectibility of man and institutions. The various efforts to create a national system of education immediately following the Revolution were largely attempts to make the principles of the eighteenth century liberal movement the determining force in the development of American character and institutions. The doctrines of the eighteenth century were: that man could progress; that the lines of human progress could be determined; and that man's nature was favorable to progress. The function of education was to aid man in the realization of the greatest possible advancement, and the state existed for the furthering of human progress in societal and individual welfare. According to this conception fixed institutions were detrimental to humanity. It was the business of the state to make possible constant readjustment by providing a proper means of education.

The fundamental principles of the American Revolution were an outgrowth of the eighteenth century movement toward freedom of thought and action. In the Declaration of Independence the doctrine of change and evolution was definitely stated and the utilitarian basis of institutions was avowed. Societal welfare dictated that as soon as institutions ceased to function for human progress others better adapted to this end should take their place. Man had a right to liberty and happiness, and it was his privilege to perfect whatever instruments were necessary for the achievement of these. The right to change any form of social controls

256

inhered within the people because they were the authors and the beneficiaries of such controls. The development of social institutions for impartial and universal progress demanded that such institutions be based upon reason. Man was no longer to look to the past for the sanctions of conduct, but was to find the sanctions in the immediate circumstances of human evolution. For the liberation of thought and action there should be evolved a science of human development. Man was a being capable of indefinite advancement, and education was the chief means whereby this advancement could be accelerated and guided. Education was the development of the capacity for growth.

Flexible institutions. In order that institutions might aid and stimulate progress rather than make it impossible, they were to be fluid, evolutionary, biological. It was the business of institutions to aid in the continuous development of the human race. To avoid the loss of any value, the youth of the nation should be made familiar with the elements of progress. The critical periods of human history in which humanity had progressed most rapidly should receive special attention in order that the principles operating in that progress might be used in the solution of present problems. Human institutions had developed through long centuries, but they had developed largely by accident of circumstances. For intelligent citizenship it would be necessary to become cognizant of how government had originated and developed, and how it had functioned at one time to retard civilization and at another to aid in its progress. It was the function of citizenship to improve government scientifically. Creative citizenship in a creative democracy demanded a flexible institutional basis that would value institutions in proportion to their present creative utility. This progressive enrichment of the life of the nation placed a new responsibility upon the citizen. Institutions were no longer sacraments or fetishes to be jealously guarded against change, but instruments to be refashioned and refined. The unique experience of the American colonists had been their common interest in subduing nature and in developing the vast resources of a virgin continent. There had been absent from the pioneer experience the class struggles that had been so destructive of the humanitarian values in Europe. The furthering of a neighbor's interest had been here consonant with the interests of each individual. Out of this there had developed an attitude of respect for and support of daring, venturesome projecting of enterprises. Initiating, refashioning, innovating, creating— all these were to be fused by the motif of societal welfare.

Prime business of the school to educate for constructive citizenship of a humanitarian character. The United States seemed to afford the best opportunity for working out a synthesis of "goods." Hitherto, the accidents of race and of geographic location had prevented any such synthesis. The United States was peculiarly free from the limitations of the racial and local prejudices that so hampered Europe. Here lay the opportunity for an integration of society. America had drawn upon the various nations for its inhabitants. It had suffered a long, common pioneer experience, and the way had been prepared for a disinterested appreciation of various cultures. Furthermore, in America there was the opportunity in a special way to make the basis of education pragmatic. The education of the child could begin and continue in worthy endeavor of a creative sort. This opportunity for creative endeavor on the part of the youth of the nation in the great enterprise of the development of its resources and the direction of its experiment in democracy, made it possible to create here a new type of life, one in which the chief value was the contribution made to national and humanitarian development. The business of the school was to help the youth of the nation to live in the enjoyment of these responsibilities. American education should be creative in character and should be centered in worthy endeavor rather than in the formal schooling that had been inherited from the past. Since the developing of the humanitarian outlook was the supreme task of the nation, the agency through which this could be accomplished to the best advantage was a national system of education that would create a coöperative spirit, in behalf of world welfare and progress.

The nation the most effective unit through which to work for societal welfare. While humanitarian or social welfare was to be the ultimate aim of education there must be emphasis laid upon national development. The nation was the largest social unit through which these common aims could be worked out. Toward this end there should be a thorough knowledge of the laws of national development. The history of the development of nationalistic cultures would be fruitful both in avoiding the evils of narrowly developed prejudices and also in gaining an appreciation of the forces that had made possible the growth of nationality. In the United States there was a pre-revolutionary basis of nationalism. We had developed here new forms of social control and we had also developed a new appreciation of the worth of the individual, regardless of his previous fortunes. Circumstances had taught the American that genius for leadership was not confined to any one social class. The nation afforded opportunities for the development of leaders through a national, democratic system of education. The new type of social control that grew out of the new duties necessitated an indigenous form of education. We could no longer depend upon local pioneer circumstances to develop activity and joint cooperative effort. The schools should cause the youth of the nation to realize that in a democracy they were not simply to obey laws imposed from above, but were to fashion the nation's policies. In 1776 Adam Smith saw this and expressed it cogently:

> "The persons who now govern the resolutions of what they call their continental congress, feel in themselves at this moment a degree of importance which perhaps, the greatest subjects in Europe scarce feel. From shopkeepers, tradesmen, and attornies, they are become statesmen and legislators, and are employed in contriving a new form of government for an extensive empire, which, they flatter themselves, will become, and which, indeed, seems very likely to become one of the greatest and most formidable that ever was in the world." [1]

A new type of education was also necessary for females. They were to be made aware of the important part that they played in the forming of American citizens. Toward this end they also were to be educated in the principles of democracy and in the laws of national development.

Advantages of a thorough national system of education. The ends of democracy could not be achieved without a system of education correlative to that form of social control. Through the establishment of a national system of education there would be universal and equal support for all grades of education; expert supervision through the training of those who were to direct the educational institutions of the nation; and there would be also a more economic and effective administration. Those who were to administer this education would be especially trained for their position. A well trained and nationally certified teaching force could alone be assured through a national system of teacher training and adequate remuneration for their services. Uniformity of educational provision for textbooks, schools, and all that appertained to effective instruction, demanded centralization of control with expert supervision. Universal and

[1] Smith, Adam, *Wealth of Nations,* Vol. II, p. 232. 1776.

equal opportunity for all grades of education depended upon a well organized national system. Public education should begin at birth and should be continued as long as it was profitable to the individual and to the nation. Provision should be made for continuation schools. Such a national system was not impracticable. It could be created as easily and be as efficient as a national system of justice, and, in the end, the expense of education would be less and the service more efficient.

Scientific control of societal welfare and development. In any adequate system of democratic government and education there should be, first, a group of specialists to gather and interpret data pertinent to effective social control. This was the basis of human happiness. Second, there should be specialists to gather and interpret data pertaining to economic development—the development of all resources. Third, there should be experimenters to make discoveries and inventions that would further human progress. Human progress depended largely upon scientific discovery and invention. Fourth, there should be an objective, impartial attitude created by the schools through science and experimentation. Until obsolete customs and institutions were destroyed and scientific controls substituted, human progress would be very limited. It was the business of the nation to create an effective national system of education that would stimulate the greatest progress of civilization. For the carrying out of this purpose, it would be necessary to instruct American youth in all that pertained to human progress and to instill in them a veneration for the contributions that had been made through the successive movements in America— especially through the Revolution and its principles.

Importance of a national system of education. One of the most scholarly and most influential writers in connection with the American Revolution was Dr. Richard Price.

In spite of virulent opposition and social ostracism because of his support of the American Revolution and its principles, he continued to be one of the chief stimuli to the liberal forces. In his work entitled *Observations on the Importance of the American Revolution,* which was published in 1784, he expressed the spirit of the foregoing plans: "With heart-felt satisfaction, I see the revolution in favor of universal liberty which has taken place in America;—A revolution which opens up a new prospect in human affairs, and begins a new era in the history of mankind." [1] Although he was writing in Great Britain, he did not hesitate to express his satisfaction in the fact that the termination of the war had prevented Great Britain from destroying the new governments, for "by providing, in a sequestered continent possessed of many singular advantages, a place of refuge for opprest men in every region of the world; and by laying the foundation there of an empire which may be the seat of liberty, science and virtue, and from whence there is reason to hope these sacred blessings will spread, till they become universal and the time arrives when kings and priests shall have no more power to oppress," no one could foresee the results of such a revolution.[2] Through the success of the Revolution a place had been provided where *"fundamental* but impartial inquiry" could furnish the basis for human progress. Again he said, "In order to introduce and perpetuate it, and at the same time to give it the greatest effect on the improvement of the world, nothing is more necessary than the establishment of a wise and liberal plan of EDUCATION. It is impossible to properly represent the importance of this. So much is left by the author of nature to depend on the turn given to

---

[1] Price, Richard, *Observations on the Importance of the American Revolution,* p. 2. 1784.
[2] *Ibid.,* pp. 2-3. 1784.

the mind in early life and the impressions then made, that
I have thought there may be a *secret* remaining to be discovered in education, which will cause future generations
to grow up virtuous and happy, and accelerate human improvement to a greater degree than can at present be
imagined." [1] The essay which contains these sentiments was
widely read. Price said further that "The end of education
is to direct the powers of the mind in unfolding themselves;
and to assist in gaining their just bent and force. And,
in order to do this, its business should be to teach *how* to
think, rather than *what* to think; or to lead into the best way
of searching for truth, rather than to instruct in truth itself." [2] Further, "Education ought to be an initiation into
candour, rather than into any systems of faith; and . . . it
should form the habit of cool and patient investigation, rather
than an attachment to any opinions." [3] While "hitherto education has been on a contrary plan. It has been a *contraction*,
not an *enlargement*. . . . Instead of . . . teaching to think
freely . . . it hath qualified for thinking only in *one*
track," [4] it was now the opportunity for America to liberate humanity through a scientific, experimental, open-minded
mode of education. This was the dynamic conception of
the state and of education that was set forth in the plans
for a national system of education.

[1] Price, Richard, *Observations on the Importance of the American
Revolution*, p. 50. 1784.
[2] *Ibid.*, pp. 50-51. 1784.   [3] *Ibid.*, p. 51. 1784.   [4] *Ibid.*, p. 52. 1784.

BIBLIOGRAPHY

PRIMARY SOURCES

1721

CARE, HENRY. English liberties, or the free-born subjects' inheritance, containing Magna Charta, Charta de Foresta, the Statute De Talagio non concedendo, the Habeas Corpus act, and several other Statutes; with comments on each of them. 1721. First edition by Henry Care, and continued with large additions by William Nelson. 6th edition. Providence, R. I. 1774. *Widely circulated during the revolution.*

MONTESQUIEU, CHARLES. Persian Letters. 1721. *Virile satire on customs in France.*

1750

MONTESQUIEU, CHARLES DE SECONDAT. Défense de L'esprit des loix, à laquelle on a joint quelques eclaircissemeus. Geneve, 1750. 80 pp. *Closely studied during early period of break with England.*

1767

DUPONT DE NEMOURS. Physiocratie. *American thinkers such as Franklin and Jefferson were charmed by the physiocratic philosophy.*

MERCIER DE LA RIVIÈRE. L'ordre naturel et essentiél des sociétés politiques. 1767. *Was read in America. Especially strong presentation of the natural basis of society.*

1768

PRIESTLEY, JOSEPH. An essay on the first principles of government, and on the nature of political, civil, and religious liberty. 1768. *Revolutionary in tone. Influenced American thinking.*

1769

American Philosophical Society. List of members of the society formed on the 2nd of January, 1769, by a union of the "American Philosophical Society," and the "American Society held at Philadelphia for the Promoting of Useful Knowledge." Philadelphia: 1769. 8 v. *Illuminating for its representative character and as an example of the attempts to get together as a unit.*

1770

BURKE, EDMUND. Thoughts on the cause of the present discontents. London: J. Dodsley. 1770. 118 pp. 3 ed. *Brought criticism upon Burke because of his American sympathies.*

1773

MONTESQUIEU, CHARLES. The Spirit of laws. London edition. 1773. 2 vols. *Brought to America immediately and widely read.*

1774

ADAMS, JOHN. History of the dispute with America, from its origin in 1754. London. 1774. Also London. 1784. *Shows evidences of the philosophy of the Declaration of Independence.*

BOLLAN, WILLIAM. The petitions of Mr. Bollan, agent for the council of the province of Massachusetts Bay, lately presented to the houses of parliament; with a brief introduction relating to the law of nature, the authority of human rulers, and the subject's common right of defence; with subsequent observations. Boston. 1774. *Eighteenth century philosophy evident.*

CAROT, A. A very short and candid appeal to free-born Britons. By an American. (Signed A. Carot.) London. 1774. *Basis of British freedom discussed.*

COOPER, MYLES. The American Querist: or some questions relative to the present disputes between Great Britain and her colonies. By a North American. New York. 1774.

DICKINSON, JOHN. Essay on the constitutional power of Great-Britain over the colonies in America; with the resolves of the committee for the province of Pennsylvania and their instructions to their representatives in assembly. Philadelphia. 1774. *Dickinson was conservative, but at this time held revolutionary principles.*

DRAYTON, WILLIAM HENRY. A letter from freemen of South Carolina, to the deputies of North America, assembled in high court of congress at Philadelphia. Charles-town. 1774. 46 pp.

FARMER, A Westchester. *pseud.* A view of the controversy between Great Britain and her colonies. . . . In a letter to the author of, A full vindication of the measures of congress. New York: J. Rivington. 1774. 37 pp. *Radical philosophy evidenced throughout.*

JEFFERSON, THOMAS. A summary view of the rights of British America, set forth in some resolutions intended for the inspection of the present delegates of the people of Virginia, now in convention. By a native and a member of the House of Burgesses. Williamsburg: Printed by Clementina Rind. 1774. London: Reprinted for O. Kearsley. 1774. 44 pp. *Natural origin of society and individual liberty made primary rather than British precedent.*

QUINCEY, JOSIAH. Observations on the act of parliament commonly called the Boston Port-Bill; with thoughts on civil society and standing armies. Boston. 1774. *Doctrine of infringement of natural rights.*

ROKEBY, MATTHEW ROBINSON. Considerations on the measures carrying on with respect to the British colonies in North America. New York re-print of London ed. 1774. Also reprinted in other American cities. *Strong presentation of rights of Americans.*

SEABURY, SAMUEL, BP. A view of the controversy between Great-Britain and her colonies. New York. 1774. *Basis of natural rights defended.*

SHARP, GRANVILLE. A declaration of the people's natural right to share in the legislature, which is the fundamental principle of the British constitution of State. London: B. White. 1774. xi, 244 pp. Philadelphia reprint of London ed. Also reprinted in other American cities. *British and natural rights the bases of freedom.*

SOMERS, JOHN (?). The judgment of whole kingdoms and nations, concerning the rights, privileges and properties of the people. A large account of the revolution of 1688; with several speeches, declarations, and addresses. Boston: Printed for I. Thomas by J. Langdon. 12th ed. 1774. 144 pp. *Revolutionary principles advocated.*

U. S. Continental Congress. Journal of the proceedings of the Congress, held at Philadelphia, September, 1774. Philadelphia. 1774. *Eighteenth century doctrines evident.*

VIATOR. *pseud.* The thoughts of a traveller upon our American disputes. London: J. Ridley. 1774. 24 pp. Reprinted in Public Advertiser. 1774.

WILSON, JAMES. Considerations of the nature and extent of the legislative authority of the British parliament. Philadelphia. 1774.

1775

ALLEN, JOHN (?). An oration, upon the beauties of liberty; or the essential rights of the Americans. Wilmington. 1775. *Defense of natural rights.*

ALMON, JOHN. Collection (A) of interesting authentic papers, relative to the dispute between Great Britain and America; shewing the causes and progress of that misunderstanding from 1764-1775. 1775. Emmet Collection. *Appeals made to natural and British rights.*

America's appeal to the impartial world. Wherein the rights of the Americans, as men, British subjects, and as colonists; the equity of the demand, and the manner in which it is made upon them by Great-Britain, are stated and considered. Hartford. 1775. *Revolutionary principles forcibly set forth.*

Authentic papers from America: submitted to the dispassionate consideration of the public. Petitions of 1774. London: J. Becket. 1775. 33 pp. *Documents show the basis of human rights.*

CARMICHAEL, JOHN. A self-defensive war lawful, proved in a sermon preached at Lancaster, before Captain Ross's company of militia . . . June 4, 1775. Corrected by the author from the copy printed at Lancaster. Philadelphia. 1775. *Principles of Locke and Rousseau supported.*

CARTWRIGHT, JOHN. A letter to Edmund Burke, controverting the principles of American government, laid down in his lately published speech on American taxation, delivered in H. C. April 19th, 1775. London. 1775.

Declaration (The) by the representatives of the United Colonies of North America, now met in general Congress in Philadelphia, setting forth the causes and necessity of taking up arms; the letter of the 12 united colonies by their delegates in Congress to the inhabitants of Great Britain; their humble petition to His Majesty and their address to the people of Ireland, collected together by lovers of peace. London. 1775. *Revolutionary principles clearly stated.*

GALLOWAY, JOSEPH. A candid examination of the mutual claims of Great Britain and the colonies, with a plan of accommodation on constitutional principles. New York: J. Rivington. 1775. 62 pp.

GROTIUS. *pseud.* Pills for the delegates; or, the chairman chastized, in a series of letters addressed to Peyton Randolph, Esq., on his conduct, as president of the General Congress held at the city of Philadelphia, September 5, 1774. New York. 1775.

JOHNSON, SAMUEL. Taxation not tyranny; an answer to the resolutions and address of the American Congress. London. 1775. *Attempts to justify forced control of the colonies.*

LEONARD, DANIEL. The origin of the American contest with Great Britain, or the present political state of the Massachusetts-Bay, in general. New York. 1775. viii, 118 pp. *Philosophical as well as economic divergences given.*

Miscellaneous pieces in prose and verse. Published in the *Pennsylvania Magazine* in the year 1775.

New Jersey, General Assembly. To his Excellency William Franklin the humble address of the representatives. Broadside. 1775.

New York, Colony. General Assembly. To the King's Most Excellent Majesty. The humble petition of the General Assembly of the Colony of New York. (Followed by the memorial to the House of Lords, and the representation to the Commons. New York. 1775. *Not as meek as the title would indicate.*

Pennsylvania Magazine. Editor, Thomas Paine. Jan. 24, 1775. *Defense of American Revolution.*

PITT, WILLIAM, EARL OF CHATHAM. The speech of the Right Honorable the Earl of Chatham, in the House of Lords, Jan. 20, 1775 (on the motion to remove the King's troops from Boston). London. (?). 1775.

REGULUS. *pseud.* A defense of the resolutions and address of the American Congress in reply to taxation no tyranny, etc. London. 1775. *Principles of natural rights defended.*

SERLE, AMBROSE. Americans against liberty; or; an essay on the nature and Principles of true freedom, shewing that the designs and conduct of the Americans tend only to tyranny and slavery. London: J. Matthews. 1775. 64 pp. *One of the most forcible statements of the opposition.*

Taxation, tyranny. Addressed to Samuel Johnson, LL.D. London. 1775.

TOPLADY, AUGUSTUS MONTAGNE. An old fox tarred and feathered. Occasioned by what is called Mr. John Wesley's Calm address to our American colonys, . . . By an Manovarian. London. 1775.

Tyranny unmasked. An answer to a late pamphlet, entitled Taxation, no tyranny. London. 1775. *Many such replies were written.*

WESLEY, JOHN. Calm address to our American colonies. London. 1775. Charged rebellion.

1776

ADAMS, JOHN. Thoughts on government: applicable to the present state of the American colonies. In a letter from a gentleman to his friend. Philadelphia: printed. Boston: reprinted by John Gill. 1776. 16 pp.

ADAMS, SAMUEL. An oration delivered at the state-house, in Philadelphia . . . August, 1776. (Urging the independence of the colonies. Philadelphia. 1776. *Principles of American life set forth.*

Affaires de l'Angleterre et de l'Amerique, Anvers. 1776-1779. Vol. I, 15-17.

BLACKLOCK, THOMAS. (Adam Ferguson ?). Remarks on the nature and extent of liberty, as compatible with the genius of civil societies; on the principles of government and the proper limits of its power in free state. Edinburgh. 1776. *Typical of European attitude—liberal.*

BRAXTON, CARTER. An address to the convention of the colony and ancient dominion of Virginia; on the subject of government. By a native of that colony. Philadelphia. 1776.

Declaration of Independence. Philadelphia. 1776.

DEMOPHILUS. The genuine principles of the ancient Saxon, or English constitution, carefully collected from the best authorities; with some observation on their peculiar fitness for the

United colonies in general, and Pennsylvania in particular. Philadelphia. 1776. *British basis of freedom shown.*

Dialogue, (A) on the principles of the constitution and legal liberty, compared with despotism; applied to the American question and the probable events of the war. London. 1776.

Exposé des droits des colonies britanniques, pour justifer le projet de leur indépendance. Amsterdam. 1776. *Some tracts were published in French although written by Englishmen. This may be one of them.*

GOODRICH, (HENRY ?). Observations on Dr. Price's theory and principles of civil liberty and government. York. 1776. 147 pp.

History of North America, containing an exact account of their first settlements, with the present state of the different colonies; and a large introduction. London. 1776.

JOHNSON, ALLEN. Readings in constitutional history, 1776-1876. Boston: Houghton, Mifflin Co. 1912. xvii, 584 pp.

LEACOCK, JOHN. The fall of British tyranny: or, American liberty triumphant. The first campaign, A tragi-comedy of five acts, as lately planned at the Royal Theatrum Pandemonium at St. James's. The principal place of action in America. Philadelphia. 1776. *The stage did its part in furthering the revolution.*

MARTIN, JOHN. Familiar dialogues between Americus and Brittanicus; in which the right of private judgment; the exploded doctrines of infallibility, passive obedience, and non-resistence; with the leading sentiments of Dr. Price, on the nature of civil liberty, &c., are discussed. London. 1776. *Bitter attack.*

MATHER, ALLYN. The character of a well accomplished ruler described, A discourse delivered at the Freeman's meeting, in New Haven, April 8, 1776. New Haven. 1776.

OLIVERS, THOMAS. A full defence of John Wesley, in answer to the reflections by Caleb Evans in his observations on Mr. Wesley's late reply prefixed to his calm articles. London. 1776.

PAINE, THOMAS. Epistle to the Quakers. 1776. *Denounced their passivism.*

PINTO, ISAAC DE. Letters on the American troubles. Translated from the French. London. 1776.

PINTO, ISAAC DE. Réponse de M. J. de Pinto, aux Observations d'un homme impartial, sur la lettre à M. S. B. dans la Jamaique, on sujet des troubles que agitent actuallement toute l'Amerique Septentrionale. La Haye. 1776.

Political thoughts of a loyal patriot. 1776.

POWNALL, THOMAS. A letter to Adam Smith. London. 1776. 2, 1, 3-48 pp.

PRICE, RICHARD. Observations on the nature of civil liberty, the principles of government, and the justice of the policy of the war with America. To which is added an appendix and postscript. London. 1776. 128 pp. *One of the ablest proponents of the revolutionary principles. This and Common Sense may be said to be the bibles of the American revolution.*

RAYNAL, GUILLAUME THOMAS FRANCOIS. A philosophical and political history of the British settlements and trade in North America. Edinburgh. 1776. *The best and most comprehensive historical analysis of that period.*

ROBINSON, MATTHEW, 2 Baron Rokeby. Further (A) examination of our present American measures and of the reason and principles on which they are founded. By the author of considerations on the measures carrying on with respect to the British colonies in North America. London, 1776.

SHEBBEARE, JOHN. An essay on the origen, progress, and establishment of national society; in which the principles of government, the definitions of physical, moral, civil, and religious liberty, contained in Dr. Price's Observations, &c., are fairly examined and fully refuted. Appendix on Mr. Burke's speech. London. 1776. *One of the most scholarly presentations of the Tory viewpoint.*

SMITH, ADAM. An inquiry into the nature and causes of the wealth of nations. London: W. Strahan. 1776. Vol. I. 510 pp. Vol. II. 587 pp. *Against mercantilism.*

United States. Continental Congress. The journals of the proceedings of congress held at Philadelphia from January to May, 1776. Philadelphia, 1776.

Watson, Richard. The principles of the revolution vindicated. Cambridge. 1776. *Became popular.*

1777

BASSU, N. Nouveaux voyages dans l'Amérique septentrionale, contenant une collection de lettres éscrites sur les lieux, par l'auteur à son amu, M. Douin . . . ci devant son camarade dans le nouveaux monde. Amsterdam. 1777. *Keen comments on American liberal tendencies.*

BURKE, EDMUND. The political tracts and speeches of Edmund Burke. Dublin. 1777.

Collection of interesting authentic papers, relative to the disputes between Great Britain and America. London. 1777.

Liberalis, *pseud,* of Almon, J. Two letters: Viz. I. a letter to the Earl of Abingdon, in which his Grace of York's notions of civil liberty are examined by Liberalis; published in the London Evening Post, November 6, 1777. II. Vera icon; or a vindication of his Grace of York's sermon, preached on February 21, 1777 in answer to a letter from Liberalis to the Earl of Abingdon by Mysteagus Candidus. London. 1777.

MONTESQUIEU, CHARLES DE SECONDAT. Complete works of Montesquieu. London. 1777. 4 vols. *Read widely.*

New England primer (The) improved for the more easy attaining the true reading of English, To which is added the Assembly of divines and Mr. Cotton's catechism. Boston. 1777.

SHERER, JEAN BENOÎT. Recherches historiques et géographiques sur le nouveau-monde. Paris. 1777.

TOPHAM, EDWARD. Address to Edmund Burke, esq., on his late letter relative to the affaires of America. London: Printed for J. Bew. 1777. 27 pp.

Unconnected (An). Whig's address to the public; upon the present civil war, the state of public affaires, and the real cause of all the national calamities. London. 1777.

Valeus, *pseud.* (Almon, J.). The letters of Valeus (which originally appeared in the *London Evening Post*) with corrections, explanatory notes, and a preface by the author. London. 1777.

1778

ABINGDON, (4 earl) WILLOUGHBY BERTIE. Thoughts on the letter of Edmund Burke, esq., to the sheriffs of Bristol, on the affairs of America. London. 1778.

CARTWRIGHT, JOHN. The memorial of common sense, upon the present crisis between Great Britain and America. London. 1778.

Conciliatory bills, the, in reference to the American colonies, considered. London. 1778.

DUBUISSON, P. U. Abrigé de la Revolution de l'Amérique anglaise, depuis le commencement de l'année 1774 jusqu-au premier janvier 1778. Par M. Americain. Paris. 1778. 1, 452 pp.

LINGUET, SIMON NICHOLAS HENRI. Political and philosophical speculations on the characteristics of the present century with reflections on the probable effects of American independency. London. 1778.

PRICE, RICHARD, and PRIESTLEY, JOSEPH. A free discussion of the doctrines of materialism, and philosophical necessity, in a correspondence between Dr. Price and Dr. Priestley. To which is added, by Dr. Priestley, an introduction, explaining the nature of the controversy, and letters to writers who have animadverted on his disquisitions relating to matter and spirit. London. 1778.

RUSSELL, WILLIAM. The history of America, from its discovery by Columbus to the conclusion of the late war. With an appendix, containing an account of the rise and progress of the present unhappy contest between Great Britain and her colonies. London: Fielding and Walker. 1778. 2 vols.

SMITH, ADAM. Fragment sur les colonies. Lausanne. 1778.

TUCKER, JOSIAH. The notions of Mr. Locke, and his followers, that all civil governments whatever, not founded on the personal choice of the governed, are so many usurpations on the unalienable rights of mankind, considered and examined. Glocester. 1778.

WASHINGTON, GEORGE. Letters from General Washington, to several of his friends in 1776. In which are set forth, a fairer and fuller view of American politicks, than ever yet transpired, or the public could be made acquainted with through any other channel. Together with Mr. Jacob Douche's letter to Mr. Washington and answer to it; by Mr. John Parke, a lieutenant in Mr. Washington's army. 1778.

WIGGLESWORTH, EDWARD. The authority of tradition considered, at the lecture founded by the Hon. Judge Dudley, in Harvard College, November 5, 1777. Boston. 1778.

1779

AUCKLAND, WILLIAM EDEN, 1. baron. Four letters to the Earl of Carlisle, on certain perversions of political reasoning; on the present circumstances of the war between Great Britain, France and Spain. On public debts: on the representations of Ireland respecting a free trade. Edinburgh: R. and G. Fleming. 86 pp. 1779.

BENEZET, ANTHONY. The Pennsylvania spelling-book; or: youth's friendly instructor and admonitor. Philadelphia. 1779.

DUCHÉ, JACOB. Discourses on various subjects. London. 1779. 2 vols.

FISHER, GEORGE. *pseud.* The American instructor: or, young man's best companion: containing, spelling, reading, writing, and arithmetic . . . instructions . to write variety of hands, with copies of both in prose and verse, . . . Also merchant's accompts, and a short and easy method of shop and book-keeping. Together with the carpenter's plain and exact rule; showing how to measure carpenters, joiners, sawyers, brick-layers, plasterers, plumbers, masons, glasiers, and painters work. Likewise the practical gauger made easy, etc. Boston: Printed for John Boyle and J. D. M'Dougall. 1779. vi, 378 pp.

FRANKLIN, BENJAMIN. Individual works: political, miscel-laneous, and philosophical pieces arranged under the following heads, and distinguished by initial letters in each leaf. (G. P.) general politics; (A. B. T.) American politics before the troubles; (A. D. T.) American politics during the troubles; (P. P.) provincial or colony politics; and (M. P.) miscel-laneous and philosophical pieces. London. 1779.

MACPHERSON, JAMES. A short history of the opposition during the last session of parliament. London. 1779. v, 60 pp.

MORRIS, GOUVERNEUR. Observations on the American revolution, by Gouverneur Morris, published according to a resolution, of congress . . . for the consideration of those who are desirous, of comparing the conduct of the opposed parties. Philadelphia. 1779. *Able discussion of leading issues philosophical and political.*

Observations on a pamphlet entitled, A short history of opposi-tion during the last session of parliament, etc. London. 1779.

PRICE, RICHARD. A sermon, delivered to a congregation of prot-estant dissenters, at Hackney. London. 1779.

SHERIDAN, RICHARD BRINSLEY BUTLER. The school for scandal. Philadelphia. 1779. 3 ed. *Rewritten around the Tory ele-*

*ment in the United States and produced with considerable
variations in American cities.*

1780

Address (An) to the free and independent voters of England.
London. 1780.

ALMON, JOHN. Address (An) to the gentlemen forming the
various committees of the associated counties, and towns, for
supporting the petitions for redress of grievances, and against
the unconstitutional influence of the Crown over parliament.
(Signed by a pleader for the rights of the people.) London.
1780.

BACKUS, ISAAC. Appeal (An) to the people of Massachusetts
against arbitrary power. Boston. 1780. 36, 8 pp.

BOWDOIN, JAMES. A philosophical discourse addressed to the
American Academy of Arts and Sciences in Boston. Boston.
1780. 35 pp.

BRISSOT DE WARVILLE, JACQUES PIERRE. Testament politique de
l'Angleterre. A Philadelphie. 1780. 100 pp.

BURKE, EDMUND. Speech of Edmund Burke, Esq. member of
parliament for the city of Bristol, on presenting to the House
of Commons (on the eleventh of February, 1780) a plan for
the better security of the independence of parliament, and the
economical reformation of the civil and other establishments.
London: J. Dodsley. 1780. 76 pp.

BURKE, EDMUND. A vindication of natural society: or, A view
of the miseries . . . arising by mankind from . . . artificial
society. By a late noble writer, i.e., E. B. London. 1780.
106 pp.

COOPER, SAMUEL. A sermon preached before John Hancock
. . . governor October 25, 1780, being the day of the commencement of the constitution and inauguration of the new
government. Boston (?). 1780.

ELLIOT, JONATHAN. The debates in several state conventions, on
the adoption of the Federal Constitution as recommended by
the general convention at Philadelphia in 1787. 1881. 5 vols.

GALLOWAY, JOSEPH. Historical and political reflections on the
rise and progress of the American rebellion. London. 1780.

KEMBLE, JOHN PHILIPS. Fugitive pieces. York. 1780. 44 pp.

LOWTH, ROBERT. A short introduction to English grammar:

with critical notes. American reprint. 1780. vi, 8-99 pp. Another edition, London. 1799. xi, 132 pp.

ODELL, JONATHAN. *pseud.* for Smith. The times a satirical poem written during the American revolution. New Jersey. 1780 (?).

PAINE, THOMAS. Public good: being an examination into the claim of Virginia to the vacant western territory and of the right of the United States to the same, etc. Philadelphia. 1780.

PERISIER, ANTIONE MARIE. Le destin de l'Amérique; or, dialogues pittoresque dans lesquels on développe la cause des événements actuels, la politique et les intérets des puissances de l'Europe relativement a cette guerre, et les suites qu'elle devroit avoir pour le honheur de l'humanité, traduit fidèlemente de l'Anglais. London. 1780. *Not translated from English and published anonymously. Apparently not printed in London.*

1781

HILLIARD, D'AUBERTEUIL, MICHEL RENÉ. Essais historiques et politiques sur les Anglo-Americaines. Bruxelles. 1781-2. 2 vols.

HUNTINGTON, JOSEPH. A discourse adapted to the present day, on the health and happiness, or misery and ruin, of the body politic, preached at Coventry, April, 1781. Hartford. 1781.

ILLINGWORTH, JAMES. The signs of the times: or, a system of true politics; humbly addressed to all His Majesties subjects. London. 1781.

Impartial (An) history of the war in America between Great Britain and the United States, from its commencement to the end of the war. With an appendix, containing a collection of interesting and authentic papers. Boston: N. Coverly and R. Hodge. 1781. v. 1.

NORTHCOTE, THOMAS. Observations on the natural and civil rights of mankind, the prerogative of Princes, and Powers of government, in which the equal and universal right of the people to election and representation, is proved by direct and conclusive arguments. London. 1781. 1, 54 pp.

RAYNAL, GUILLAUME THOMAS FRANCOIS. The revolution of America—new edition. Translation of his "Révolution de l'Amerique," issued in 1781. Dublin. 1781. xx, 244 pp.

United States, Constitutions (The) of the several independent states of America; the Declaration of Independence! the Articles of Confederation . . . the treaties between His Most Christian Majesty and the United States of America. Philadelphia. 1781. *Very widely circulated.*

WEBSTER, NOAH. Letter from Noah Webster to George Washington, and from George Washington to Noah Webster, Brooklyn, New York. Historical Printing Club, Yorktown, 1881.

1782

Essay on the origin and progress of government. London: T. Cadell. 1782. 35 pp.

Indépendance (L') des Anglo-Américains démontrée utile à la Grande-Bretagne. Londres (?). 1782.

PAINE, THOMAS. A letter addressed to the Abbe Raynal, on the affairs of North America. Philadelphia. First edition. 1782.

Proposals to amend and perfect the policy of the government of the United States of America; or, the fulfilling of the prophecies in the latter days, commenced by the independence of America. Containing a new mode of elections; with a method of supporting government without taxing or fining the people. 1782.

RAYNAL, GUILLAUME THOMAS FRANCOIS. The revolution of America. Norwich. 1782. 10-94 pp.

TOD, THOMAS. Consolatory thoughts on American independence; showing the great advantages that will arise from it to the manufactures, the agriculture, and commercial interest of Great Britain and Ireland. Edinburgh: J. Donaldson. 1782. 68 pp.

TRUMBULL, JOHN. M'Fingal; a modern epic poem; in four cantos. Hartford. 1782. First complete edition. Philadelphia: from the press of Mathew Carey. 1791. 95 pp.

WILLIAMS, DAVID. Letters on political liberty. Addressed to a member of the English House of Commons. London. 1782.

1783

Boston Magazine. 1783-1786.

Case (The) and claim of the American loyalists impartially stated and considered; printed by order of their agents. 1783.

GALLOWAY, JOSEPH. Political reflections on the late colonial governments: royal, proprietary, and charter governments of the American colonies, etc. London: G. Wilkie. 1783. 259 pp.

RAYNAL, GUILLAUME THOMAS FRANCOIS. The revolution of America. Edinburgh. 1783. vi, 11-191 pp.

Rudiments of law and government, deduced from the law of nature; particularly addressed to the people of South Carolina, but composed on principles applicable to all mankind. Charlestown: Printed by John M'Iver, jun. 1783. xiii, 16-56 pp.

STOKES, ANTHONY. A view of the constitution of the British colonies, in North America and the West Indies . . . down to the present period. London. 1783.

TAYLOR, HANNIS. A memorial in behalf of the architect of our federal constitution, Peletiah Webster. Philadelphia. 1783. 48 pp.

TULLIUS. *pseud.* Three letters addressed to the public on the following subjects: I. The nature of a federal union . . . II. The civil and military powers . . . III. The public debt. Philadelphia. 1783.

WEBSTER, PELETIAH. A dissertation on the political union and constitution of the thirteen United States of North America: which is humbly offered to the public, by a citizen of Philadelphia. Philadelphia: T. Bradford. 1783. 47 pp.

1784

ALLEN, ETHAN. Reason the only oracle of man, or a compenduous system of natural religion. Bennington, Vt.: Haswell and Russell. 1784. xxi, 23-477 pp.

BELL, ROBERT. Illuminations for legislators and for sentimentalists. Philadelphia. 1784. 2, 52 pp.

CHALMERS, GEORGE. Opinions on interesting subjects of public law and commercial policy; arising from American independence. London. 1784. 200 pp.

Constitutions (The) of the several independent states. London. 1784.

DILLWORTH, THOMAS. The schoolmaster's assistant . . . To which is prefixed an essay on the education of youth. New York and other places. 1784.

FRANKLIN, JAMES. The philosophical and political history of the thirteen United States of America . . . etc. . . . London: J. Hinton and W. Adams. 1784. 156 pp.

Letters to a young nobleman, upon various subjects, particularly on government . . . wherein occasion is taken to remark on the writings of Dr. Price. London. 1784.

MABLY, GABRIEL BONNOT DE. Observations sur le gouvernement les loix des Etats-Unis d'Amerique. Amsterdam. 1784. Translated London. 1784.

MANDRILLON, JOSEPH. Le spectateur américain, ou, remarques générales sur l'Amérique Septentrionale, et sur la république des trieze Etats-Unis . . . Suivi de recherches philosophiques sur la découverte du nouveau monde. Amsterdam. 1784.

MORSE, JEDEDIAH. Geography made easy. Being a short but comprehensive system of that very useful and aggreable science. Calculated particularly for the use and improvement of schools in the United States. New Haven. 1784. Other editions consulted: 1789, 1790, 1791, 1792, 1793, 1794, 1800. *More than a geography; history and geography combined; increasing emphasis on American history.*

PRICE, RICHARD. Observations on the importance of the American Revolution and the means of making it a benefit to the world. London. 1784. 109 pp.

WEBSTER, NOAH. A grammatical institute, of the English language, comprising, an easy, concise, and systematic method of education, designed for the use of English schools in America. Hartford. 1784. *Many other editions.*

1785

WEBSTER, NOAH. Plan for the union of the American states. (From the fourth section of . . . Sketches of American Policy). 1785, Old South Leaflets. Vol. VII. No. 197.

WEBSTER, NOAH. Sketches of American policy under the following heads: I. Theory of government. II. Governments on the Eastern continent. III. American states; or the principle of the American constitutions contrasted with those of European states. IV. Plan of policy for improving the advantages and perpetuating the union of the American states. 1785.

1786

American Philosophical Society. Transactions, of the American Philosophical Society, held at Philadelphia, for promoting useful knowledge. Philadelphia: Printed by William and Thomas Bradford 1771-86. 2 vols. Vol. 2 has imprint. Philadelphia: Printed and sold by Robert Aitken, 1786.

PAINE, THOMAS. Dissertations on government. Philadelphia: printed by Charles Cist and sold by Messrs. Hall and Sellers, Robert Aitken, and William Pritchard. 1786. 53 pp.

Patterson, B. F. Description of New York in 1786. (In New York Directory for 1874) iii-xxii pp.

RUSH, BENJAMIN. A plan for the establishment of public schools and the diffusion of knowledge in Pennsylvania; to which are added, thoughts upon the mode of education proper in a republic, addressed to the legislature and citizens of the state. Philadelphia: Printed for Thomas Dobson. 1786. 36 pp.

1787

CAREY, MATHEW. The Is In Yon (Signed Tom Thoughtful). Reprinted in the American Museum, on Repository of Ancient and Modern Fugitive Pieces, Prose and Poetical. 1782. Vol. I, No. 2, pp. 116-119. (Phila.).

RUSH, BENJAMIN. Thoughts upon female education, accomodated to the present state of society, manners, and government, in the United States of America. Philadelphia: Printed by Pritchard and Hall. 1787. 32 pp.

WEBSTER, NOAH. Examination into the leading principles of the federal constitution proposed by the late convention held at Philadelphia. With answers to the principal questions. *Note on flyleaf in Webster's handwritings and signed by him: "This is a hasty production—written at the request of Mr. Fitsimmons of Philadelphia—a member of the convention. N. Webster."* Philadelphia: Pritchard and Hall, 1787. 41 pp.

1788

JEFFERSON, THOMAS. Notes on the state of Virginia; written in the year 1781, somewhat corrected and enlarged in the winter of 1782, for the use of a foreigner of distinction. Paris. 1788. 2, 224 pp.

SULLIVAN, JAMES. Thoughts upon the Political situation of the United States of America . . . With some observations on the constitution for a federal government. Worcester, Mass.: Printed for Isiah Thomas. 1788. 209 pp.

WEBSTER, NOAH. An introduction to English grammar. Being an abridgement of the Second Part of the Grammatical Institute. Philadelphia. 1788. 36 pp.

1789

WEBSTER, NOAH. Attention! or new thoughts on a serious subject; being an enquiry into the excise laws of Connecticut; addressed to the freemen of the state. By a private citizen. Hartford. 1789. 18 pp.

WEBSTER, NOAH. Dissertations on the English language; with notes, historical and critical, to which is added, by way of an appendix, an essay on a reformed mode of spelling, with Dr. Franklin's arguments upon that subject. Boston: Printed for the author by Isiah Thomas and Co. 1789. xvi, 18-410 pp.

1790

WEBSTER, NOAH. Journal (A) of the transactions and occurances in the settlement of Massachusetts and the other New-England colonies, from the year 1630 to 1644; written by John Winthrop, Esq. first governor of Massachusetts. Edited by Noah Webster. Hartford. 1790. 364 pp.

WEBSTER, NOAH. A collection of essays and fugitiv writings. On moral, historical, political and literary subjects. Boston. 1790. xvi, 414 pp.

WEBSTER, NOAH. The little reader's assistant. Contains American history stories and "A federal catechism." Hartford: Printed by Elisha Babcock. 1790. 2 parts in 1 vol.

WEBSTER, NOAH. The prompter; or a comentary on common sayings and subjects, which are full of common sense the best sense in the world. Boston. 1790. Other editions, 1791-1849.

WEBSTER, NOAH. A short view of the origin and progress of the science of natural philosophy; with some observations on the advantages of science in general. Delivered at the public examination of the candidates for the first degree, in the chapel of Yale College. In New York Magazine. 1790. Vol. I, June, pp. 338-40. July, pp. 383-84.

1791

Constitutions (The) of the United States, according to the latest amendments: to which are annexed, the Declaration of Independence; and the federal constitution; with the amendments thereto. This edition contains the constitution of Vermont, not in any former one. Philadelphia: Carey, Stewart and Co. 1791. 2, i, 176 pp.

CORAM, ROBERT. Political inquiries: to which is added a plan for the general establishment of schools in the United States. Wilmington: Printed by Andrews and Brynberg. 1791. viii, 10-107 pp.

Delaware Gazette. 1791.

PAINE, THOMAS. Rights of man: being an answer to Mr. Burke's attack on the French Revolution. Philadelphia: Reprinted by Samuel Harrison Smith. 1791. 2 ed. 105 pp.

PRIESTLEY, JOSEPH. The proper objects of education in the present state of the world. London. 1791. 2, 1. 52, 4 pp.

PRIESTLEY, JOSEPH. A discourse on the occasion of the death of Dr. Price; delivered at Hackney, on Sunday, May 1, 1791. A short sketch of the life of Dr. Price; a catalogue of books written by Dr. Priestley. London. 1791. 46 pp.

PRIESTLEY, JOSEPH. Lectures on history and general policy; to which is prefixed, an essay on a course of liberal education for civil and active life. Dublin. 1791. 2 vols. London editions 1793 and 1803.

ROUSSEAU, JEAN JACQUES. An inquiry into the nature of the social contract; or, principles of political right. London: G. G. J. and J. Robinson. 1791. 387 pp.

SULLIVAN, JAMES. Observations upon the government of the United States of America. Boston: Printed and sold by Samuel Hall. 1791. viii, 10-55 pp.

1792

BARLOW, JOEL. Advice to the privileged orders in the several states of Europe, resulting from the general necessity and propriety of a general revolution in the principle of government. Part I and II. London and New York. 1792-94.

DELACROIX, JACQUES VINCENT. A review of the constitutions of the principal states of Europe and of the United States of America. London. 1792. 2 vols.

PAINE, THOMAS. The crisis: in thirteen numbers. Albany: Printed and sold by Charles R, and George Webster. 1792. 186 pp.

PAINE, THOMAS. The writings of Thomas Paine. Containing: Common sense. 2. The crisis. 3. Letter to the Abbe Raynal. 4. Public good. 5. Letter to the Earl of Shelburne. 6. Letter to Sir Guy Carlton. 7. Letter to the Abbe Seyeys. 8. Letters to the authors of the Republican. 9. Rights of Man. Albany. 1792. 616 pp.

1793

CHIPMAN, NATHANIEL. Sketches of the principles of government. Rutland. 1793. xii, 292 pp.

FRANKLIN, BENJAMIN. Collected works: Vaughn. Works of the late Dr. Franklin; consisting of his life, written by himself, together with essays, humorous, moral and literary chiefly in the manner of the Spectator. Dublin. 1793. vi, 303 pp.

TRUSTAFF, SIR GEORGE JEOFFREY. *pseud.* A foreigner's scribble for amusement, or, constitutional notions of the powers of the national and state governments of the United States, respectfully submitted to the public in his own strange way. New York. 1793. 20 pp.

WATTS, ISAAC. Edited by David West. The improvements of the mind; or a supplement to the art of logic, In two parts by Isaac Watts. To which is added a discourse on the education of children and youth. Boston: Printed by J. Lamson and T. Odiorne for David West. 1793. 2 parts.

WEBSTER, NOAH. Effects of slavery on morals and industry. Hartford: Printed by Hudson and Goodwin. 1793. 56 pp.

1794

CLARK, JOSIAH. The parent's monitor: or an address to parents and teachers, concerning the education of youth in several particulars by Josiah Clark, Philomath. Boston. 1794.

France (1792-95). Convention nationale. Comité d'instruction publique. Report on the organization of national schools: to complete a republican education made in the name of the committee of public instruction. April 1794. By Bouquier. Translated from an authentic original. Philadelphia: Printed and sold at No. 112 Market Street. 1794. 12 pp.

PAINE, THOMAS. Letter to the people of France. Third year of the French republic.

PAINE, THOMAS. Age of reason. 1794.

WEBSTER, NOAH. Bill of mortality. With remarks on the history of the town of Hartford in Connecticut. (In collections of the Massachusetts Historical Society). Vol. 3, pp. 4-6. 1794.

WEBSTER, NOAH. The revolution in France. New York: Printed and published according to act of congress by George Bunce and Co. 1794 ed. 72 pp.

1795

COBBETT, WILLIAM. Observations on the emigration of Dr. Joseph Priestley, and on the addresses delivered to him, on his arrival at New York, with additions. Philadelphia. 1795. 88 pp.

CONDORCET. Tableau historique des progrès de l'esprit humain. 1795. viii, 389 pp.

HODGSON, WILLIAM. The commonwealth of reason. London: the author. 1795. xvi, 17-104 pp.

KNOX, VICESIMUS. The spirit of despotism. Philadelphia reprint of London edition. 1795. 5, 319 pp.

PAINE, THOMAS. Dissertation on first principles of government. Paris: Printed at the English Press. Third year of the French republic (1795). 40 pp.

SMITH, ADAM. Essays on philosophical subjects by the late Adam Smith. Life of Smith by Dugald Stewart. London: T. Cadell jr. and W. Davies. 1795. xcv, 244 pp.

SULLIVAN, JAMES. The French nation defended. Boston: From the Chronicle-press by Adams and Larkin. 1795. 31 pp.

WEBSTER, NOAH. Vindication of the treaty of amity, commerce, and navigation, with Great Britain. Signed Curtius. 1795. In Treaty of amity, commerce, and navigation . . . Philadelphia. 194-276 pp.

WEBSTER, NOAH. Contributions to the memoirs of the Connecticut Academy of arts and sciences. 1795, 1799, 1804.

1796

BARLOW, JOEL. The political writings of Joel Barlow; containing advice to the privileged orders. Letter to the national convention. Letter to the people of Piedmont. The conspiracy of kings. A new edition corrected. New York. 1796. xvi, 18-258 pp.

CLARKE, JOHN. Letters to a young student in the university of Cambridge, Massachusetts. Boston. 1796. iv, 6-148 pp.

DOGGETT, SIMEON. A discourse on education, delivered at the dedication and opening of Bristol Academy, the 18th of July, 1796. Newbedford, Mass. 1797. 28 pp.

GODWIN, WILLIAM. An enquiry concerning political justice, and its influence on general virtue and happiness. Dublin. 1793. Philadelphia. 1796. I vol.

PRIESTLEY, JOSEPH. Miscellaneous observations relating to education. The first American edition. New London. 1796. x, 102 pp. English edition. 1778.

RUSH, BENJAMIN. An eulogium, intended to perpetuate the memory of David Rittenhouse, late president of the American Philosophical Society. Philadelphia: Printed for J. Ormrod by Ormrod and Conrad. 1796. 46 pp.

SMITH, SAMUEL H. Remarks on education: illustrating the close connection between virtue and wisdom, to which is annexed a system of liberal education, which having received the premium awarded by the American Philosophical Society, December 15th, 1797, is now published by their order. (Written 1796). Philadelphia: Printed for J. Ormrod. 1798. 10-92 pp.

VOLNEY, CONSTANTIN FRANCOIS, CHASSEBREUF COMTE DE. The law of nature, or principles of morality deduced from the physical constitution of mankind and the universe. Philadelphia: Printed for T. Stephens by F. and R. Bailey. 1796. viii, 161 pp.

1797

GODWIN, WILLIAM. The enquirer. Reflections on education, manners, and literature. In a series of essays. Phila. 1797. viii, 387 pp.

JOHNSON, JOHN I. Reflections on political society. New York. 1797. 19 pp.

LAFITTE DU COURTEIL, AMABLE LOUIS ROSE DE. Proposal to demonstrate the necessity of a national institution in the United States of America, for the education of children of both sexes. To which is joined, a project of organization. Philadelphia. 1797.

PAINE, THOMAS. A letter to the Honourable Thomas Erskine. Paris: Printed for that author. 1797. iv, 6-31 pp.

PAINE, THOMAS. The works of Thomas Paine, secretary for foreign affairs, to the congress of the United States, in the late war. Philadelphia. 1797. 2 vols.

ROUSSEAU, JEAN JACQUES. A dissertation on political economy: to which is added, a treatise on the social compact; or, the principles of politic law. First American edition. Albany: Printed and sold by Barber and Southwick. 1797. 72, 214 pp.

WASHINGTON, GEORGE. Farewell Address. 1797.

WEBSTER, NOAH. Mr. Noah Webster's attack on Porcupine. From Minerva of New York. March 21, 1797. Reprinted in Porcupine's Political Censor, March 1797.

1798

GIRARDIU, LOUIS HUE. Education: circular relating to the formation of a school at Dumfries, Virginia, for teaching languages and other subjects belonging to a course of liberal education. Richmond. 1798.

RUSH, BENJAMIN. Essays: literary, moral and philosophical. Philadelphia. 1798. 378 pp.

SULLIVAN, JAMES. An impartial review of the causes and principles of the French Revolution. Boston: Printed by Benjamin Edes. 1798. 101 pp.

WEBSTER, NOAH. A letter to the governors, instructors and trustees of the Universities, and other seminaries of learning, in the United States, on the errors of English grammar. New York: Printed by George F. Hopkins for the author. 1798. 36 pp.

WEBSTER, NOAH. An oration pronounced before the citizens of New-Haven on the anniversary of the Independence of the United States, July 4, 1798. New Haven. 1798. 16 pp.

1799

KNOX, SAMUEL. An essay on the best system of education, adapted to the genius of the government of the United States. Comprehending also, an uniform, general plan for instituting and conducting public schools in this country, on principles of the most extensive utility. To which is prefixed, an address to the legislature of Maryland, on that subject. Baltimore: Warner and Hanna. 1799. iv, 173 pp.

ROBERTSON, WILLIAM. The history of America, books ix and x, containing the history of Virginia to the year 1688; and of New England to the year 1652. Philadelphia: Reprinted from the London edition by James Humphreys, and sold by him. 1779 ed. xiv, 18-196 pp.

1800

DUPONT DE NEMOURS, PIERRE SAMUEL. Du Pont, Bessie Gardner, translator. National education in the United States of America, by Dupont de Nemours; translated from the second French edition of 1812 and with an introduction by B. G. Du Pont. Newark, Del.: University of Delaware Press. 1923. v-xxi, iv, 161 pp. First edition in New York, 1800.

WEBSTER, NOAH. A letter to General Hamilton, occasioned by his letter to President Adams. New York (?). 1800. 8 pp.

1801

EDGEWORTH, MARIA and R. L. Practical education: the second edition in three volumes. London: Printed for J. Johnson by J. Crowder. 1801. 3 vols.

New England primer. Improved and adapted to the use of schools. Designed as an introduction to the American spelling book. Embelished with cuts. Hudson. 1801. 94 pp.

1802

WEBSTER, NOAH. Miscellaneous papers on political and commercial subjects. New York: Printed by E. Belden and Co. 1802. viii, 227, 48 pp.

WEBSTER, NOAH. The rights of neutral nations in time of war. Reprinted in miscellaneous papers. 1802.

1803

Parent's friend, or extracts from the principal works on education, from the time of Montaigne to the present day. Methodized and arranged with notes. Philadelphia. 1803. 2 vols.

1806

WEBSTER, NOAH. Elements of useful knowledge. Hartford: Printed for O. D. Cooke by Hudson and Goodwin. 1806 ed. 4, 206 pp. Vol. 1.

WEBSTER, NOAH. Elements of useful knowledge. New Haven: From Sidney's press for I. Cooke and Co. 1806 ed. Vol. 2. 224 pp.

WEBSTER, NOAH. Elements of useful knowledge. Containing a historical and geographical account of the empires and states in Europe, Asia, and Africa, with their colonies. To which is added a brief description of New Holland, and the principal islands in the Pacific and Indian Oceans. For use of schools. 1806 ed. Vol. 3.

1807

WEBSTER, NOAH. A letter to Dr. David Ramsay, of Charleston (S. C.) respecting the errors in Johnson's dictionary, and other lexicons. New Haven: O. Steele and Co. 1807. 28 pp.

1812

WEBSTER, NOAH. History of animals; designed for the instruction and amusement of persons of both sexes. New Haven: Howe and Deforest. 1812. 247 pp. (This is a part of Webster's plan of universal knowledge series. Vol. IV of the series.)

1817

WEBSTER, NOAH. A letter to the Honourable John Pickering on the subject of his vocabulary; or, collection of words and phrases supposed to be peculiar to the United States of America. Boston: West and Richardson. 1817. 60 pp.

1819

DESTUTT DE TRACY. Commentary of Montesquieu's Spirit of laws. Paris. 1819 edition. xv, 480 pp.

1823

WEBSTER, NOAH. Letters to a young gentleman commencing his education: to which is subjoined a brief history of the United States. New Haven. 1823. 335 pp.

1824

American Philosophical Society. Catalogue of the library of the American Philosophical Society, held at Philadelphia for promoting useful knowledge. Published by order of the society. Philadelphia. 1824. xv, 290 pp.

1832

WEBSTER, NOAH. History of the United States: To which is prefixed a brief historical account of our English ancestors, from the dispersion at Babel, to their migration to America; and of the conquest of South America, by the Spaniard. New Haven: Durrie and Peck. 1832. 324 pp.

1835

WEBSTER, NOAH. Instructive and entertaining lessons for youth with rules for reading with propriety, illustrated by examples; designed for use in schools and families. New Haven: S. Babcock. 1835. 7-252 pp. (Substantially part III of the Institutes.)

1840

American Philosophical Society. Laws and regulations of the society together with the charter of the society, and a list of its members. Philadelphia: J. C. Clark and Son. 1840. 80 pp.

1843

PATTERSON, ROBERT MASKELL. Early history of the American Philosophical Society: discourse at the celebration of its 100th anniversary; with introductory address by the president, Du Ponceau. Philadelphia. 1843. 3-196 pp.

To the friends of American literature. Vindication of Webster. 1843 (?).

WEBSTER, NOAH. A collection of papers on political, literary, and moral subjects. New York. 1843. 4-373 pp.

1846

CHIPMAN, DANIEL (Brother). Life of Honourable Nathaniel Chipman LLD. with selections from his papers by Daniel Chipman. Boston. 1846. xii, 5-402 pp.

QUESNAY, FRANCOIS. Le droit naturel;—analyse du tableau economique. (In Daire, E. Physiocrates. 1846.)

1850

ADAMS, JOHN. The works of John Adams, 2nd president of the U. S.: with a life of the author, notes and illustrations by his grandson, Charles F. Adams. Boston: Little, Brown and Co. 1850-56. 10 vols.

1853

JEFFERSON, THOMAS. The writings of Thomas Jefferson. Being his autobiography, correspondence, reports, messages, addresses, and other writings, official and private. H. A. Washington, editor. 1853 edition. 10 vols.

1854

PAINE, THOMAS. The works of Thomas Paine, a hero in the American revolution. With an account of his life. Philadelphia. 1854. 3 vols.

1882

SCUDDER, HORACE ELISHA. Noah Webster. Boston: Houghton Mifflin and Co. 1882. vi, 302 pp., 1 part.

1889

American Philosophical Society, Philadelphia. Subject Register of papers published, in the transactions and proceedings of the American Philosophical Society. Compiled by Henry Phillips, Jr. Philadelphia: MacCalla and Co., printers. 1889. 75 pp.

1890

SMITH, ALBION WOODBURY. The beginnings of American nationality. Baltimore: Johns Hopkins University Series. 1890. 77 pp.

1894

QUESNAY, FRANCOIS. Tableau economique; first printed in 1758 and now reproduced in fac-simile for the British economic association. London. 1894.

1898

RIDDLE, WILLIAM. Nicholas Comenius; or, ye Pennsylvania schoolmaster of ye olden time. Lancaster: T. B. and H. B. Cochran. 1898. vii-xxi, 469 pp.

TURGOT, ANNE ROBERT J. Reflections on the formation and distribution of riches by Turgot, 1770. New York: The Macmillan Co. 1898. xxii, 112 pp.

1899

JEFFERSON, THOMAS. The writings of Thomas Jefferson. Collected and edited by P. L. Ford. New York; G. P. Putnam's Sons. 1899 edition. 10 vols.

1900

American Philosophical Society. Proceedings—memorial volume. Philadelphia. 1900.

MADISON, JAMES. The writings of James Madison including letters and documents. Edited by G. Hunt. G. P. Putnam's Sons. 1900. 10 vols.

1906

FRANKLIN, BENJAMIN. Life and writings of Benjamin Franklin. New York: Smyth Macmillan Co. 1906 edition. 10 vols.

1907

ROSENGARTEN, JOSEPH GEORGE. The early French members of the American Philosophical Society. Philadelphia. 1907. 87-93 pp.

1914

DU PONCEAU, PETER STEPHEN. An historical account of the origin and formation of the American Philosophical Society held at Philadelphia. . . . With the communication of J. Francis Fisher. Philadelphia; American Philosophical Society. 1914. iii, 3-196 pp.

Date (?)

WEBSTER, NOAH. Dissertation on the English language. Reprinted from Old South Leaflets. Vol. VIII. No. 196.

WEBSTER, NOAH. History of the United States. From an American selection of lessons in reading and speaking. Boston. Old South Leaflets. Vol. VIII. No. 198.

SECONDARY SOURCES

Political, Social, and Economic Theory

BOGARDUS, EMORY STEPHEN. *A History of Social Thought.* Los Angeles: University of Southern California Press. 1922. 510 pp.

BOGART, EARNEST LUDLOW. *The Economic History of the United States.* New York: Longmans, Green and Co. 1912. 597 pp.

BOUCKE, OSWALD FRED. *The Development of Economics* (1750-1900). New York: The Macmillan Co. 1921. vi, 248 pp. Bib. Pp. 329-342.

BOUCKE, OSWALD FRED. *A Critique of Economics, Doctrinal and Methodological.* New York: The Macmillan Co. 1922. ix. 305 pp. Bib. pp. 289-301.

BURY, JOHN BAGNALL. *The Idea of Progress: an Inquiry into Its Origin and Growth.* London: The Macmillan Co. 1920. xv, 377 pp.

BURY, JOHN BAGNELL. *A History of the Freedom of Thought.* London: Williams and Norgate. 1913. v, 7-256 pp.

DEALEY, JAMES QUAYLE. *Growth of American Constitutions from 1776 to the End of the Year 1914.* Boston: Ginn and Co. 1915. viii, 308 pp.

DUNNING, WALTER ARCHIBALD. *A History of Political Theories from Rousseau to Spencer.* New York: The Macmillan Co. 1920. ix, 446 pp.

FISHER, SYDNEY GEORGE. *The evolution of the constitution of the United States, showing that it is a development of progressive history and not an isolated document struck off at a given time or an imitation of English and Dutch forms of government.* Philadelphia: J. B. Lippincott Co. 1900. 3-398 pp.

GRAY, J. C. *The Nature and Sources of Law.* New York: The Macmillan Co. 1921. 2nd edition. xviii, 348 pp.

HAYES, CARLTON, J. H. *A Political and Social History of Modern Europe.* New York: The Macmillan Co. 1921 edition. 2 vols. (Vol. 1.)

HAZEN, CHARLES DOWNER. *Contemporary Opinion of the French Revolution.* Baltimore: Johns Hopkins Press. 1897. x, 315 pp. Johns Hopkins University Studies in history and political science.

HILL, MABEL. *Liberty documents with contemporary exposition and critical comments drawn from various writers.* New York: Longmans, Green and Co. 1901. xxviii, 458 pp. Albert Bushnell Hart Series.

LEVY-BRUHL, LUCIEN. *History of Modern Philosophy in*

France. Chicago: Open Court Publishing Co. 1899. x, 500, 23 pp.

LEWINSKI, JAN ST. *Founders of Political Economy.* London: P. S. King and Co. 1922. viii, 173 pp.

MERRIAM, CHARLES EDWARD. *History of the Theory of Sovereignty since Rousseau.* New York: Columbia University Press. 1900. x, 11-232 pp.

MERRIAM, CHARLES EDWARD. *A History of American Political Theories.* New York: The Macmillan Co. 1910. xv, 364 pp.

THORPE, FRANCIS NEWTON. *The Constitutional History of the United States.* Chicago: Callaghan and Co. 1901. 3 vols.

THORPE, FRANCIS NEWTON. *The Constitutional Work of the States in the Eighteenth Century.* Chicago: A. C. McClurg and Co. 1901. 168-202 pp.

WALSTON, SIR CHARLES. *Aristodemocracy, from the great war back to Moses, Christ, and Plato;* an essay by Sir. Charles Waldstein. London: J. Murry. 1916. xviii, 434 pp.

WEULERSSE, G. *Le mouvement physiocratique en France de 1756 à 1770.* Paris: F. Alcan. 1910. 2 vols.

Nationalism

BABCOCK, K. C. *The Rise of American Nationality 1811-1819.* New York: Harper and Bros. 1906. xvi, 339 pp. American Nation Series.

BARNES, HARRY ELMER. "Nationalism; Its Origin and Development." New York: *Encyclopaedia Americana.* 1919. 743-765 pp.

BASSERR. *The Federalist System.* New York: Harper and Bros. 1906. xviii, 327 pp. American Nation Series.

DEWEY, JOHN. "Nationalizing Education." National education association of the United States. *Journal of Proceedings and Addresses.* 1916. 183-189 pp.

DI BERARDINO, LOUIS. *The Nationalism of the New Democracy.* Philadelphia: 1914. 25 pp.

FARRAND, LIVINGSTON. "Basis of American History 1500-1900." New York: Harper Bros. 1904. xi-xviii, 303 pp. (*Am. Nation: A History.* vol. 2.)

HERBERT, SYDNEY. *Nationality and Its Problems.* London: Methwen and Co. 1920. viii, 173, 31 pp.

KREHBIEL, EDWARD BENJAMIN. *Nationalism, War and Society: A Study of Nationalism and Its Concomitant, War, in their Relation to Civilization.* New York: The Macmillan Co. 1916. xxxv, 276 pp.

MUIR, RAMSAY. *National Self-Government, Its Growth and Principles; the Culmination of Modern History.* New York: Henry Holt and Co. 1918. xi, 312 pp.

MUIR, RAMSAY. *Nationalism and Internationalism: the culmination of Modern History.* London: Constable and Co. 1917. 229 pp.

PILLSBURY, WALTER BOWERS. *The Psychology of Nationality and Internationalism.* New York: D. Appleton and Co. 1919. 11, 314 pp.

ROSE, JOHN HOLLAND. *Nationality in Modern History.* New York: The Macmillan Co. 1916. xi, 202 pp.

SLOSSON, PRESTON W. "What is Nationality." *Unpopular Review.* 1915. Vol. 5. pp. 40-50.

WOLSTON, SIR CHARLES. *Patriotism: National and International.* New York: Longmans, Green and Co. 1917. xlvi, 155 pp.

Education

ALEXANDER, FREDERICK MATTHIAS. *Man's Supreme Inheritance: Conscious Guidance and Control in Relation to Human Evolution in Civilization.* New York: E. P. Dutton and Co. 1918. xvii, 254 pp.

CUBBERLY, ELWOOD PATTERSON. *Changing Conceptions of Education.* New York: Houghton Mifflin Co. 1909. viii, 69 pp.

DEWEY, JOHN. *Creative Intelligence; Essays in the Pragmatic Attitude.* New York: Henry Holt and Co. 1917. iv, 3-467 pp.

DEXTER, EDWIN GRANT. *A History of Education in the United States.* New York: The Macmillan Co. 1906. xxi, 656 pp.

FITZPATRICK, EDWARD A. *The Educational Views and Influence of De Witt Clinton.* New York: Columbian Series, No. 44. 1911. 157 pp.

HART, JOSEPH KINMONT. *Democracy in Education: A Social Interpretation of the History of Education.* New York: Century Co. 1918. ix, 3-418 pp.

KNIGHT, EDGAR WALLACE. *Public Education in the South.* Boston; New York, etc.: Ginn and Co. 1922. xii, 482 pp.

PARSONS, ELSIE W. CLEWS. *Educational Legislation and Administration of the Colonial Governments.* New York: The Macmillan Co. 1899. xi, 7-524 pp.

REISNER, EDWARD HARTMAN. *Nationalism and Education since 1789; a Social and Political History of Modern Education.* New York: The Macmillan Co. 1922. xiii, 575 pp.

REISNER, EDWARD HARTMAN. *Democracy and Nationalism in Education; Syllabus and Readings.* New York: Columbian Press. 1919. 29 pp.

RIDDLE, WILLIAM. *One Hundred and Fifty Years of School History in Lancaster, Pennsylvania.* Lancaster: the author. 1905. vii-xix, 442 pp.

SLOSSON, EDWIN EMORY. *The American Spirit in Education; a Chronicle of Great Teachers.* New Haven: Yale University Press. 1921. x, 309 pp.

INDEX

Absolutism gives way to relativism, 10

Adams, John, for separation from England, 22; on the Representative Assembly, 29; on remote causes of American Revolution, 31; *Defense of the American Constitution*, 31; on education of youth, 43; on necessity of proper education, 49; Webster's acquaintance with writings of, 204

Administration of Education, compulsory, and the Physiocrats, 19; of women, according to Rush, 57-60; for open-avenues ahead, 67; for change, 67; by the state, 71; of support of students, 71, 72, 74, 195; cost of, private and public schools, 77, 78, 193, 194; of bureaus of research, 82, 84; in state and nation, 102, 103; in colleges, 127, 128; in universities, 130-135; in schools, 150; supervisory powers of board, 159; resident students, 165; in national system, 173, 175; council of public instruction at head of national system, 196, 197; time distribution of college curriculum, 195

Agrarianism, 169, 186

Aims of Education, for control of social progress, 8, 14, 15, 50, 51, 67, 72, 89, 90, 91, 92, 125, 126, 138-139, 150, 261; for constructive citizenship and intelligent public opinion, 16, 56, 87, 88, 112, 258, 259; for political reform, 19; for integration, 46, 72, 80, 171-173, 233, 234, 258; for nationalistic culture, 45, 56, 80, 81, 235, 237, 240-241, 242, 247; for candid, experimental, scientific attitude and improvement, 45, 53, 82, 83, 112, 141, 150, 151, 157, 250-251; for homogeneity, 49; for friendships, 49; for supreme regard for country, 49, 50, 251, 252; for instilling of republican principles, 50; for democracy, 51, 52, 64, 67, 68, 69, 72, 82, 90, 91, 100, 101, 231, 236, 237; for broad culture, 52, 102, 237-254; for development of national resources, 53, 80, 81, 118, 152, 153; Christian, 56; for progress of liberty, 56; practical legislation and sense of political responsibility, 56, 259, 260; for greater enlightenment, 56; for advancement of agriculture and manufacture, 62; for independence, 66; for inner control, 66; for freedom and open-avenues-ahead, 67; for equal opportunity, 69; for effective social control, 80, 139-140; for evolution of morals, 83, 84, 141, 142, 144; for forming the man, 86, 87; for stability and prosperity of American institutions, 87, 93, 182; to free from religious and political dominance, 87, 88; for intelligent criticism of democracy, 83, 88; general objectives, 115, 116, 121; universal values of mankind, 116; for destruction of class distinctions, 116, 232; for preparation for college and for life, 116;

297